Citizen Spy

Citizen Spy

Television, Espionage, and Cold War Culture

Michael Kackman

Commerce and Mass Culture Series

University of Minnesota Press
Minneapolis • London

An earlier version of chapter 2 was published as "Citizen, Communist, Counterspy: *I Led 3 Lives* and Television's Masculine Agent of History," *Cinema Journal* 38, no. 1 (1998): 98–114. Copyright 1998 by the University of Texas Press. All rights reserved. Reprinted with permission.

Published by the University of Minnesota Press
111 Third Avenue South, Suite 290
Minneapolis, MN 55401-2520
http://www.upress.umn.edu

Library of Congress Cataloging-in-Publication Data

Kackman, Michael.
    Citizen spy : television, espionage, and cold war culture / Michael Kackman.
        p.   cm. — (Commerce and mass culture series)
    Includes bibliographical references and index.
    ISBN 0-8166-3828-4 (hc : alk. paper) — ISBN 0-8166-3829-2 (pb : alk. paper)
    1. Spy television programs—United States—History and criticism.   I. Title.
II. Series.
    PN1992.8.S67K33   2005
    791.45'6—dc22   2005002138

Printed in the United States of America on acid-free paper

The University of Minnesota is an equal-opportunity educator and employer.

12 11 10 09 08 07 06 05   10 9 8 7 6 5 4 3 2 1

For Darlene,
who taught me to read

Contents

Preface: Doing Television History

This project was sparked by my interest in the peculiar cultural politics of the Cold War. In part, my fascination was marked by a sense of distance and wonder—the hyperbolic anti-Communism of the early 1950s seemed so anachronistic as to be comically naïve. Television, of course, is central to this too-common assumption about the superiority and sophistication of the present. Shifting social norms, enhanced production values, the dated grammar of popular culture, and today's ubiquitous reruns and remakes all make 1950s and 1960s television seem quaint, its representations diminished, its politics more charming than prescient. But this tendency to contain the past through nostalgia and irony overlooks two interlocking principles that have shaped the development of this book. First, the cultural Cold War's underlying questions about national identity and citizenship, and the privileged means of representing them, are very much with us today. We need look no further than the daily headlines to see deeply impassioned arguments about who or what qualifies as "American." Next, while the past is gone and buried, history tethers it to the present. Our ability to recognize citizens and national subjects hinges on our mobilization of history—on an articulation of values, ideologies, and identities that together cohere around the idea of America. Television, this book argues, is central to both these issues.

Television is difficult to make sense of historically. This seemingly omnipresent medium might be described as an economic institution, a form of narrative entertainment, an electronic public sphere, a mechanism of globalization, a cultural forum, a domestic technology, or a marketing device—and each such choice would foreground different historiographic priorities. Television doesn't offer easily isolable, discrete objects of study. Does one study a particular program, an episode, a network, a studio, an advertising agency, an audience, a star? The methods of textual analysis that film scholars adapted from literary criticism don't quite fit newer media. Whereas a given film might be studied as a relatively bounded narrative, television is complicated by episodic seriality and what Raymond Williams described as flow: an ongoing stream of information, in which individual programs, commercial messages, news, and public service announcements collide and combine.[1] And not only is television broadly intertextual, its texts are impermanent. While the historical significance of the most popular programs is disproportionately magnified by being preserved in the electronic amber of cable network syndication, countless important broadcasts now survive only as written transcripts or as residues in other historical accounts. Similarly, the supporting materials (scripts, production notes, correspondence, and so on) that offer insights into the circumstances of production are often discarded. This is in part due to the fact that television generates a vast amount of material, but it is also a product of the general low esteem in which this medium is often held—both by audiences and producers. Ironically, because television is seemingly "everywhere," much that is important about it is at risk of disappearing from the historical record.

But just as television is ephemeral, so too is the past. Ultimately unknowable, a foreign country, the past lingers out of sight, conjured only in the histories we write.[2] Hayden White suggests that the common assumption that crucial explanatory facts lie dormant—in the archive, in memories, in some endless public record—like little nuggets eager to be found (a-ha!) is a beguiling fallacy. We'd like to think that history is a sage process of first gathering data, then stringing it together in the most natural, coherent way—as if filling in the pieces of a precut jigsaw puzzle, 500 or 1000 to a box. White insists that narrative comes first; facts only become visible when placed in a covering framework within which they are rendered factual.[3] That's not to say that history is arbitrary, but a host of assumptions—in the case of this book, about the development of the television industry, its place within a national and/or global culture, its relationships to other media artifacts and practices, and so on—lead toward certain kinds of facts and away from others. Furthermore, it is not only the historian's narrative frameworks that shape this process; unspoken assumptions also guide those who (whether at the studio, the network, or the archive) had to select what kinds of materials to keep. Many TV collections in highly respected archives consist solely of final drafts of scripts—a ringing endorsement of the singular value of the final literary product if there ever was one. Much rarer are collections that include information that hints at the kinds of decisions (representational and otherwise) that shaped the production process.

As a result, it's impossible, in this history or any other, to gather comprehensive data that are completely consistent from program to program, producer to producer, and network to network. It's also impossible to make a singular unified argument that conclusively encapsulates all aspects of every program discussed here. The data available vary from program to program; some production companies retained exhaustive notes regarding script and casting decisions, others multiple script revisions, still others vital external correspondence, and some kept only kinescopes and release prints. Few kept everything; some kept nothing. How could they know that historians would want to root through their garbage? (This is, of course, the charitable interpretation; perhaps they wanted to make sure that their detritus went safely to the landfill via the shredder. Concerns over intellectual property have made some copyright holders increasingly reluctant to allow scholars to peer into the machine.)

This book is thus not what Carlo Ginzburg calls a serial history, a broad narrative examining that which is homogeneous and consistent in a search for an underlying unifying structure.[4] In that sense, this isn't a genre study. Though it is very much concerned with the aggregate accumulations of meanings in texts that share certain narrative preoccupations, it doesn't attempt to explain the evolution or devolution of a form that exceeds, or preexists, its individual expressions. Nor is it what Foucault calls a total history, which "draws all phenomena around a single centre—a principle, a meaning, a spirit, a world-view, an overall shape."[5] Rather than the "polished surface" of total history, this book's sympathies lie toward what Ginzburg calls microhistory, a mode of historical inquiry that moves between levels of analysis, and in which "the hypotheses, the doubts, the uncertainties became part of the narration; the search for truth [becomes] part of the exposition of the (necessarily incomplete) truth attained."[6]

This isn't to say that my selection of methods and objects of study is random or idiosyncratic, but to acknowledge that the book's shifting modes of analysis are part a matter of what evidence was empirically available, and part a matter of what historical traces opened up fruitful lines of inquiry about TV's place within American popular culture. This book explores the continuities between television espionage programs and both official and popular discourses of national identity. In some cases the connections between TV's fictional representations and state institutions were overt and intentional. In others, these linkages are more oblique, formed not through prescriptive policy but through common claims about national identity. The first chapter, for example, lays out the broad discursive framework of connections between official state politics and semidocumentary spy narratives in the 1950s, while the second is more narrowly focused on one program's negotiation between documentarism and narrative. Chapter 3 explores two largely forgotten programs that scarcely can be said to have a direct influence on what followed. Their place in this history is not causal, but rather illustrative of what would turn out to be remarkable transformations in the U.S. television industry, American popular culture, and narratives of national identity in the late 1950s and early 1960s. Chapter 4 addresses how parodic espionage narratives turned inward on their own discourses of national authority amid a cultural climate responsive to self-referentiality and satire. The programs discussed in chapters 5 and 6 aired largely simultaneously with the parodic programs discussed in chapter 4, and thus can't be said to respond to the parodies in a linear or dialectic fashion indicative of a transformation in a genre. But even while the parodies exposed the vulnerability of the rigidly reductive version of nationalism that was popularized in the 1950s, other spy programs offered new realist narratives of national identity more amenable to the cultural contexts of the mid- to late-1960s America. Chapter 5 explores this through the intertextual connections that linked *I Spy* to broader debates over civil rights and its relationship to the American national body, while chapter 6 is more industrial in focus, examining the research practices that guided the representational decisions made by a diversifying and increasingly globally minded television studio.

It is in the very nature of history to exclude; the historian continually balances the equally compelling demands of breadth and depth. In navigating those demands, I have chosen to use each program as a case study of a given issue that reflects on the book's larger arguments as a whole. The chapters of this book are thus not entirely symmetrical in approach: some draw particular attention to industrial strategies, others to matters of representation or televisual narrative, others to specific cultural contexts or political references. While there is no "unified field theory" that governs this historical account, the book's chapters are meant to be additive. Arguments advanced and evidence marshaled in one chapter about one program might productively be extended elsewhere, and I want to draw attention to these shows' cumulative layering of discourses and meanings. This project uses a particular subset of programs from a fascinating twenty-year period to chart the interconnections among the television industry, political institutions, popular culture, and discourses of national identity. But while U.S. espionage television programs of the 1950s and 1960s are its central object of study, this book aims to enter into a broader conversation about how, why, and in what circumstances something so indescribably vague—yet so passionately immediate—as national identity takes shape. The political Cold War has long since passed, though its successors are forming; the cultural struggle over the boundaries, limits, and responsibilities of citizenship and nationhood is ongoing.

Acknowledgments

There is always a tinge of hubris in acknowledgments; the longer the litany of appreciation, the more it resembles a giddy declaration of wealth. Still, my sister always tells me that it's a kindness to allow people to help you, and to not let one's creeping sense of unworth stand in the way of good will. I suspect she's right, so I'll start there: thank you, Lari, for your enthusiasm and curiosity. I'm also grateful to be part of a family that wasn't required to do, think, and believe the same things in the same way at the same time. Edwin Lau was my first intellectual colleague; Jane Shattuc was my first mentor.

The Media and Cultural Studies Program in the Department of Communication Arts at the University of Wisconsin–Madison was a remarkably inviting home. The faculty and graduate students there often showed a rare combination of compassionate community, quick laughter, and the well-placed follow-up question. No one embodies all three of these characteristics as fully as Jason Mittell, unless it's Kevin Glynn. Daniel Marcus and Derek Kompare offered thoughtful comments on works in progress, as did Darrell Newton, Norma Coates, Chris Smith, and Doug Battema. Jo Ellen Fair and Vance Kepley were gracious readers. Our weekly colloquia and hallway conversations were deeply enriching, and the Red Shed to which we regularly adjourned is a last great grubby Third Place. Throughout graduate school, Lisa Parks was my best friend and critic, and she helped shape what this project would become. John Fiske taught me to care about cultural theory and to love teaching it. Michele Hilmes patiently read endless speculative pages and guided me toward more interesting questions; she also gave me my first experience teaching television and introduced me to the musty pleasures of the archive. Julie D'Acci read each sentence of my dissertation, often far more carefully than I had written them. In my final months of work, her diligence was a great kindness. How to thank enough?

At DePaul University, the financial support of the University Research Council and College of Liberal Arts and Sciences was invaluable and much appreciated. Dean Michael Mezey and Associate Dean Charles Suchar made the experience of adjusting to life as a new faculty member in a rapidly growing university as painless as possible. Julie Artis, Craig Miller, Lexa Murphy, Barb Willard, Greg Scott, Kimberly Moffitt, Caroline Bronstein, and Eileen Cherry shared generously of their ideas and friendship. Jackie Taylor and Anna Vaughn-Clissold of the DePaul Humanities Center created a thriving intellectual community, and I benefited from participating in the NEH critical race theory seminar they sponsored. Particular thanks are also due Amanda Ladas, for her research assistance and insight.

Much of my research was conducted in a number of archives. I'm especially grateful to the State Historical Society of Wisconsin, the Wisconsin Center for Film and Theater Research, the UCLA Library Department of Special Collections, the National Archives, and the American Heritage Center at the University of Wyoming. Though little of their work reaches bookstore shelves, archivists may be the most important historians of all. Thank you for saving those scraps of paper, snapshots, and ephemera. Jerrold Zacharias and Ellis Zacharias Jr. kindly shared their father's unpublished papers and photographs.

Many others helped in ways small and large. Vicky Johnson shared her expertise and video collection, Toby Miller offered important insights about the manuscript, and series editor Justin Wyatt read multiple drafts and offered invaluable constructive criticism along the way. Much of this work was presented at the annual conferences of the Society for Cinema and Media Studies and Console-ing Passions, where I benefited from comments and ongoing conversation. My colleagues and graduate students in the Department of Radio–Television–Film at the University of Texas at Austin offered helpful comments and encouragement, and a Jesse H. Jones Fellowship in Communication from the University of Texas College of Communication provided crucial support.

Mary Kearney helped me not just to see this project through to completion but to see what lay beyond. Thank you.

Introduction
The Agent and the Nation

It trains men, as part of their civic, fraternal grant, to internalize national imperatives for "unity" and "sameness," recodifying national politics as individual psychology and/or responsibility.

—DANA NELSON, *NATIONAL MANHOOD*

In 1966, amid an explosion of espionage programming on American television, the men's magazine *Esquire* devoted a special issue to "Spies, Science, and Sex." The issue begins with a full-page image of Robert Vaughn, newly famous as secret agent Napoleon Solo of *The Man from U.N.C.L.E.* Vaughn slouches self-confidently, shoulders thrust back, his hands in the pockets of his crisp shark-skin suit. Above his head is printed simply "Spies..." with the ellipsis trailing off before his gaze. Turning the page, we follow his eyeline match, completing the image. Sprawled out before him is an attractive woman in a negligee, caressing and kissing a metallic robot.[1] On the first page, Vaughn is the very picture of cool detachment and latent masculine power. But on turning the page, the erotic encounter that he (and we) might have assumed to be his birthright has been denied; the anonymous woman has turned her back to him, instead devoting her affections to a mechanical man. Vaughn is but a voyeur, stripped of his reward.

In a sidebar, the taunting text begins, "A spy knows what's going on. You don't. He knows who's after us. You don't. He knows why. You don't. And, without penalty, he can do what he wants to about it—kill, steal, maim, rape, lie, cheat, travel, live it up. But you can't."[2] This introduction—to a collection of some dozen or more articles on spying in America circa 1966—captures the central tension surrounding the figure of the secret agent. The spy, the article suggests, is an "agent" in the fullest sense of the word—self-possessed, resourceful, independent, "a man in control of himself, capable of taking action, an old-fashioned freeman." But at the same time, that myth of agency is an impossible ideal, utterly unattainable, not only for the reader *(you don't... you don't...*

Esquire magazine, May 1966.

you don't . . . but you can't) but even for the hyperbolically masculine Napoleon Solo himself. The myth of his agency is complete only so long as it is isolated, stripped of context; when we turn the page, when he is brought into cultural relations with that which he desires, it crumbles.

The spy in 1960s America was thus more than just an iconic masculine hero. Invested with the power to act on behalf of the state, he represented the possibility of limitless willful action, but his agency was also circumscribed and limited by the apparatus he served. As much an anonymous bureaucrat and piece-work technician as a superhero, the spy embodied a wide range of often deeply conflicting discourses about masculinity, American national identity, and its ideal citizen-subject. The spy was both the ultimate "freeman" and a symbol of the wrenching anonymity of life as a corporatized postwar American "organization man." The figure of the spy is an index of profound transformations in American television in particular, and popular culture more generally, in the first two decades of the Cold War.

Though the glamorous programs of the mid-1960s featured the most remembered American TV spies, espionage programs first emerged in the earliest years of the Cold War. Heavily influenced by the semidocumentary crime films and television programs of the late 1940s and early 1950s, *I Led 3 Lives* (syndi-

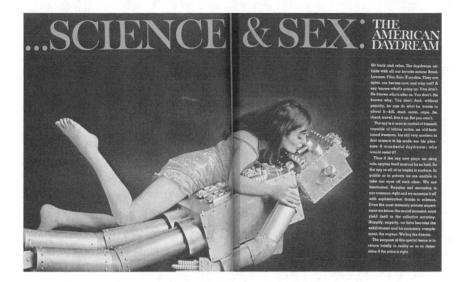

cated, 1953–56), *Treasury Men in Action* (ABC/NBC, 1950–54), *Behind Closed Doors* (NBC, 1958–59), and *The Man Called X* (syndicated, 1955–57) were promoted as tell-all glimpses into the real practices of government agents.[3] Dealing with cases drawn from the headlines of the day, these shows won the approval of the FBI, State Department, and Department of Defense, and were heavily promoted as being based on the lives of, or supervised by, actual spies and federal officials. Such programs were called "documentary melodramas" within the television industry, a seemingly incongruous phrase that nonetheless captured these shows' interplay between the fictional and the civic. Through such devices as on-screen narrators, official endorsements in the credits, and overt references to contemporary political events, these programs allowed portions of the nascent television industry to demonstrate their civic responsibility to both audiences and the federal government. From its earliest incarnations, the American spy drama was about more than nationalism in an abstracted, general sense; these programs offer explicit meditations on the challenges, possibilities, and limitations of dominant conceptions of U.S. citizenship.

Within these espionage dramas, the figure of the individual secret agent is the principal site through which "appropriate" American citizenship is modeled. Symbolically embodying the prerogatives of the American nation, the secret agent was initially constructed as a highly conventional white male protagonist.

Political and cultural conditions, together with the economics of television production, led to a kind of representational shorthand by which complex historical and political conditions were transformed into a series of narrative challenges faced by heteronormative masculine agents. In programs like *I Led 3 Lives,* the protagonist's agency is founded in discourses of historical continuity; the ideal citizen emerges out of a mythic American past that legitimates and reinforces his authority.

These programs' combination of narrative and documentary realism, however, wasn't always stable and coherent. The stylistic conventions of realist narrative were sometimes directly at odds with the documentarist address by which these programs claimed to be authoritative sources of vital political information. Like much fictional television, these shows are usually centered around an individual protagonist, who is invested, more or less, with the ability to resolve whatever challenges are posed by the narrative. This ideal figure is constructed according to an ultimately ahistorical model of heroic American citizenship that is imagined as somehow preceding—and outlasting—immediate instabilities. This idealized agent, however, was often at odds with the programs' claims to be realistic accounts of important social and political events. These two discursive influences on spy programs—mythic conceptions of nationhood and the official imprimatur of the state—don't always neatly fold in upon one another. In the 1950s programs, this tension often produces a crisis of confidence in the secret agent himself. Herb Philbrick of *I Led 3 Lives* is faced with the dilemma of the organization man—he struggles to find some sense of masculine individuality within an increasingly bureaucratized culture, one in which men's work is performed at the behest of faceless governmental or corporate institutions. In *Behind Closed Doors*—airing in 1958–59, among the last of the documentarist spy shows—this tension generated pragmatic problems for the show's producers. Poised between a strictly documentary account of bureaucratic state institutions and a heroic narrative of an idealized spy, the show was both and neither; dismissed as "unbelievable" and "hokey," *Behind Closed Doors* was canceled during its first season. This basic ideological problematic would continue to mark spy programs; who or what was to be the voice of the nation—the agent or the agency?[4]

While a few espionage and intrigue programs aired on American television during the early 1960s, they were sporadic and generally imported—most

notably NBC's British-produced anthology series *Espionage* (1963) and a few
locally syndicated runs of the British programs *The Avengers* (1961–65) and *The
Saint* (1963). A dramatic surge in espionage programs didn't begin until mid-
decade. The first widely popular espionage program of the 1960s, *The Man
from U.N.C.L.E.* (NBC, 1964–68), revisits the authoritative 1950s semidocumentary, but reconfigures the agent's relationship to the state as an implausible
farce. The program mocks earlier shows' authoritative address to the citizen-
viewer, and instead of the CIA and the FBI, it substitutes a set of quasi-official
bureaucracies: U.N.C.L.E. and T.H.R.U.S.H. This narrative motif is continued
in the half-hour comedy *Get Smart* (NBC/CBS, 1965–70), which similarly suggests that bureaucratic state authority and individual agency are irreconcilable—
the show's protagonist is a clumsy antihero, hopelessly hobbled by his own
bureaucratic parochialism. By the mid-1960s, the notion that the spy was an
uncompromising symbol of American moral leadership began to fray as well.
After a series of public relations fiascos for the U.S. government—the Soviet
downing of Francis Gary Powers's U2 spy plane in 1960, a botched 1961 counter-
revolutionary invasion of Cuba at the Bay of Pigs, and mounting evidence that
the CIA was violating both international and U.S. law in its Third World operations—spy programs became sites for the popular reevaluation of the spy as
an American ideal. *Get Smart* not only portrayed a bumbling agent, unable to
live up to the national ideal; the show was also one of the first public forums that
registered a growing public dismay over the interventionist tactics of the CIA.

The boom in espionage percolated across other television formats, including opportunistic spy-themed episodes of *Bewitched, Gilligan's Island,* and other
sitcoms.[5] In the final season of *77 Sunset Strip* (ABC, 1958–64), investigator Stu
Bailey returned to his past career as a World War II OSS agent, and began to
take on international cases. The show's star, Efrem Zimbalist Jr., went on to the
lead role in *The F.B.I.* (ABC, 1965–74); though more closely associated with the
Bureau than the 1950s semidocumentary spy programs, it rarely dealt with espionage and instead focused almost exclusively on domestic crime. The detective
drama *Burke's Law* (ABC, 1963–66) was transformed into *Amos Burke—Secret
Agent* for its final season, and it generated a spinoff detective series, *Honey West*
(ABC, 1965–66) that was popularly compared to other spy programs and Bond
films. The spate of spy-tinged programs also included *It Takes a Thief* (ABC,
1968–70), *The Man Who Never Was* (ABC, 1966–67), and the spy/western hybrid

Wild Wild West (CBS, 1965–70). Also on the air were several British imports, which were both popular and very economical purchases for the U.S. networks.[6] These included *The Avengers* (ABC, 1966–69), *Secret Agent* (CBS, 1965–66), *The Saint* (ABC, 1967–69), and *The Prisoner* (NBC, 1968). Throughout the mid-1960s, espionage emerged not so much as a genre unto itself, but rather as an inversion of other, more established generic narrative forms. Whether explicitly comic or linked to action and crime dramas, by the mid-1960s the spy was often a mechanism for disrupting and sometimes reconfiguring assumptions about televisual narrative, the coherence and stability of heroic protagonists, and the relationship between individuals and institutions.

This is not to say that the figure of the spy was stripped of its ideological pull as an ideal national citizen. In *I Spy* (NBC, 1965–68), this ideal is reinvigorated by a turn toward cultural relevance, diffracting spy programs' interrogation of agency onto ongoing cultural debates over African American citizenship and civic responsibility. In the program, the first dramatic series to star an African American actor, the civil rights movement and pan-Africanism collide; *I Spy* tests the geopolitical implications of black American travel and social mobility. In *Mission: Impossible* (CBS, 1966–73), longest running and last of the period's spy dramas, the notion of individual agency is nearly completely evacuated; its agents are anonymous mercenaries in service to the bureaucratic state. *Mission: Impossible* was also one of the first American television programs crafted specifically so as to ensure success on the international syndication market. The result is a contradictory text that is both intensely nationalistic and carefully circumspect about how its racial and cultural representations might interfere with its commercial viability. Spiraling outward from domestic postwar containment through the international "development decade," by the end of the 1960s these programs offered a model of American national identity that increasingly diverged from official state institutions, and instead was articulated alongside consumption, class privilege, and global mobility.

The shifts in these shows' representations of American national identity were closely tied to the changing political, cultural, and ideological landscape of the Cold War. Popularized by journalist Walter Lippman's 1947 book of the same title, the term "Cold War" has since become a kind of structuring shorthand, an endlessly expansive phrase that has come to encapsulate the zeitgeist of an era. The term's origins, though, lay in the postwar geographic and political tensions between the United States and the Soviet Union, whose wartime alliance had been tenuous at best. The 1945 Yalta Conference partitioned Germany, ceded control of Poland to the Soviets, and laid the foundations of the United Nations, but it didn't resolve the conflicts between the emerging superpowers. Instead, within a year of the war's end, Stalin had pronounced capitalism and Communism incompatible, and Winston Churchill had visited the United States and declared that "a shadow has fallen upon the scenes so lately lighted by Allied victory. From Stettin in the Baltic to Trieste in the Adriatic, an iron curtain has descended across the continent."[7] Also within that year conflicts over the control of Turkey and Iran prompted both superpowers to begin to remilitarize.[8]

The Cold War was never simply a political struggle, however; from its earliest moments, it was also characterized by profound restrictions of political and cultural expression in everyday American life. What we now in shorthand refer to as the Red Scare was a broadly dispersed anxiety that spread throughout American culture in the late 1940s and 1950s (although it must be noted that the term doesn't solely apply to this period—the American right reacted similarly to the creation of the Soviet state at the end of World War I, with a concomitant antagonism toward social movements such as women's suffrage and Garveyism that paralleled the containment culture of the post–World War II period).[9] Though Wisconsin senator Joseph McCarthy is among the most memorable of its antagonists, other figures and groups arguably had more direct political influence. The hearings convened by the House Un-American Activities Committee (HUAC) certainly had the most immediate impact upon the entertainment industry.[10]

The creation of HUAC in 1938 was as much a response to the institutionalization of progressive social programs of the New Deal as to a direct Communist threat. To be affiliated with the Communist Party of the U.S.A.—both before and during World War II—wasn't necessarily to be labeled an insurgent; the party's membership and influence grew throughout the 1930s, buoyed by the left politics of the New Deal and the liberal anti-Fascist movement. The two-year period between the Hitler-Stalin nonaggression pact and the German invasion of the Soviet Union, however, provoked renewed suspicion of Communists, leading to increased power for the Committee and the passage of the Smith Act that outlawed subversive political organizations. The Committee's first target was the Works Progress Administration (WPA), which provided federal jobs in rebuilding and expanding civil infrastructure and cultural institutions. Chairman Martin Dies, a fierce anti-Communist, charged that the "WPA was the greatest financial boon which ever came to the Communists in the United States. Stalin could not have done better by his American friends and agents."[11] Dies directed his wrath at the WPA-funded Federal Theater Project; ironically this lesser-known HUAC investigation was likely the most accurate in its accusations. It was the series of investigations that the Committee began after the war, however, that would shake the motion picture and television industries.

In October 1947, HUAC began its interrogation of high-profile witnesses in its search for Communists and sympathizers, or "fellow travelers." Among the first friendly witnesses were studio chiefs Jack Warner and Walt Disney, Screen Actors Guild president Ronald Reagan, novelist Ayn Rand, and actor Gary Cooper. Based upon their testimony and that of others, the Committee questioned dozens of suspected Communists. The Committee's scrutiny was particularly directed toward writers and the Screen Writers Guild, in part because of their association with the theater groups that had been investigated before the war. Those who acknowledged their association would be excused if they submitted the names of other Communists; those who refused to answer were almost invariably blacklisted by the motion-picture studios, who were keen to preserve their relationships with the Committee. The Hollywood Ten— including prominent screenwriters Ring Lardner Jr. and Dalton Trumbo— refused to cooperate, were held in contempt of Congress, and jailed. Some of those scrutinized were recently discharged veterans, but that wasn't sufficient proof of patriotism. Those who had supported or enlisted in the Abraham Lincoln Brigade in the Spanish Civil War earned a special label—that of "premature anti-Fascist."[12]

By 1950 tensions were continuing to rise. The Soviets had successfully tested a nuclear weapon, the Chinese revolution had brought Mao to power, the Rosenbergs were arrested on suspicion of nuclear espionage, and President Truman had created the CIA and NSA and initiated loyalty oaths for federal employees.[13] Early that year, Senator McCarthy appeared before a West Virginia Republican women's group and announced that he held the names of 205 Communists within the State Department, considered by the right to be a stronghold of

"Red" influence in the Democratic administration.[14] As McCarthy began his investigations in the Senate, HUAC renewed its interrogation of Hollywood writers, directors, and actors, asking them the infamous question: "Are you now or have you ever been a member of the Communist party?" The Committee's investigations in 1951 and 1952 were even more exhaustive than those of 1947, and their work was supplemented by *Red Channels: The Report of Communist Influence in Radio and Television.* The publication was the work of a private anti-Communist group formed by former FBI agents; for fear of boycott or political pressure, the motion-picture studios refused to employ anyone named in its pages. The Republican presidential victory in November 1952 somewhat tempered HUAC's zeal. McCarthy was censured by the Senate in 1954, having failed to produce any evidence to support his claims. HUAC's influence had peaked (its most noteworthy subsequent hearings were its 1956 investigations of playwright Arthur Miller and African American actor Paul Robeson), but its paranoid chill pervaded the film and television industries for years to follow.

The broader cultural climate of Red-baiting suspicion and pressures toward political conformity extended well beyond the hearing rooms of the Senate and House. America in the 1950s was characterized by a conflation of popular definitions of domestic life with the political ideology of containment—the policy first articulated by diplomat George Kennan that called for the economic and political isolation of the Soviet state. The principle of containment prompted President Truman's decision to extend military and economic aid to Greece and Turkey in 1947, the creation of NATO in 1949, and the U.S. commitment to rebuild the western European economies under the Marshall Plan. It also underlay the U.S. decision to enter the Korean and Vietnam wars to prevent the spread of Communism via the "domino theory." But while containment's origins lay in official politics, it was more directly felt by most Americans as a constriction of social norms. The postwar period was one of tumultuous transformations—it saw the rapid development of the planned suburb and the ascendance of the white middle classes that largely inhabited them, the professionalization and bureaucratization of work, and deep social anxieties over the status of millions of women who had flooded the American workplace during World War II. The period was characterized by retrenchment of gender roles, the valorization of a "traditional" nuclear family (though such a thing scarcely existed, then or now), and intense pressures to conform. Political loyalty and loyalty to social norms were in many cases equated; women who dared challenge the ideology of domestic motherhood ran the risk of being labeled unnatural, insurgent, or both.[15] Cold War political struggles were mapped onto the domestic sphere not just through gender norms, but also through a blend of consumerism and technological utopianism; when he visited the 1959 American National Exhibition in Moscow, Vice President Richard Nixon debated Soviet premier Nikita Khrushchev about the merits of the time-saving conveniences to be found in the modern suburban home.[16]

The U.S.-Soviet political tensions that were at the heart of the Cold War continued to escalate throughout the 1950s. In 1954 the CIA overthrew the elected governments of Guatemala and Iran to install pro-Western regimes, and by 1956, the Soviets had crushed a Hungarian rebellion and created the Warsaw Pact to oppose NATO. In 1957 America's worst fears of Soviet nuclear power were seemingly realized when the successful Sputnik satellite launch demonstrated that two oceans weren't enough to guarantee safety. Castro's assumption of power in Cuba shortly thereafter only exacerbated these anxieties, and led to the disastrous CIA-sponsored invasion at the Bay of Pigs. The Soviets' successful downing of an American U2 spy plane and the construction of the Berlin Wall further eroded diplomatic relations between the superpowers, which reached a point of maximum crisis over the Soviet installation of nuclear missiles in Cuba in 1962.

The resolution of the missile crisis marked the first thawing of U.S.-Soviet relations. The Kremlin–White House telephone hotline was installed, and the first nuclear test ban was signed in 1963. Alan Nadel has suggested that the gradual thawing of the social strictures of containment culture was linked to these political transformations. The conflation of geopolitics with all aspects of American everyday life represented, to Nadel, an impossibly tight master narrative whose convoluted logic simply could not hold. Certainly, the early 1960s saw the reemergence of the political left that had been in hiding for over a decade. So, too, did the period see the broadening popularity of political movements once defined as dangerously dissident: Betty Friedan's *The Feminine Mystique* bespoke the corrosive frustration of the "illness that had no name," the U.S. civil rights movement was making concrete steps toward national acceptance, and an emerging youth culture began to articulate a voice of political opposition.[17]

This is not to say, however, that the American political landscape was shifting uniformly or linearly. Though they supported domestic social programs, Presidents Kennedy and Johnson were also adamant Cold Warriors; the lines of conflict simply shifted. When in 1964 the People's Republic of China tested its first nuclear weapon, the "Red menace" was relocated to Asia; the Gulf of Tonkin Resolution and the escalation of the war in Vietnam only contributed to this anxiety. And though the passage of the Civil Rights and Voting Rights Acts in 1964 and 1965 marked a distinct turning point in American racial politics, these gains also circumscribed the range of acceptable black political expression, and were arguably as much a public relations move to demonstrate American progressivism to the decolonizing Third World as they were an ethical act of civic conscience.[18] The Cold War was not simply an external conflict that was the province of official politics; instead, it was a persistent presence that shaped immediate questions of national identity, civic responsibility, and the limits of cultural expression.

Still, by the late 1960s the terms of political and cultural debate in America were clearly changing. In 1966 the magazine *Ramparts* revealed the CIA's extensive use of academic departments at American universities to funnel arms and money to covert operations around the world.[19] Subsequent revelations exposed the Agency's infiltration and surveillance of student organizations and black activist groups across the country. By 1968—the year of the My Lai massacre and the Tet Offensive—the U.S. antiwar movement was widespread and vocal, and even Walter Cronkite, the leading voice of legitimate journalism, had declared the Vietnam War an unwinnable quagmire. Popular media that had been so central a component of containment culture began to show signs of embracing the counterculture; the blacklisted folk singer Pete Seeger appeared on network television for the first time in over a decade when he sang the thinly veiled antiwar allegory, "Waist Deep in the Big Muddy." While *The Smothers Brothers* variety program on which he appeared was scrutinized and eventually cancelled by CBS, it was nonetheless a point of rupture that, as Aniko Bodroghkozy writes, showed that "popular culture could have radical implications at certain historical moments when every institution and facet of the social order suddenly become possible grounds for the unmasking and overthrowing of delegitimized power."[20] That same year, Abbie Hoffman appeared before HUAC in his American flag shirt, turning the hearing chamber into a spectacle; Robert Vaughn (himself a prominent symbol of the shifting cultural and political environment) wrote that the once-omnipotent Committee "sat mute while they were lectured to by hippies, yippies, old Marxists and young radicals."[21] The lasting implications of these changes are anything but clear, however; the Vietnam War dragged on for several more years, including the expansion into Cambodia in 1970 that sparked the fatal protests at Kent State University in Ohio. The period also saw the conservative retrenchment of Nixon's "silent majority," and by the end of the 1970s the "new" Cold War with the Soviets was escalating, even as the CIA's Third World meddling was publicly condemned by the Senate's Church Committee in a climate of post-Watergate reform.[22]

Perhaps one of the most noteworthy transformations within American culture after the restrictive environment of the Red Scare 1950s was the reclamation of relatively sanctioned zones of skepticism within popular culture. It is overly simplistic to suggest that the 1950s was univocally restrictive or that it excluded all dissent, or conversely that by the late 1960s dissent was systemically or uniformly accepted. Even the seemingly unstoppable political juggernaut of McCarthyism was, after all, directly challenged at its height by Edward R. Murrow's *See It Now,* and the work of blacklisted writers often found its way onto television through various circuitous means.[23] Still, though, the ideological containment of the early Cold War was matched by a relatively young television industry, weakened by the blacklist, and in which the centralization of network power contributed to a relatively narrow range of cultural discourses. What is fascinating about the shifts in American culture in general—and in narrative television in particular—over this roughly twenty-year span is not some sort of progress narrative of liberalization, but rather the shifting ways in which popular culture gives voice to national identity. The first decade of the Cold War was often characterized by a tight correspondence between state institutions, the television industry, and the representations it circulated. By the end of the 1960s, however, a more politically independent and internationally minded TV industry aired programs that increasingly articulated national identity not through official state politics, but rather through liberal pluralism, class mobility, and consumerism.

Espionage programs were and are central to such a conversation. The earliest programs articulate what might be termed a kind of vulgar nationalism. In them, the meanings of national identity, patriotism, and subversion are seemingly self-evident; redolent of smug confidence, the iconic mid-1950s espionage drama *I Led 3 Lives* offered authoritative lessons in how one might identify a closet Communist or "parlor pink." Due to a variety of influences—political, economic, and cultural—such representations gradually gave way to programs in which the national interest was a bit more ambiguous, even opaque. The apparent amorality of *Mission: Impossible* (its agents were, after all, little more than soldiers of fortune) could not be farther from the forthright moral logic of *I Led 3 Lives* and its contemporaries *The Man Called X* and *Behind Closed Doors*. *The Man from U.N.C.L.E.* and *Get Smart* often directly challenged the legitimacy of the authoritative nationalist narratives that preceded them; by doing so, they didn't render nationalism obsolete, but they spoke of the national in a way that was self-conscious, even playful. The Cold War still mattered; it just mattered in less overt, more malleable ways. As Frederick Dolan writes,

> The Cold War was *constitutive* of American national identity. While it prevailed, its vocabulary shaped the nation's tasks, policies, and pursuits, forming a frame through which issues as different from one another as civil rights, dissent, culture, education, and the economy could be weighed together in terms of their significance for the nation's struggle with a worldwide communist movement.[24]

David Brown begins his book *Contemporary Nationalism* with the observation (borrowed from the second Psalm, via Handel) that the nation is a "vain thing"—an artifice, fleeting and impermanent. So, too, did Benedict Anderson observe that the nation is imagined—a product not of natural law or divine order, but of human history, politics, and systems of communication. Still, this imaginary community is not just a potent political force, but a personal one as well. National identity is deeply felt, often as profoundly and innately as race or gender identification. This is the irony of nations—their historical transience is continually elided through discourses of timeless essence and innate belonging. As Slavoj Zizek notes, these discourses aren't easily dismissed: "To emphasize in a 'deconstructionist' mode that Nation is not a biological or transhistorical fact but a contingent discursive construction, an overdetermined result of textual practices, is thus misleading: such an emphasis overlooks the remainder of some *real,* nondiscursive kernel of enjoyment which must be present for the Nation qua discursive entity-effect to achieve its ontological status." The nation's political and cultural salience—its effectiveness as discourse—is founded on its own claims of prediscursive presence. National identity isn't experienced as a discursive practice; it's experienced as a concrete relationship to a real thing.[25]

Despite—or because of—the powerful pull of national identity, "nationalism" is something of a dirty word, both popularly and critically. In part, this is because of distinctions that are made between what Brown calls civic and ethnic or ethnocultural nationalisms. He characterizes civic nationalism as "the belief that residence in a common territorial homeland, and commitment to its state and civil society institutions, generate a distinctive national character and civic culture, such that all citizens, irrespective of their diverse ancestry, comprise a community in progress, with a common destiny." Civic nationalism is the ideal of Rawlsian political liberalism, of a common public culture, of participatory democracy and Habermas's public sphere. Ethnocultural nationalism, on the other hand, "refers to a sense of community which focuses on belief in myths of common ancestry; and on the perception that these myths are validated by contemporary similarities of, for example, physiognomy, language, or religion." Ethnocultural nationalism, which often has little to do with official state political boundaries, is the nationalism of birthright, heritage, and—in the extreme case—ethnic cleansing. Ethnocultural nationalism essentializes and privileges difference; civic nationalism pretends it isn't there.[26]

Civic nationalism is also the nationalism of nation-building, posited in the language of international development as an alternative, even antidote, to what is characterized as the crude xenophobia and violence of ethnic nationalism. From this perspective, for example, Monroe Price seeks to "determine how the state can generate, sustain, or encourage narratives to communal well being and remain true to democratic values." For such critics, the public sphere and the nation are both imagined as relatively unified wholes—zones of conflict but still dedicated to the liberal goal of the public sphere as a zone of Habermasian "ideal speech situations" where autonomous citizens might debate in a climate of egalitarian respect. Maurizio Viroli similarly attempts to reclaim a form of nationalism he calls republican patriotism, formed through "attachment to the laws, the constitution and the way of life of a particular republic.

Republican patriotism is also distinct from ethnic nationalism because it does not attach moral or political relevance to ethnicity; on the contrary, it recognizes moral and political relevance, and beauty, in the political values of citizenship, particularly republican equality, which are hostile to ethnocentrism."[27]

The degree to which we can avoid attaching "moral or political relevance to ethnicity," though, remains open to question. Nancy Fraser and others have critiqued the Habermasian public sphere in part because it assumes equality of participation and access and undervalues the importance of competing subcultures and alternative manifestations of the public sphere. Furthermore, advocates of civic nationalisms assume that ethnic, regional, class, and gender identities can be subsumed within, or bracketed distinctly from, one's citizenship. "The central claim," Margaret Canovan writes, "is that patriotism means the political loyalty of citizens to the free polity they share, whereas nationalism is a matter of ethnicity and culture. . . . Unlike nationalism (it is argued), patriotism is not exclusive, uncritical or bellicose, and is therefore compatible with commitments to universal humanity. Unlike nationalism, patriotism does not expect or demand ethnic and cultural homogeneity, and is therefore tolerant of diversity." But, as Canovan insists, civic nationalisms make much the same exclusions as the cruder, more "bellicose" versions: "even the most apparently cosmopolitan constitutional patriotism does not alter the fundamental truth that citizenship is first and foremost an inherited privilege . . . [a] commitment to the persistence of a polity belonging to a privileged subsection of humankind—'our people.'" Nationalism excludes.[28]

The most powerful expressions of nationalism blend the civic and the ethnocultural, constructing a modern political subjectivity on underlying discourses of ethnic and/or cultural heritage.[29] George Mosse's *Nationalization of the Masses,* for example, discusses how German politicians and other cultural leaders promoted a "national liturgy" formed around a combination of monumental architecture, pagan and Christian religious traditions, and classical Greek ideals of beauty and form.[30] By lionizing the masculine valor and heroism of generals and political leaders, Nazi monumentalism helped contribute to a nationalistic pride that centered around ancestor worship. This century's most prominent expression of ethnocultural nationalism by a modern state, Nazi Germany didn't completely eliminate civic participation—instead, it promoted it, while also establishing violent and essentialist prerequisites for the recognition of civil subjects. Where the two intertwine is in the appropriative process of history; when civic nationalism appeals to a shared heritage, it borrows from and reinforces ethnocultural distinctions. And when Price seeks to develop modern nations by reinforcing the "historic values which reinforce community," he necessarily invokes mechanisms of exclusion; whether the product of a liberal state or an ethnic subculture, the nation is a difference engine.[31]

The machine of nationalist identification churns ever on—crafting and recrafting its histories to recenter the present, continually rewriting narratives of internal coherence and externalized difference. While discourses of nationalism often insist that the nation is an inherent, natural expression of collective will and sentiment, it is continually being reshaped and reformed. This is what prompts Andrew Parker et al. to write, "Hence, on the one hand, the nation's insatiable need to administer difference through violent acts of segregation, censorship, economic coercion, physical torture, police brutality. And hence, on the other, the nation's insatiable need for representational labor to supplement its founding ambivalence, the lack of self-presence at its origin." The ongoing representational work of defining that which is national doesn't dissipate in the hybrid, multiethnic, liberal states of late capitalism; instead, the sometimes rapid demographic and cultural upheavals of contemporary society make narratives of belonging ever more in demand. Pondering the question of whether nations have an essential origin or are purely imagined, Ernest Gellner writes, "Some nations have navels, some achieve navels, some have navels thrust upon them. Those possessed of genuine ones are probably in a minority, but it matters little. It is the need for navels engendered by modernity that matters."[32]

Media of various forms are central to the constitution of a national identity. For Benedict Anderson, the rise of the modern nation-state is closely intertwined with the development of print media, which unite disparate communities around an "imagined" collective center.[33] This culminates in the development of the concept of "meanwhile," the notion that geographically disparate groups might engage in moments of simultaneous mediated cultural interaction. While Anderson has been critiqued for perhaps drawing too neat a distinction between the premodern and the modern state (overlooking different trajectories of media development in the colonial world, for example), *Imagined Communities* continues to exert an enduring influence upon contemporary broadcast media scholarship. Anderson's model has influenced the work of scholars like Michele Hilmes, who has discussed the ways in which radio and television have contributed to the formation of national cultures by casting the immigrant experience as central to a shared American heritage.[34] Similarly, Nina Liebman and Alan Nadel have shown how postwar American television bridged the gulf between the private and public spheres—in part by linking norms of gender and class to national political concerns—and George Lipsitz has shown how media representations of ethnicity helped ameliorate post–World War II tensions surrounding suburbanization and consumerism.[35]

At stake in these representations is citizenship—that authorized subject position that is the seemingly natural product of national history and beneficiary of state institutions and processes. Historically, this privileged position has been both gendered and racialized, with full agency reserved for white men, though the specific terms and boundaries of that privilege have continually shifted. In *National Manhood: Capitalist Citizenship and the Imagined Fraternity of White Men,* Dana Nelson charts the influence of race and gender on ideals of citizenship during the late eighteenth and early nineteenth centuries, exploring "how and under what conditions 'white' manhood came to 'stand' for nation, how it came to be idealized as a 'representative' identity in the United States." Through an analysis of official political texts, medical journals, and nineteenth-century ethnographies, she discusses how white masculinity became established as an American national norm and ideal. "National/'white' manhood," Nelson writes, "however effective for certain [cultural] purposes, is not a 'unified' identity. It is an impossible identity—impossible in the sense that it is an always-agonistic position, making it difficult for any human to fit into a full sense of compatibility with its ideal construction." National manhood not only works to exclude women and people of color from full citizenship and agency; it also is an impossible ideal for white men themselves.[36]

It is overly simplistic, then, just to identify the normative impulses within a particular set of representations or discourses. While dominant norms of citizenship do largely mirror the race, gender, and class hierarchies that suffuse American society, the ways in which those norms are articulated—and the externalized threats against which they are measured—vary considerably. In *Being Political: Genealogies of Citizenship,* Engin Isin argues that citizenship, while constituted in discourses of exclusion—of those various strangers and

outsiders who are deemed unworthy of fully vested social and political agency—
cannot ever fully exclude that which it denies. Indeed, the ongoing cultural struggles of "being political"—making demands upon the social body to change in
some systemic way—require a sense of otherness, of marginality. Isin "considers citizenship as that kind of identity with a city or state that certain agents
constitute as virtuous, good, righteous, and superior, and differentiate it from
strangers, outsiders, and aliens who they constitute as their alterity via various
solidaristic, agonistic, and alienating strategies and technologies. Citizenship
exists through its alterity and strategies, and technologies of citizenship are
about the dialogic constitution of these identities via games of conduct."[37] Citizenship, in other words, is constitutive—not just of the idealized category of
"citizen," but of its others as well.

   This book thus explores not just the normative impulse within these programs, but also the movement across the boundaries of acceptable citizenship
that continually redefined American national identity during the Cold War. In
her analysis of the political protests of turn-of-the-century women garment
workers, Nan Enstad writes, "Relying on a range of cultural theories, scholars
explore the political significance of culture in the daily lives of historical actors
whom they position in a field of cultural contradictions and limited agency. . . .
[But] while scholars show identities to be historically constructed rather than
essential, they often present them as fixed and stable." The danger, for Enstad,
of historical scholarship that ascribes relatively fixed identities to past political
and cultural movements is that some of the most progressive potentials of those
movements can be too easily overlooked. Following Judith Butler, she writes
that "when individuals are constructed to match the ideal of the rational political subject, they become recognizable as such to others. But this subjectivity is
not the only historical possibility. We need a more sophisticated inquiry into
the diversity and range of political subjectivities and how they form." By
exploring not just spy programs' norms, but rather their mechanisms of normalization, this book questions the foundations of national agency—how it is
that an individual comes to speak and act for a culture and a nation. In chart-
ing such a history of political subjectivities, it attempts to follow through on
Enstad's charge that we trace "the ways some identities become widely culturally intelligible and seem as natural and self-evident, while others recede into
epistemological obscurity."[38]

Given the transformations within American culture during the Cold War, espionage shows provide a rich opportunity to explore television's participation in the formation of a national culture. This book situates the spy programs of the 1950s and 1960s as part of the representational labor that maintained and redefined dominant definitions of American national identity during the period. It looks at how, in Homi Bhabha's phrase, the nation is narrated; that is, how the nation is constructed through ongoing discourses of cultural, racial, and gender difference, inscribed in trajectories of historical continuity. As E. Ann Kaplan puts it, "Viewing nation as narrative puts emphasis on how nation is articulated in language, signifiers, textuality, rhetoric. It emphasizes the difference between the nation-state as a set of regulations, policies, institutions, organization and *national* identity—that is nation as *culture*."[39]

This book begins with the early spy dramas that emerged as extensions of the semidocumentary crime format. Chapter 1, "Documentary Melodrama: Homegrown Spies and the Red Scare," explores how reality-based espionage programs of the 1950s established close relationships between producers and official political institutions. The FBI, the State Department, the Treasury Department, and the Department of Defense each contributed to, or were invoked by, programs during this period, and many of these shows were based on the exploits of current or former government agents. Such close correspondences helped to establish strict narrative conventions that framed Cold War ideological conflict as a gendered battle over the authority of a nationalistic, and masculinist, protagonist. In such narratives, the legitimating force of the state was never far from sight, and national authority was conflated with a highly reductive vision of an ideal postwar citizen. Chapter 2 examines the syndicated Ziv program *I Led 3 Lives* in detail, paying particular attention to how the agent draws his authority from domestic gender norms. In the show, Herb Philbrick's legitimacy as anti-Communist and federal agent is expressed through his intelligibility as a suburban patriarch. Rather than offer neatly enclosed fictional narratives, these 1950s programs regularly blurred the distinction between television as entertainment and television as a technologized extension of the public sphere. They directly cultivated a sense of civic nationalism by encouraging viewers to participate in neighborhood and city activities as a patriotic local corollary to the national efforts of the on-screen spies. Good citizens, they asserted, watched television.

Chapter 3 examines how documentarist narrative began to unravel in two transitional programs of the 1958–59 season. Neither *Behind Closed Doors* nor *World of Giants* was commercially successful, and each lasted just a single season. These shows nonetheless reveal an industry, and a culture, in transition. Last of the reality-based programs, *Behind Closed Doors* was based loosely on the book of the same title by a retired senior military intelligence officer, and the show's production methods, narrative format, and stylistic cues closely resemble semidocumentaries of the early 1950s. But due to a number of influences—including shifting relationships with sponsors, a complicated and often cumbersome coproduction environment, and sinking audience credulity in the format, *Behind Closed Doors* was canceled in its first season. The Ziv production of *World of Giants* that same year was a similar commercial disappointment. The show is fascinating, though, in how it blends documentarism with a narrative device drawn straight from nuclear paranoia films; its protagonist has been shrunken to six inches tall in an experimental jet-fuel accident. The result is a convoluted mix of authoritative nationalism and science fiction. Together, these two shows are important not just because they reveal the limits of the semidocumentary narrative, but more specifically because they reveal the incongruities between divergent modes of narrative credibility: those of documentary facticity and classical realist narrative.

Chapter 4, "Parody and the Limits of Agency" explores how spy shows' origins in officially sanctioned realism contributed to a countervailing tendency toward satire. After the 1962 release of the first Bond film, *Dr. No,* many espionage programs quickly incorporated elements of self-referentiality, parody, and humor. *The Man from U.N.C.L.E.* was a self-conscious send-up of both the Bond films and earlier American espionage dramas, while *Get Smart* was a spoof created by Mel Brooks. These programs parody the authoritative address of the earlier "documentary melodramas," and in them the tight correspondence between nation and gendered representations begins to fray. In these shows, the very notion that the masculine agent might act directly on behalf of the state becomes the principal source of humor and critique. These programs were central to the emergence of self-conscious camp in mid-1960s American television, which plundered the popular culture past, inverting and sometimes subverting its norms, narratives, and authoritative truth claims.

The final two chapters are case studies of two of the most critically and commercially successful spy programs of the 1960s. Though neither invokes the authoritative documentary discourses of the previous decade, both participate in important redefinitions of American identity in the context of the international 1960s. Chapter 5 explores how the American civil rights movement was folded into dominant definitions of American national identity. Airing alongside the spy parodies *U.N.C.L.E.* and *Get Smart*, *I Spy* straddles a tumultuous period for both the civil rights movement and the decolonization of the developing world. As African American activists began to look outside the United States for political and cultural affiliations — to anticolonial movements in Africa, to the Marxist theories of Albert Memmi and Frantz Fanon, and to Islam — *I Spy* contributed to the formation of a black American political sensibility that was resolutely American in origin. Far from being exhausted of its nationalistic pull, here the figure of the spy is mobilized amid shifting social conditions to reassert the viability of a historically constituted ideal American subject. At a moment of anxiety over pan-Africanism, *I Spy* constructs a distinctly American black subjectivity, founded in discourses of American liberalism and enriched by class mobility and leisure. The program was one of the earliest instantiations of what Herman Gray calls the "civil rights subject," a reductive trope of African American identity that is detached from international political and cultural movements and anchored instead to foundational American national ideals of self-determination and individual liberties.[40] In a sense, then, *I Spy* represents a new form of containment narrative, one that symbolically incorporates African Americans into the American national body in order to mitigate pan-African critiques of American racism.

Issues of internationalism and the implications of U.S. interventionism converge in *Mission: Impossible,* which is discussed in chapter 6. The program, itself only the second network drama with an African American costar, navigates a delicate path between jingoistic American paternalism and benevolent internationalism. During this period of newly emergent nations and pluralized global identities, the program devoted prodigious energy to researching its representations of cultures abroad. As global media infrastructures developed in the 1960s, international distribution became increasingly important to U.S. television networks and studios. This growing market led producers to craft each episode carefully in order to avoid offending or alienating international audiences, while continuing to present a normative view of U.S. supremacy. *Mission: Impossible* offers a unique opportunity to examine the strategies employed by the show's producers in forging their representations of international "others." The program was a highly productive source of cultural representations that recentered American identity in new global contexts.

Last among the U.S. spy dramas of the period, *Mission: Impossible* was also indirectly but significantly influenced by the Vietnam War. The program's narratives of American technocratic superiority and its agents' disregard for international law provoked criticism from audiences in the United States and abroad, a generalized sentiment that led to the virtual disappearance of spy programs by the early 1970s. At a time when America's "real" international agents abroad were the young men dying in a highly televised and ill-defined conflict in Vietnam, the romantic appeal of suave globe-trotting agents began to lose its luster. By 1970 *Mission: Impossible*—the show whose agents most directly matched the covert and illegal practices of the CIA at the time—was converted into a domestic crime drama. Just as the spy programs emerged out of domestic "true crime" programs in the early 1950s—marking the onset of an important period of international possibility and expansion—by the end of the 1960s spy programs collapsed inward, back toward domestic settings and conflicts.

These programs sit on the cusp between two very different forms of truth-telling—sometimes contradictory, sometimes complementary. The first is the truth of the undeniable fact, of the newscast, of documentary evidence, authoritatively revealed. The second is that of realist narrative, compelling because the desires and motivations of its characters seem natural, commonsensical, inevitable. One way to explain the shifting discourses of TV spy programs is that they emerge out of the former and gradually evolve toward the latter. The process of transformation isn't exactly linear, though, and the boundaries between the two are indistinct. Even the most rigidly factual documentary is also a narrative, complete with protagonists, antagonists, rising conflict, and a resolution, whether tragic or comic. At the same time, the legitimacy of realist narrative derives from its verisimilitude; we lend it credibility because it seems, more or less, to be an analog of the world as we know and assume it to be. What makes spy shows particularly noteworthy, though, is the relative force of *both* these standards of realism. Authenticated not just by documentary evidence, but by powerful authority figures (military leaders, political figures, popular heroes), these shows are also intensely affective, psychologically fraught narratives of personal transformation.

The result is a specifically televisual kind of realism, what John Caughie calls "an *aesthetics* of immediacy... exploiting the illusion of the real for political ends." In such narratives, "the two discourses, of documentary and drama, are integrated to produce a self-confirming system of images and looks, a self-authenticating discourse of truth."[41] From the Red Scare programs' unitary white paternal agent to *I Spy*'s black cultural emissary and *Mission: Impossible*'s fascination with masquerading as the Other, these programs were mechanisms through which American national identity could be continually renegotiated amid destabilizing political and cultural conditions. Nations are constructed in the popular imaginary as timeless entities, marked by continuity and permanence. But in the face of social changes—shifting race relations, domestic work patterns, geopolitics, economics, and so on—nations and their nationalisms are faced with an ongoing historicist problem. Oscillating between what Frederick Dolan describes as the "two poles of, on the one hand, solid foundations or grand narratives and, on the other, the ever present threat of the collapse of absolutes," they must keep some notion of a unified past centered squarely in the rear-view mirror even as they plummet down the winding road of the present.[42] As nations change, so too do their histories, citizens, and subjects.

Documentary Melodrama
Homegrown Spies and the Red Scare

Dear Lou:

I think the time is ripe for the Bureau to get into television.

—LETTER FROM CHARLES C. BARRY, NBC EXECUTIVE, TO LOUIS
NICHOLS, ASSISTANT TO THE DIRECTOR OF FBI, JUNE 1953

Spies were everywhere in 1950s American media culture. Villains and heroes, they emerged from the shadows just long enough to affirm America's worst fears of Communist infiltration. The Red Scare of the late 1940s and early 1950s insisted that Communist spies lurked behind every curtained window and at the corners of every film set, as Senator Joseph McCarthy and the House Un-American Activities Committee proclaimed that a vast Communist conspiracy threatened to undo American democracy. J. Edgar Hoover's FBI stretched its net widely for subversives, and Hoover used popular media to extend his reach. While only a few documented cases of espionage made it to trial, those that did sparked significant media attention. Dramatic cases like those of Julius and Ethel Rosenberg fueled further investigations and contributed to popular anxiety over the possibility that the friendly neighbor next door might really be a Communist spy or a "parlor pink." Most of the spies in postwar America, however, were fictional.

Books, magazines, film, radio, and television were filled with the exploits of secret agents, real and imagined. Popular biographies documented the lives of spies like Mathilde Carré, a World War II double agent whose alias, "the Cat," was attributed to her green eyes, her "somewhat fang-like teeth," and her habit of "curling up in a leather chair and nervously scratching its arms with her fingernails."[1] Communists like Matt Cvetic, Herbert Philbrick, and Winston Burdett testified against their former comrades and became American heroes overnight. Popular magazines such as *Coronet, Reader's Digest,* and *The Saturday Evening Post*—as well as the news weeklies *Time, Newsweek,* and *U.S. News and World Report*—ran lengthy articles about the adventures of real spies. In "Spies in U.S. Told Russia All," *U.S. News* insisted that "tales of espionage, intrigue are not just dream stories. They're the real thing. Here, taken from court records, are details on how spies work, as supplied by the spies themselves."[2] Films like *Walk East on Beacon* (1952) brought the threat of Communist infiltration to American shores; *I Married a Communist* (1949) and *My Son John* (1952) found subversion within the family itself.[3] The line between "real" espionage and Hollywood "dream stories," however, was blurry at best. Informer Matt Cvetic's experiences were adapted into the fictional radio serial *I Was a Communist for the FBI* in the late 1940s, and in 1951 Warner Brothers released a feature film under the same title that earned an Oscar nomination as, remarkably, "Best Documentary."

Many of the most popular representations of spies in the 1950s appeared on television, where the distinctions between documentary and fiction grew even dimmer. These programs emerged directly out of breathless biographical accounts of intrigue during World War II. In the late 1940s and early 1950s, a number of "spymasters" and operatives capitalized on their daring past lives and wrote widely popular books. Television producers snatched up several of these books and put them in series production. Herbert Philbrick, an FBI informer, wrote an account of his years as a secret Communist (and double agent) in Boston during and after the war. In 1953 Ziv Television Productions adapted that book, *I Led 3 Lives,* into a highly successful syndicated series. In 1955 Ziv also capitalized on a memoir by Ladislas Farago—an espionage enthusiast and journalist who did a wartime turn with the Office of Naval Intelligence. The independent production company turned Farago's book, *War of Wits: The Anatomy of Espionage and Intelligence* (1954), into another series, *The Man Called X* (1955–57). One of the highest-ranking American spies to go public was Rear Admiral Ellis Zacharias, who as former head of Naval Intelligence cowrote a memoir with Farago entitled *Behind Closed Doors: The Secret History of the Cold War.* In 1958 that book became the basis of yet another series, NBC's *Behind Closed Doors.*

The nonfiction, "based-in-fact" truth claims of popular espionage narratives were extensions of the true crime genre that was already a mainstay of pulp fiction and late-1940s cinema, and which was becoming increasingly popular in television as well.[4] By invoking this "semidocumentary" narrative style, these programs articulated a kind of civic nationalism linked to the institution of television itself. Exploiting the factual basis of their source material, such programs as *Treasury Men in Action, I Led 3 Lives,* and *The Man Called X* were part of broader efforts to harness the private, domestic practice of television viewing as a civic responsibility and a public practice. Amid social anxieties over the invasive new medium, networks and independent producers alike sought to burnish their public service credentials, showing that television viewing could be a responsible civic activity. "Documentary style" crime, war, and espionage shows invited the viewer to participate in the protection of the American state. NBC, for example, aired a number of based-in-fact programs in the early 1950s, including *Dragnet, Medic, The Big Story,* and *American Inventory,* as well as the World War II documentary *Victory at Sea. Medic* won industry awards as an outstanding "documentary dramatic series" that traced the exploits of a top-notch medical rescue team, and *Dragnet* was promoted as "an engrossing, behind the scenes dramatization of your police force in action."[5] According to NBC, such "prestige programming" served "a profitable two-fold purpose: to build maximum audience . . . and widespread community goodwill."[6] The earliest espionage shows emerged from this cycle of programs, and their reality basis was for producers both an effective marketing device and a symbol of their civic responsibility.

Reality-based programs provided an economical ready source of storylines for a growing new medium. Producers culled the back files of police and military cases and assigned stories to a pool of staff writers who quickly produced half-hour scripts. As a promotional tool, these shows' low-budget production was an asset rather than a liability, and technical inconsistencies like uneven lighting, sparse sets, and botched dialogue were dismissed as evidence of their "documentary" status. Promotion materials and credit sequences reminded viewers that these were harrowing tales of real valor, not simply the fabrications of a screenwriter. As an NBC press release was quick to point out, "*Treasury Men in Action* is based on actual cases taken from the Department's closed files, and each script has its official approval."[7] *I Led 3 Lives* was similarly promoted as "fantastically true," and "not just a scriptwriter's fantasy."[8] Thus while produced on the cheap, these shows relied on their documentary status to gain credibility as quality television with a civic function.

These programs also gave federal agencies an important contact point with the public. While the federal government has always had a regulatory influence on television, in the case of 1950s espionage programs there was a textual connection as well. Many of these shows were produced with the cooperation of either the federal government or former agents, which gave the state a direct presence in fictional narratives of national identity. The close relationship between state institutions and broadcasters served several purposes: for broadcasters, it gave a much-needed legitimacy to the fledgling medium; for producers, state endorsement was an important promotional tool; for the FBI and other agencies, it was an opportunity to help shape a powerful new medium that bridged the public and private spheres. Though the FBI, in particular, was cautious about too close an association with the networks and studios (the motion-picture and television industries were rocked by accusations of Communist infiltration, and its workers were often under direct investigation), television's potential for collective cultural address offered an important point of contact between the state and the private lives of Americans. The HUAC hearings were far from the only significant media events addressing the relationship between espionage and citizenship in the 1950s; each week fictional TV programs provided further lessons about what it meant to be a good citizen.

Television's preoccupation with "real" events and scenarios wasn't limited to purely documentary news programming. More important is the medium's broader investment in the everyday and the "real" as a mode of civic public address—what John Corner terms its *documentarism*. From stars who play "themselves" (as with *Burns and Allen* and *The Adventures of Ozzie and Harriet*) to reality-based reenactments of crimes and major public events, "programs which offer depictions of actuality, with or without exposition, have always been central to television's appeal." Such depictions, according to Corner, bridge the public and private spheres by projecting an idealized public spectator, together with their civic identity, into a dramatic narrative. It is not necessary to insist or even assume that the viewer accepts that the particular television narrative at question is completely, unerringly true. Instead, through reality-based programs, television "elicits from its viewers certain kinds of *investments of self*.... This capacity is an important aspect of its 'public' character—to call viewers into empathy and understanding; to create a 'virtual community' of the commonly concerned, of vicarious witness; to cut through accommodating abstraction with the force and surprise of 'things themselves.'"[9]

Through their documentarism, programs like *Treasury Men in Action, I Led 3 Lives,* and *The Man Called X* also established a televisual mode of civic nationalism. Commended by such groups as the American Legion, the Daughters of the American Revolution, and the Freedom Foundation as educational resources in the cultural battle for American democracy, these shows equated anti-Communism with civic involvement. By appealing to viewers to participate in their communities, support churches and local government, and maintain a vigilant lookout for subversives, they linked the act of television viewing to state authority, national identity, and local civic responsibility.

Finally, although documentary realism was crucial to these programs' "virtual community of vicarious witness," the conventions of narrative television drama were as well. The industry developed a curious term for precisely these types of shows—"documentary melodrama."[10] This seemingly contradictory term is nonetheless an apt one for the early espionage programs. While they professed to be documentary accounts of verifiable historical fact, these shows also drew upon the dramatic conventions of crime and action genres. They took great liberties with historical information, and instead relied heavily upon the narrative persona of the star agent to provide both a narrative and a historical anchor. As melodramas, they translated distant geopolitical events into familiar, and often familial, everyday incidents. In *I Led 3 Lives,* for example—the spy program most centered on everyday domestic life—much of the drama comes from tensions surrounding the insubordination of a child, uncontained or "misguided" female sexuality, or an "inappropriate" distribution of gendered power within the home. In these programs, the individual masculine protagonist becomes the literal embodiment of state and national interests, whose future depends upon the maintenance not only of a democratic social order and capitalist economic system, but also on the perpetuation of stable gender identities. Thus while their documentarism marked them as virtual organs of the state, espionage programs also reduced the state to the figure of a white masculine protagonist, establishing narrative television itself as a means of constituting American national identity.

Spy Culture: Popular Espionage, "Documentary Melodrama," and NBC's "FBI Project"

The earliest espionage television programs emerged from a media culture fascinated with spies and fearful of Communist subversion. Tales of World War II adventure permeated the press well into the 1950s, and magazines ran serialized accounts of wartime espionage, under titles like "I Was a Woman Spy," the true story of a French Canadian woman knighted by the British government for her service during World War II. Transcripts from Senate and House committee testimony were reprinted in mainstream magazines. Winston Burdett told his tale of personal involvement with the Communist Party before and during World War II to the 1955 Senate Internal Security Subcommittee, and *U.S. News and World Report* published his testimony under the title, "Onetime Spy Tells His Story: How U.S. Press Was Infiltrated by Communists." The nuclear espionage scandal that culminated in the execution of the Rosenbergs was a similar source of fascination; *Reader's Digest* called it the "Crime of the Century."[11]

Newspaper editors competed for compelling stories—the more salacious the better. When Don Whitehead wrote *The FBI Story* in 1956, competing newspapers clamored to serialize the book. An account of the FBI's role in counterespionage, the book was serialized by the Associated Press, and United Press and the *Chicago Tribune* Press Service quickly launched multipart series of their own. These serials borrowed heavily from one another, prompting scandals over plagiarism and copyright infringement. According to *Time,* the "*Tribune* hastily put together its own nine-part FBI story, [and] beat the AP's release date on using material from Whitehead's book. Though the *Tribune* claimed FBI cooperation, the series drew heavily on Whitehead's book for the first three installments, then turned to rewriting FBI stories in the *Trib*'s morgue." This enthusiasm spilled over into fictional accounts of espionage as well. Serials were popular in magazines like the *Saturday Evening Post,* whose "Spy and Counterspy" told of a scientist's brush with American Communists spying for Russia. These serial narratives influenced the early television espionage programs, which were often adapted directly from the printed page.[12]

With the exception of World War II memoirs, the accounts of espionage in American media during the 1950s were for the most part domestic in scope. Few articles discussed international spies, focusing instead on homefront subversives. As Cold War cultural historians Elaine Tyler May, Alan Nadel, and Nina Liebman have suggested, the media of the period often reinforced discourses of nationalistic containment, conflating Cold War political conflicts with struggles over shifting domestic gender roles.[13] Within this context, espionage— the most visible symbol of submerged Cold War political instabilities and a source of intriguing adventure narratives—also represented a means of regulating cultural and gender difference. For at precisely the time when suburbanization atomized urban communities and replaced them with a veneer of uniformity, and when sociologists decried the erosion of normative masculinity as the workplace became a bureaucratic machine staffed by anonymous "organization men," espionage sought out the hidden pockets that evaded homogeneity. During this era of containment, in which popular discourses proclaimed the civic virtue of nationalist conformity, domestic espionage was a mechanism for policing internal deviance. It is little wonder, then, that the espionage programs of the 1950s were often focused on ferreting out spies at home. Television, which linked the national public and the private home, was enlisted to help accomplish this task.

The federal agency responsible for domestic espionage and counterespionage was the FBI, and its outspoken director, J. Edgar Hoover, was a prominent media figure at the time. According to one account, "To U.S. newspaper readers, the FBI is such a familiar story that J. Edgar Hoover has supplanted the vacuum cleaner as a household word for efficiency." Hoover aggressively promoted both the Bureau and himself, writing book forewords, popular magazine articles, and selectively endorsing films and television programs. In articles like "What Makes an FBI Agent," Hoover wrote of his agents' valor and dedication to the public good. Mindful of the cultural and economic power that accompanied an official endorsement, Hoover doled out quotes and built a small industry around true stories of the FBI. As one journalist observed, "While editors scrapped, J. Edgar Hoover happily churned out 'exclusive' quotes and prefaces for competing sagas, and let each editor boast that the FBI had 'opened its files' wide." Always keen to shape the national character, the director wrote in the foreword to Whitehead's book that the FBI "is never very far from the crossroads of America, either spiritually or physically."[14]

When espionage made its way onto television, the first spy programs bore more similarity to the "true crime" detective and police shows of the early 1950s than they did to the dashing Bond films of the 1960s. One of the earliest American television programs to present its viewers with factual cases of deviance and espionage was *Treasury Men in Action* (ABC and NBC, 1951–54).[15] The show was based on the files of the Treasury Department, which oversaw the Secret Service and Customs Service, and each episode was a reenactment of a particular case. Episodes often dealt with tax fraud, bootlegging, or counterfeiting, and began to incorporate elements of international espionage. All the stories were taken directly from the files of the Treasury Department. In 1951 the show received the Sylvania Award for best "documentary melodrama," an industry prize that honored the show for tackling issues of pressing national concern.[16]

Most *Treasury Men* episodes began in the office of the Chief, played by actor Walter Greaza. The program was a live anthology series with a changing cast that reenacted particular crimes on a studio set. The Chief, in direct address, would invite viewers to take part in—simply by watching—a civic investigation of "anti-American" crime. "This is Secret Service," he would declare, "and tonight, in the role of the chief enforcement officer of the United States, I want to tell you one of the strangest and most extraordinary cases we have ever had on our records."[17] At the close of the episode, the Chief would summarize the story and remind viewers that this was "one more job well done by your Treasury men in action."

On *Treasury Men* Walter Greaza mediates between the state, the narrative, and audiences. His authority as arbiter of national truths is based on the combination of the show's use of official state records, his fictional role as "Chief" of a federal agency, and a more generalized persona as a community leader outside the diegesis of any given episode. While the facts of the case may come from the files of the American *state*, the real "we" spoken through the program is a more diffused one of American *national* community. When Greaza addresses the public viewer in direct address to the camera, he steps partially out of his role as head of an enforcement agency and speaks as a citizen. The character of the Chief changed slightly from episode to episode—in some cases, he might announce "Tonight, in my role as Chief Enforcement Officer of the Alcohol and Tobacco Tax Division . . . ," while in others he plays the "Chief of the Division of Customs," and in still others he is the "Chief of the Secret Service." In this way, the program's continuity comes from Greaza's citizenship rather than his character's fixed identity. Greaza claimed in an interview, "For the young-sters, it is graphically true evidence that crime does not pay. For the parents, it offers dramatic illumination of where some of their tax dollars go."[18] *Treasury Men in Action*'s "dramatic illumination" is part documentary record, part ad-venture tale, and also something more; the show encourages viewers to invest themselves in a community of common concerns that find their fullest, *truest,* expression in a *fictional* narrative. In this way, "documentary melodrama" be-comes a means of constructing that most intangible, yet steadfastly "real," artifact—the national character.

Although *Treasury Men in Action* was more preoccupied with domestic crime-solving than explicit espionage, the show is nonetheless relevant—both as an early experiment in the narrative adaptation of government sources and as a text redolent with suspicions of underground subversion. Like other films and programs of the Red Scare era, *Treasury Men* reveals a profound mistrust of any activity that takes place outside the glare of full daylight. Many of the show's episodes were concerned with underground economies lingering from World War II, portrayed as tantamount to Communist subversion. The show tackled "black markets" as aggressively as it did "red" citizens, suggesting that alternative economies were arguably as threatening to a capitalist democracy as Communism itself. "Bookie parlors," bootlegging, customs fraud, tax evasion, and peddling in military secrets were all anti-American crimes of a similar order, for they each threatened to undermine the American economic system.

In "The Case of the Honorable Men," for example, a clan of hillbilly moon-shiners is producing illegal whiskey in a tight-knit and secretive organization.[19] Clan leader Cousin Albert says in a family meeting, "We're goin' to start makin' a new batch of whiskey. And bein' all kinfolk, we're goin' to share in it. That's the way us Allens are. That's what makes us strong. We stay together." The group is suspicious of outsiders, and it operates according to rigid rules imposed by the family leader. The Chief explains to viewers that this creates a "difficult problem for undercover work by our investigators. To combat these men and break into their circle, a clever and courageous investigator was required." The only way for the Treasury men to thwart the bootleggers is through espionage, and a special investigator infiltrates the group to dismantle it. Although the family's collectivism, authoritarian leadership, and secrecy are much like popu-lar portrayals of Communist cells, the Allens' real crime is one of class; hostile to modernization, they cling to an underground white ethnic economy that is tantamount to subversion. Ultimately, though, the family members see the error of their ways after the Treasury agents' purge, and they're returned to a state of "honorable" citizenship. This episode became a particularly direct lesson in patriotic service, for at its conclusion the commissioner of the IRS appeared on-screen,

> [to] present the Treasury Department's civilian Service Honor Award to investigator Charles S. Nicholson, Jr., of the Alcohol Tax Division, whose case [was] dramatized on the program. The true story, titled "The Case of the Honorable Men," relates how the agent's courageous single-handed work resulted in the dissolution of a band of moonshiners and the arrest of two of its ringleaders. At the risk of his life, Nicholson went up into the hills alone, to break up the bootleggers' operations.[20]

Acting as a state agent, Nicholson exposed an underground economic activity, staving off the disintegration of America from within.

In "The Case of the Iron Curtain," *Treasury Men* turned explicitly to Communist espionage, in the story of "a man who would sell anything for a price, including . . . his own country."[21] As in "The Case of the Honorable Men," this episode is about how a basically honest man can stumble into criminal behavior when he maintains a secret life. Jean, a Parisian with a failing import/export business, is wracked by a guilty secret—that during the Holocaust he revealed secrets of a planned escape to Nazi guards, leading to the deaths of several Jewish detainees. Ostracized by his fellow French citizens, Jean nearly commits suicide after the war. Jean's guilt and loneliness make him an easy target for a Communist spy who entraps him in a plot to smuggle airplane parts into the Soviet bloc. A victim of his own past, Jean eventually undergoes a transformation of character by publicly coming to terms with his cowardly actions. Like a former Communist, it is only when he first fully confesses his inadequacies to the authorities, and then names the agent who tricked him, that Jean is able to regain his standing as a good citizen.

While "documentary melodrama" might have been an expedient way of blending state interests with series narrative, it posed certain problems for producers who were concerned with their relationship with the federal government.

Shows like *Treasury Men* were rife with anti-Communist rhetoric and nation-alistic appeals to civic responsibility, but networks were nonetheless circum-spect about fictionalizing official state institutions. Fearful of the opprobrium of the U.S. government at whose whim they were able to broadcast, network continuity acceptance departments forbade producers to refer to such agencies as the CIA, FBI, and the State Department without explicit agency approval.[22] Even *Treasury Men,* which was produced with the endorsement of the Treasury Department, was not allowed to refer to other federal agencies. Network cen-sors deleted such references or changed the names of agencies to make them intentionally vague.[23]

The effect of such network censorship was to make officially sanctioned fictional representations of the federal government on TV much more promi-nent when they did appear. When producers had the approval of a federal agency, they incorporated it into the show's promotional materials. *Treasury Men, I Led 3 Lives,* and *The Man Called X* were promoted as tell-all glimpses into the secret operations of the federal government. Government agencies them-selves exploited their close relationships to such programs, using such moments as the Service Honor Award presentation during a live *Treasury Men* broadcast as free publicity.[24] As a *Variety* reviewer commented, Greaza's closing line at the end of each episode of *T-Men,* "One more job well done by your Trea-sury Department," was "one of the biggest booster lines for a Government agency."[25] Such shows likely put a human face on the bureaucracies of the fed-eral government, linking them to the daily lives of American citizens, and establishing a continuity between official state institutions and "private" family entertainment.

Noting the successes of such documentary crime shows as *Dragnet* and *Treasury Men in Action,* and seeking to capitalize on popular interest in anti-Communism and espionage, NBC attempted in the early 1950s to combine the two. From 1952 to 1954 NBC executives sought to produce a show with the direct involvement of the FBI. NBC saw official FBI participation as a lucrative promotional opportunity, and they were also wary about attempting to present a reality-based espionage show without Bureau approval. NBC vice president Charles Barry oversaw the effort, and he pitched the idea to the FBI, writing, "I think the time is ripe for the Bureau to get into television. . . . NBC, of course, is highly interested. I believe that the arrangement should definitely be between the Bureau and NBC. In this way, the program would be built under NBC supervision, with the cooperation and advice of the Bureau and would, I think, make an ideal arrangement."[26] The show, which was to be modeled in part after *Dragnet*, would allow the network to air reality-based narratives of homefront espionage and subversion. Internally, NBC executives were confident that such a show would be a huge financial success. Barry claimed, "If NBC gets the official FBI program—they get a winner. This program could run for years and years and rank with *Dragnet, Treasury Men in Action*, or the *Racket Squad*. The show is automatically good for 30 to 40 points."[27] "A top flight FBI series," according to Barry, "would also make a real dent in *Lucy*."[28]

For two years NBC discussed the possibility of an FBI program with Director Hoover and his senior staff. By 1953 the talks became more formalized, and NBC called in recently retired NBC president Niles Trammell to negotiate the deal. Trammell had maintained close relations with the FBI, the Army, and the State Department during his tenure at the network, and he was to act as a consultant on the deal. In promoting their offer, NBC stressed

> It would be our desire to bring to the public not only entertaining programs but programs high in public service value which would present a true picture of the great work done in the public's behalf by their FBI. We hope you will agree with us that the National Broadcasting Company has the resources and creative know-how to bring the finest reflection of the FBI accomplishment to television.[29]

Banking on their success with *Dragnet, Treasury Men in Action,* and other documentary-based programs, NBC hoped the show would be a popular and profitable series that would simultaneously reinforce the network's relationship with the U.S. government.

In order to appease Hoover and maintain the show's official credentials, NBC was willing to accept several FBI conditions. NBC assured Bureau heads that they "would have unequivocal script approval, approval of the main actors in the series and approval of the sponsor."[30] A direct nod to the ongoing HUAC investigations and resultant blacklist, the Bureau would be allowed to investigate and reject any members of the NBC creative team.[31] The FBI was particularly concerned about the choice of sponsor, as they felt that this decision would reflect upon the bureau. NBC proposed that the program be sponsored solely by Campbell's Soup, which, after conducting an investigation, the FBI found agreeable.[32]

Some of the FBI's requests, however, were difficult for the network to meet. Hoover wouldn't commit to an agreement with NBC before Campbell's or another approved sponsor had signed a long-term contract, but he also wouldn't allow an audition pilot to be shot for marketing purposes. NBC found itself in a difficult predicament—without a sample episode, they were unable to gain a commitment from a sponsor, and without a sponsor they could not secure the FBI's approval. For several months NBC tried to work around the FBI's demands, but without success.[33]

The NBC/FBI project eventually fell through. It wasn't until a decade later that the FBI signed an agreement with ABC to produce *The FBI*, starring Efrem Zimbalist Jr., which aired from 1965 to 1974. The show was a commercial success, sponsored by the Ford Motor Company, and Zimbalist became something of a public ambassador for the Bureau. By that time, however, the FBI itself was focused on domestic crimes (particularly, at Attorney General Robert Kennedy's insistence, organized crime), and *The FBI* had little of the espionage and anti-Communist Red-baiting that would likely have marked a 1950s FBI program. Furthermore, spy programs changed considerably over the course of that decade, and their undercover operatives bore little resemblance to the dour law enforcement professionals of *The FBI*. Although network and public interest was high, none of the 1950s espionage programs were produced directly from Bureau files. Instead, they relied upon the personal memoirs of former spies. Ziv Television was particularly invested in this style of production, creating *I Led 3 Lives* in 1953 and *The Man Called X* in 1955. *I Led 3 Lives* preceded *X*, and its blend of documentarism with family melodrama is the subject of chapter 2. The latter program, though, is particularly important in how it introduced international settings and plots to 1950s espionage drama.

The Man Called X:
The American Agent Goes Global

A knotty problem confronts the producer of a series dealing with esoteric matters. If he hokes up the subject matter for dramatic purposes, he is sure to hear from irate experts, both real and self-appointed. But if he succumbs to their blandishments for detailed accuracy, he may wind up with a half-hour of gobbledygook and no audience.

—VARIETY REVIEW OF *THE MAN CALLED X*

A syndicated program based on the files of a former spy, *The Man Called X* starred Barry Sullivan as Ken Thurston—known only as "X"—who traveled the globe to support a range of American espionage causes. The program was inspired by Ladislas Farago, an American journalist who eventually managed to turn his interest in espionage into a career. During World War II Farago took a position working for U.S. Naval Intelligence, a predecessor to the CIA. After the war, he returned to journalism and wrote several books about espionage, including *War of Wits: The Anatomy of Espionage and Intelligence* (1954) and *Burn After Reading: The Espionage History of World War II* (1961). In 1959 he co-wrote *Behind Closed Doors* with former boss Rear Admiral Ellis Zacharias (the book was later adapted for television by NBC). A popular source of expert information about international espionage, in 1960 Farago also prepared a special issue of *Confidential Magazine,* entitled *Spies Confidential,* an enthusiastic compilation of spy stories culled from his own books and other media accounts.[34]

The Man Called X began as a radio drama that aired from 1947 to 1952; the reality-based promotional device, however, was unique to the television adaptation. Based on Farago's 1954 book *War of Wits,* the show was produced with Farago's participation, and he was prominently featured in its promotional materials. *War of Wits* was a manual of technique, describing particular espionage practices in detail. Major sections of the book described the differences between intelligence, espionage, sabotage, counterespionage, and propaganda, and explained how each was used by intelligence services throughout the world. Farago himself had never really operated as a spy, instead working in propaganda and counterespionage at "clandestine Desk X" through a fictional alter ego, "Balint Boda, an omniscient and ubiquitous Hungarian forever moving surreptitiously behind the Iron Curtain, whose hypothetical body gained substance by the effectiveness of his patriotic appeals."[35] Balint Boda was a pure fabrication, the product of an elaborate paper trail designed to mislead German intelligence. Farago was never fictionalized in the series; instead, he was one of TV's first technical advisors.

Ziv produced *The Man Called X* according to much the same pattern they had developed for *I Led 3 Lives,* but while *3 Lives* focused on domestic cases of Communist subversion, each episode of *X* was set in a different foreign country. The producers solicited story ideas from Farago and then prepared script outlines that were assigned to writers working out of the New York or Los Angeles office. After another round of comments and recommendations from Farago, the episode was hurried into production. By the mid-1950s, Ziv had developed an extremely efficient, low-cost production system, and they were able to produce at least two episodes per week.[36] Ziv's assembly-line production and low budgets left little room for careful deliberation about individual episodes, and like most Ziv programs, *X* is highly formulaic. Farago was likely thus far more valuable to Ziv as a promotional ploy than as a source of historical data. Nonetheless, the program's producers attempted to follow Farago's suggestions as closely as was possible given the demands of syndicated production.[37]

In part Ziv exploited Farago's contributions in order to assure that *X* would be differentiated from other crime or adventure programs.[38] It was apparently a challenge to get scriptwriters to reinforce this distinction, likely because they were also writing for Ziv detective shows like *Boston Blackie* and *Martin Kane.* Dick Dorso, Farago's principal contact at the Ziv New York office, advised,

> bear in mind that our government has spent about a million dollars training X in all the fields of espionage so that he is not only a valuable asset to our country but in addition is prepared to meet emergency situations fully equipped to cope with them. . . . The tendency on the part of most of the writers is to regard X as sort of a Sam Spade type of private eye rather than a man highly skilled in the techniques of espionage.[39]

Thus while the show capitalized on the interest generated by detective shows and pulp-fiction novels like Mickey Spillane's highly popular Mike Hammer series, producers sought to frame the program as a source of accurate technical and political information. Further, this show was a pivotal point at which producers sought to distinguish espionage from true crime. While *Treasury Men* was a direct extension of the domestic crime genre, and *I Led 3 Lives* was principally concerned with how Communism infiltrates the private home, *The Man Called X* was characterized by international settings, globe-trotting spies rather than federal police, and by an increasing reliance on deception through technology and masquerade. *The Man Called X* thus prefigures the popular internationalist spy dramas of the 1960s: *Mission: Impossible, I Spy,* and *The Man from U.N.C.L.E.*

Farago offered tips on a wide range of topics, including industrial espionage, uses of military aircraft, political assassination, safecracking, wiretapping, and other methods of "proper espionage technique," which the producers believed added "authenticity to the show."[40] Farago's role as technical consultant was an important part of the program's credit sequences, which opened with a voiceover that stated, "These are the stories of America's intelligence agents, our country's first line of defense. These stories are based on material from the files of one of America's foremost intelligence experts." In the final credits, Farago is listed as a technical advisor and as "Former Chief of Research and Planning, Special Warfare Branch, Office of U.S. Naval Intelligence." The show thus foreshadows a shift in future spy programs' conventions of realism—away from documenting the experiences of actual spies to an emphasis on technological verisimilitude.

Each episode of *The Man Called X* was set in a different foreign country in which X assisted or directed the operations of a particular secret mission. This series disrupts many common understandings of 1950s television and its relationship to American culture—that the 1950s was essentially a domestic decade, a period of insular isolation, and that television was an ideological mechanism for the normalization of domestic family relations.[41] Scholars have convincingly shown that early television was marked by tensions surrounding its new invasive presence in the home, and that one of the ways those tensions were negotiated was through reassuring portraits of American family life.[42] At the same time, the period's transformations in American urban and suburban living patterns, shifting relationships between gender and work, and concerns over young women's reproductive and sexual practices made the nuclear family a valorized ideal within 1950s culture.[43] *The Man Called X,* however, is the flip side of the suburban family sitcoms; it put a concrete face on the outside world that was increasingly seen as terrifying. For despite dominant patterns of domestic containment, the U.S. government (as well as the growing television industry itself) was asserting itself in a sphere of international political and cultural expansion. The establishment of the Truman Doctrine of Communist containment (1947) and the U.S. involvement in the Korean War (1950–53) had already demonstrated the U.S. government's goals of global intervention. While internationalism within both American politics and media representations is more often associated with the 1960s, some media texts of the 1950s began to reflect the growing interest in global culture as well. *X* is one of the earliest American spy programs to concern itself consistently with international contexts.

Episodes of *The Man Called X* were set in Iran, Vietnam, Honduras, Nicaragua, Romania, Austria, and China, among other foreign locales. Each episode began with an establishing shot of the Washington headquarters of "the Bureau," an intentionally ambiguous government agency that employed X. As a voiceover explained the details of the case, the viewer saw a shot of an airplane in flight, and then aerial establishing shots of the country in which the episode takes place. Though shot in the United States (supplemented with stock footage of international locations), all of the program's action was set in foreign locales, and never on U.S. soil; the only scenes set in the United States are the debriefing meetings between X and the head of the Bureau. Although its international setting was an important part of the show, it also aroused some political sensitivities for the producers. As one Ziv executive pointed out,

> Officially, our government has no foreign espionage system in peacetime. Therefore, it is important in our stories that when X goes to a foreign country, it must not be for purposes of official or unofficial espionage. The easiest angle to use is because of potential involvement, our government is asked to cooperate in an endeavor to accomplish something of importance. If for some reason we cannot use such an angle, then we must find an equally acceptable substitute. The thing to avoid is anything that sounds like the tone of "one of our espionage agents in Europe, etc., etc."[44]

As a result, X was generally portrayed as an invited guest of the country where he operated, and Ziv producers were careful to position the spy as an aide to the more direct actions of American allies.

In "Extradition Story," for example, the opening voiceover informs us that "three friendly nations protested that subversive groups in their countries were armed with stolen U.S. Army weapons purchased somewhere in Central America. With the help of the Nicaraguan government, a plan was promptly put into action."[45] Once there, X lures Mr. Kalergis, an international arms dealer, out of Honduras and into Nicaragua where he can be legally arrested. Much of the episode centers on the elaborate ruse X employs so that he would not violate another country's laws. In another episode, X travels to Eastern Europe at the request of a "small group of responsible and patriotic officials [who] had dispatched a secret and urgent request to Washington" to aid in the defection of a famous ballerina who "was a symbol of liberty and represented their hope for a decent democracy."[46] In this way, X was constructed as following through on the spirit of the Truman Doctrine, first elaborated in the 1947 speech to Congress in which the president declared, "I believe that it must be the policy of the United States to support free peoples who are resisting attempted subjugation by armed minorities or by outside pressures."[47] Like the Truman and Eisenhower administrations' "domino theory" protectionism, X's intervention in the internal politics of other countries was portrayed as a welcome gesture that encouraged the global spread of democracy.

Many of the cases portrayed in *The Man Called X* were taken from the day's headlines. Some storylines were altered, however, in order to provide as uncomplicated a picture of American benevolence as possible. In one instance, producers were inspired by Farago's suggestion to look into U.S. manufacturers' manipulation of international politics to build markets. "Fact: A great deal of trouble is being caused in Morocco by the fight between Coca Cola and Pepsi Cola," Farago wrote. "Coca Cola and Pepsi Cola are both seeking exclusive franchises in Morocco. Coca Cola is backing the Istivqlel group and Pepsi Cola is backing the Pasha of Marakeech [*sic*]. To accomplish this, both companies are pouring in money in unlimited quantities." These companies were subsidizing local political conflicts in Morocco in an effort to dominate that country's beverage market. In order to make such a tale palatable at home, Farago suggested they "switch the firms to Belgian and Dutch, and add X."[48] Thus by displacing U.S. economic imperialism onto Western European nations, producers obscured the practices of American corporations and presented an uncomplicated portrait of American benevolent international leadership.

In "Provocateur," *The Man Called X* fictionalized a recent event in American international relations. In the episode, X ventures to Iran to foil a Communist plot to disrupt an American-Iranian oil export treaty. Iran had been one of the first testing grounds for U.S.-Soviet "domino" struggles. During World War II the Allies had used Iran as a corridor through which to supply the Soviet military, and Britain, the United States, and the USSR all maintained a presence there. In 1941 the United States helped to install Shah Reza Pahlavi (the same leader who was permanently overthrown in 1979). When World War II ended, however, tensions over Iran grew between the United States and the USSR, nearly leading to a proxy war like those in Vietnam and Korea. Iran underwent a significant upheaval in the early 1950s, and the Shah was overthrown when Iran nationalized the formerly British-held oil industry. Fearful of Soviet influence, the United States intervened in 1953, reinstalling the Shah and solidifying U.S. power in the region.[49] The incident was one of the first major operations of the newly formed Central Intelligence Agency.

"Provocateur" fictionalizes this delicate period. In the episode, the "Krimm Economic Mission," which represented a Soviet-led international investment group, goes to Tehran to attempt to negotiate an oil-export deal. Such a contract would threaten U.S. interests in Tehran, and X is dispatched to monitor the situation. X learns that Communist military officials in the mission are planning to assassinate their own diplomat and blame it on the Americans in order to manipulate the Iranians to sign with the Soviet bloc. Thus X finds himself in a an awkward position, as the narrator explains, "X, assigned to protect American interests, strangely finds that he has to protect the life of the head of the unfriendly mission in order to carry out his assignment."[50] After a complicated series of deceptions in which he leads the Communists to think they have successfully completed the assassination, X scuttles the deal. Just as the program drew inspiration from the illegal operations of U.S. companies but shifted the blame to foreign governments, this episode is inspired by real political conditions but recrafts them in a sanitized portrait of American benevolence. While the United States had just recently intervened in Iranian politics in order to force the Soviets out, *The Man Called X* suggests that the U.S. presence in Iran was at Iranian behest in order to help rid the country of Soviet treachery.

The program's realist representations of international political environments were not without restrictions, however. As with earlier programs, like NBC's *Treasury Men in Action*, Ziv took great care in its portrayals of the U.S. government. While X was originally to have worked for "the Bureau," Ziv first changed this to "the Department," because, as one producer said at the time, "We'd rather be investigated by the State Department than the FBI."[51] Eventually, X's official affiliation was made even more vague, when a Ziv executive directed the writers "to duck the situation of pinpointing it this carefully and refer to 'Washington,' i.e., 'See if Washington has any further information on this subject.'"[52] When in the episode "U.S. Planes," X poses as a U.S. Air Force officer, producers first secured the permission of the Air Force and then cited that permission in the episode's voiceover narration.[53]

Although *The Man Called X* was highly specific in its references to developing countries, including precise descriptions of such details as Vietnamese geography or Moroccan currency, Ziv producers were more circumspect in the representations of nations thought to arouse more volatile audience reactions. While most episodes were positioned as a clash between Communism and democracy, producers were reluctant to "pinpoint the Russians as heavies." And consistent with their policy of aligning X with the legitimate governments of the countries in which he operated, Ziv's censor insisted that producers "make sure the country we are using is not improperly involved. It is of course important for any local government official to be straight and the heavies will either be local Communists, local racketeers, or people of communistic background who merely happen to be using the country involved as a physical locale."[54] In part, these precautions helped Ziv maintain cordial relations with the U.S. government. During the production of *The Man Called X*, Ziv was also airing *I Led 3 Lives* with tacit FBI approval, and their program *West Point* was produced with the full participation of the U.S. Army, and the production company took care that its fictional TV programs not meddle in matters of national security. As in later programs like *Mission: Impossible*, the spy operates out of a fictional and ambiguous agency but remains responsive to political sensitivities, in part to avoid conflicts with official government institutions.

Equally important, however, was the more immediate requirement to keep audiences and advertisers happy. Most Ziv programs were sold directly to individual stations and local sponsors by traveling salesmen. As a result, the company was responsive to small advertisers and sought to avoid representations that might cause repercussions. Because of such concerns, the production company was in one case particularly cautious about arousing controversy over representations of Germany. As a senior Ziv executive declared,

> This particular outline highlights a danger point for us. That danger point is Germany! Undoubtedly, this program will be sold to breweries, in certain markets, and I am thinking particularly of Milwau-

kee, Cincinnati, St. Louis, etc., there are large German populations who will react badly to anything unfavorable about Germany. On the other hand, there are large liberal sections of our population which will react equally badly to anything favorable about Germany. In think this is one country where we will be walking a tightrope. I believe it would be wise to avoid Germany wherever possible, and if we feel that we must do it, we must use extreme caution and care. The only purpose of this memo is to put up a red flag! This is dynamite![55]

Thus while the show's documentarism was an important part of Ziv's promotional strategies, a variety of influences—in this case the Holocaust and World War II—placed firm limits on the show's representation of international settings. Because of governmental pressures and advertiser concerns (not to mention the demands of shooting two episodes a week for around $15,000 apiece), the program's realism was more a stylistic and promotional device than a strictly documentary account of verifiable events.

Throughout the espionage and intrigue programs of the 1950s, there is an ongoing dedication to citing the nation in concrete form; these narratives repeatedly—and enthusiastically—invoke the "real": the real agent, real locations, real techniques, and real, verifiable expertise. In the earliest programs like *Treasury Men in Action* that emerged out of reality-based police dramas, this realism is authenticated primarily by citing official law enforcement institutions. By the mid-1950s, however, this institutional authentication is supplemented by the prominent role of personal historical accounts by former spies. In addition, *The Man Called X* presages a kind of espionage realism that was to become more common in programs of the 1960s and beyond—an emphasis on specific international locales and "proper espionage technique." This general movement—from government institutions to individual spies to technical accuracy—is an important consequence of the difficulties of fitting the prerogatives of governmental institutions to a television narrative. But despite these shifts in representational strategies, each of these programs uses conventions of documentary realism to craft a discursive community of common national concern. In these "documentary melodramas," voiceover narration and direct address are devices of ideological closure, for they mitigate the possibility of alternative interpretations. That is, these shows claim to speak for—and shape the definitions of—American national identity and citizenship.

Civic Television:
Cold War Nationalism and Direct Address

Real realism pays.

—*TIME*, AUG. 2, 1954

Each episode of *The Man Called X* ends back at the Washington headquarters, where X has presumably just been debriefed by his superiors. As in other reality-based espionage shows, the protagonist turns to the camera and delivers a brief address that was reminiscent of the integrated ads on single-sponsored programs of the 1950s.[56] But rather than advertise a particular consumer product, X offers a patriotic testimonial. Typically, this direct address begins with a quote from a famous American statesman, and then ties their patriotism to that of the audience and the program. In "Extradition," for example, X fervently proclaims, "The great American statesman Daniel Webster once stated, 'Nothing will ruin the country if the people will undertake its safety, and nothing can save it if they leave that safety in any hands but their own.' No one knows this better than the men of the intelligence service."[57] In other episodes, the epilogue includes quotes from such prominent American heroes as Douglas MacArthur, Thomas Paine, and John Calhoun.

This moment of direct address is reminiscent of the closing sequences of *Treasury Men in Action* and *I Led 3 Lives,* each of which ended on a similar appeal to American nationalism. Like Walter Greaza and Richard Carlson, stars of *Treasury Men* and *3 Lives,* X star Barry Sullivan addresses his audience not as a dramatic character, but as a civic spokesman. In each of these programs, the lead actor steps partially out of his fictional role, linking the television narrative to the ongoing political and cultural processes of American life. This partial detachment from the fictional narrative is not a comment on the artifice of the drama, but rather is a means of reinforcing its ideological message. For here, when the actor qua citizen addresses the national television audience with utter sincerity and patriotism, the gulf between fiction and documentary is seamlessly bridged, bound together through the figure of the nationalistic hero. In a particularly forceful declaration of civic pride, Sullivan as X entreats his audience:

> In every corner of the world, the government of the United States
> —your government—is working ceaselessly with other democra-
> cies to make this a *better* world. There's also a big job to be done

> here at home—a job in which you can render great assistance. Be a
> *real* member of your community. Cooperate in all civic activities.
> Aid the efforts of your local school system by taking an active inter-
> est in parent-teacher groups. Attend and support the church of your
> choice. Remembering always—a democracy can be as strong as the
> people who elect it.[58]

Here, the fictional narrative, the governmental institution, the television apparatus, the citizen-actor, and the citizen-viewer converge, united by a common
American nationalism that blends geopolitics with everyday life in a tight ideological package of containment.

   These programs' realism is far more than a clever and profitable means of
promotion. More important, these 1950s reality-based espionage programs were
part of early television's processes of self-legitimation—part of an ongoing effort to establish the new medium as a sustaining civic institution. These programs establish discursive continuities between civic community, the nation,
the state, and television itself. In doing so, they became part of broader attempts
to ameliorate anxieties about the new medium by nestling it comfortably into
everyday American cultural life. Indeed, popular mid-1950s articles like "Television: The New Cyclops" called the TV an invading "monster," worrying that
"in less than ten years, TV has become one of the most powerful social forces
in the U.S."[59] Such comments speak to concerns over how TV was transforming social relations, replacing face-to-face interaction with mediated communication. In the face of these worries, the overt civic appeals of semidocumentary crime and espionage programs were a palliative, marking television not as
a threat to, but as an extension of, traditional civic life.

   Leftist and liberal critics, however, were skeptical of these new realist modes
of 1950s television. An *Atlantic Monthly* critic wrote, "The sure-fire topics are
sin, sex, and subversion, not presented abstractly but pepped up with live witnesses. . . . After all, are we trying to protect the American home, or aren't we?"
Blacklisted screenwriter Ring Lardner Jr. joined in, writing that "in a mass
medium where writers' work is consumed at a ravenous rate, the lure of the
socially significant becomes more than the veriest hack can resist. . . . He begins
to suffer from third-act trouble, and he is ready to try anything. He turns to
reality."[60] Such critics lamented the loss of the anthology dramas of television's
"golden age" of "quality" live programming, dismissing reality-based programs

as formulaic adventure narratives akin to "hard-boiled" crime fiction.[61] One particularly opportunistic Los Angeles producer would likely have earned the ire of such critics: *Confidential File* offered a "sharp look at a rugged profession," giving TV audiences "a closeup look at some extremely fancy shenanigans: they watched two collection-agency men in a fascinating demonstration of the techniques of repossessing an automobile." The show was produced by a former *Dragnet* writer and print journalist who wanted to capitalize on the "stark reality in dialogue and faces. I wanted to do a show with real realism."[62]

Despite such criticisms, documentarist televisual realism was well suited to the brand of right-wing nationalism fostered by the Red Scare. More conservative media critics saw television as a means of reaching viewers who might otherwise be swayed by Communist rhetoric. *The Saturday Evening Post*, which capitalized on anti-Communism with both fiction and nonfiction serials, editorialized that "there is good evidence that the [Communist] propaganda is succeeding, especially among the ignorant masses in Europe, Asia, and Africa whom the Russians are cultivating. Others say it is beneath our dignity to stoop to a reply. But dignity can be purchased at too high a price."[63] Television, *Post* editor Bruce Bliven suggested, was a key forum for public information and should not be surrendered to the subversives. At home, the producers of documentarist spy programs were quick to fill the gap. For not only did "real realism pay," it also helped ensure official approval of a medium that was arousing considerable uneasiness within American society at large.[64]

That espionage programs took broad liberties with their "documentary" material isn't surprising. Their interplay between official state politics, documentary, direct address, and dramatic narrative, though, is ultimately less directed toward proving the viability or accuracy of the specific event represented than it is toward reaffirming the program's civic legitimacy. As John Corner writes of docudramas, "As a documentary project, the reconstruction therefore has its justification not so much in terms of the immediate circumstances dramatized but in terms of the general skills, commitment and fortitude for which it provides evidence."[65] Their realism generalized rather than specific and concrete, these documentary melodramas are most important as broad narratives of state institutional authority. The veracity of each individual element is less important than these programs' claims of immutable nationhood. These shows' shifting relationship to realism is thus related to the paradoxical transience of "the national." For while national identity is not inherent, it nonetheless operates culturally as having a stable, fixed, essential character. In other words, national identity is more than just an imagined community—it is an imagined community whose coherence depends upon the collective acceptance of a discourse of irreducible materiality. In the earliest programs, like *Treasury Men in Action,* the realist representation of the nation is supported through close relations with official state institutions, and in *The Man Called X,* national realism is encoded in politically precise settings and specific uses of technology. Though the tactics shift, these shows share an ongoing commitment to the realist portrayal of state institutions, global politics, and technological accuracy.

The espionage programs of the 1950s also raise important questions about the relationship between TV producers and the state. Produced at a time when television as a public institution was under intense scrutiny, and when anti-Communism sought to unravel the truth of subversive infiltration, 1950s espionage programs invoked a community of civic participation, nationalistic patriotism, and domestic containment. These shows likely tell us as much about how American society spied TV as an emerging political, economic, and cultural institution as they do about what spies themselves saw. Because they so directly narrativized official state institutions, these shows perhaps more than others of the period demonstrate producers' concerns about their relationship to the federal government. Such concerns likely led to these programs' rigid ideological closure through such textual devices as authoritative voiceovers, direct address, and appeals to civic pride. Still, though, the very textual features that so closely linked these programs to state institutions were unstable, and eventually collapsed under the weight of their own inconsistencies. The title of *The Man Called X* is telling; the program's protagonist has surrendered his name, and perhaps his identity, to the federal government. Increasingly this surrender becomes a source of narrative tension, and eventually comedy. *The Man Called X* hints at a growing conundrum: the notion that an invisible, nameless, faceless spy might be an "agent" of national authority. For how, we might ask, is one to be a proper citizen without a name?

2

I Led 3 Lives and the Agent of History

In May 1949 Herbert Philbrick, an advertising executive for a Paramount Pictures theater exhibition chain in Boston, stepped out of the shadows and into the witness box to give the star testimony in a widely publicized case against eleven Communist leaders. Through banner headlines, the nation learned that for nine years Philbrick had been a secret member of the Communist Party. Throughout that time, he had supplied the FBI with thousands of documents that exposed the operations of the Communist Party of America. Overnight, Herbert Philbrick became an outspoken anti-Communist and a hero of the political right. In 1952 he wrote a best-selling book that was quickly adapted into a successful television series. Both went by the title *I Led 3 Lives.*

Ziv Television developed *I Led 3 Lives* as a syndicated program, producing 117 episodes from 1953 to 1956. For over a year, the show was America's top-rated syndicated series. Throughout its production, *I Led 3 Lives* remained closely tied to the figure of Herbert Philbrick, using his life as the primary source of material for its episodes. The program declared its authenticity through voiceover pronouncements at the beginning of each episode which invoked the authority of Herbert Philbrick, the "real" counterspy and author of the initial autobiography. As a paid staff member, Philbrick read and revised scripts, suggested potential plotlines, and verified the accuracy of the show's representations of Communism and the FBI. But despite Philbrick's involvement, the program freely adapted his experiences to fit the conventions of narrative television and the economic demands of syndicated production.

It is hardly remarkable that *I Led 3 Lives* might make truth claims that didn't exactly conform to the lived experiences of those it purported to represent.

But while other espionage programs of the period drew their authority from official state endorsement, the truth claims of *I Led 3 Lives* depend upon narratives of personal historical accountability that conflate the public persona of the real Herb Philbrick with the narrative conventions of 1950s domestic drama. *I Led 3 Lives* is thus more than just another site at which the nascent TV industry capitalized on popular interest in Communism and inscribed factual reality into a popular series narrative. The show here serves a historiographic function, weaving the act of writing history into the narrative structure of a program. Indeed, the program's realism is based as much upon the narrative authority of its masculine protagonist as it is upon the legitimacy of the "real" Herbert Philbrick's lived experiences. Where other shows foregrounded their link to state institutions, this show relied on its status as personally verifiable "history" for its credibility.

Although the program draws its discursive authority from the former spy Herb Philbrick, it relies less on his involvement with the Communist Party than on his intelligibility as a traditionally masculine father and husband. As a result, this "true" history of Communism is framed as a gendered struggle over the integrity of the home and the authority of its patriarch. In this way, the narrative structure of each episode—as well as the structure of the white nuclear family that centers that narrative—is strongly reminiscent of the suburban sitcoms that grew in popularity during the 1950s. As Nina Liebman has suggested, such family melodramas worked to contain feminine agency and reinscribe the patriarchal authority of the father.[1] Indeed, *I Led 3 Lives* negotiates two of the period's most contentious sites of cultural struggle—gender and Cold War politics—displacing anxieties over shifting gender norms onto global politics. Faced with the dual threats of feminine agency and Communist subversion, *I Led 3 Lives* conflates the two, feminizing Communism in relation to Philbrick's masculine agency, and constructing any expression of feminine self-determination as a threat to the American state. Among Cold War spy programs, *I Led 3 Lives* is particularly revealing since it is one of the very few that positions its protagonist in the domestic sphere; *I Led 3 Lives* locates its most profound crises not just in the home, but in the family itself.

What is at stake in this doubled narrative of gender norms and nationalist ideology is history—that of the state, of the nation, and of the citizen-subject. The program reminds us of this continually—in promotional materials, in testimonials by J. Edgar Hoover and other prominent anti-Communists, and within the text itself. Indeed, the Communist women of *I Led 3 Lives* challenge not only Philbrick's masculinist nationalism, but his claim to historical truth as well. Historical knowledge, this program asserts, is the rightful domain of the patriarch, and it is the program's masculine protagonist who is valorized as the source of historical knowledge and the agent of historical change.

The program's masculinist narration produces a history that situates the hero's agency in his individualism and his private home life, rather than in his institutional affiliation. Philbrick, enmeshed in the dual bureaucracies of the FBI and the American Communist Party, finds his agency in a turn inward, toward his sense of individuality and his identity as a family man living a private, domestic life. The key question surrounding this program is that of who was to be the privileged subject of history; that is, at this particular moment on early American television, who would be allowed to narrate a history that negotiated the dangerous minefields of both international politics and gendered family relations? Gender is central to the show's logic, for the installation of Philbrick as the historical anchor of a decidedly ahistorical account of Communism depends upon the feminization of Communism and the establishment of the home and a patriarchal vision of the private sphere as Philbrick's center of authority and agency.

Will the Real Herbert Philbrick Please Stand Up: Comrade Herb Tells the Historical Truth

As the opening credits introduced each episode of *I Led 3 Lives,* a voiceover intoned,

> This is the story, the fantastically true story, of Herbert A. Philbrick, who for nine frightening years did lead three lives . . . average citizen, high level member of the Communist Party, and counterspy for the Federal Bureau of Investigation. And who, for the first time, has released his secret files concerning not only his own activities, but the activities of other counter-espionage agents. For obvious reasons, actual names and places have been changed, but the story is based on fact.[2]

This voiceover is accompanied by a slow zoom in to the cover of Philbrick's autobiographical book. Quite literally, the television program begins with an assertion of authenticity—the history about to be presented is one that is supported by a written record of truth that garnered the praise of such groups as the American Legion and the Daughters of the American Revolution. As the voiceover continues, however, television's effacement of the "real" emerges as the announcer reminds us that "for obvious reasons, actual names and places have been changed." Nevertheless, it is the written text's status as an incontestable factual record—together with the implied unassailability of Philbrick's patriotism—that provides the necessary precondition for the "fantastically true" televisual narrative to follow.

Faced with the challenge of transforming the complex historical realities of Philbrick's life as spy and counterspy within the American Communist Party into a weekly thirty-minute television program, *I Led 3 Lives*' producers exploited the authenticity of Philbrick's espionage entanglements in order to lend credence to their fictionalization of "historic" events. Philbrick submitted hundreds of pages of notes and suggestions to the show's producers, who deferred to his expertise, particularly in matters of the wording of dialogue and accounts of FBI strategies. In a memo to the show's writing staff, Maurice "Babe" Unger, vice president of Ziv TV, recommended,

> We are insistent that all of the material which we use in these stories be on an authentic basis and double checked in this regard by Philbrick. Therefore, it is extremely important on all the scripts that we follow Philbrick's suggestions, criticisms, etc., one-hundred percent to the letter.[3]

Just as the opening credits of *I Led 3 Lives* declared its truthfulness, the show's promotion materials, which targeted both audiences and potential sponsors, declared its status as historical truth:

> *I Led 3 Lives:* Tense because it's Factual! Gripping because it's Real! Frightening because it's True! . . . Not just a script writer's fantasy— but the authentic story of the Commie's attempt to overthrow our government! You'll thrill to the actual on-the-scene photography . . . factual from the records dialogue. . . . Authentic sets and scripts personally supervised by Herbert Philbrick, the man who for nine agonizing years lived in constant danger as a supposed Communist who reported daily to the FBI! Never before has such a dramatic document appeared on TV![4]

The show's realist public-service claims earned it wide praise as a valuable source of historical knowledge.[5] In 1955 Admiral Arthur Radford, chairman of the Joint Chiefs of Staff, presented the Freedom Foundation Top Award to the show's producers.[6] *I Led 3 Lives* also won the blessing of Reverend Edwin R. Broderick, director of the Radio and Television Communications Office of the Archdiocese of New York, who felt the program would "promote a stimulating, enthusiastic, and sympathetic public reaction, and, therefore, be of inestimable value to all who believe in and hope for the continuance of our American way of life. I wholeheartedly recommend it and feel it will do credit to any organization under whose sponsorship it appears."[7] The program was even used as a U.S. Army training film, and on at least one occasion producers helped to change the show's scheduling so that the soldiers on a nearby military base could view it at a convenient time.[8]

In keeping with their strategy of positioning *I Led 3 Lives* as verifiably "real," Ziv producers also emphasized the program's documentary-style location shooting. The show's "actual on-the-scene photography" cultivated a realist aesthetic, but it also kept production costs low. As Jon Epstein, a senior writer for the series, explained, "We shot the hell out of Hollywood.... Ziv did it because it was cheaper to shoot Hollywood and Vine than it was to try and build a set of something." The producers also saved money and reinforced the show's realism by choosing not to use makeup. According to Epstein, "the reason for that, they said, was 'well this is very documentary and we want to keep it documentary in style.' But I tell you ... one of the things they were trying to do was to save the cost of a makeup man every week ... they rationalized these things to the point where they believed it themselves." Rationalized or not, though, these production techniques were hailed in advertisements and press materials to further substantiate the program's claims to truth.[9]

These cost-cutting strategies were symptomatic of the pressure to condense complex historical material into a form that would be profitable in a growing television industry. Ziv TV, a low-budget syndicator, produced *I Led 3 Lives* for roughly $18,000 per episode—only 10 percent of the cost of a typical network filmed series—and often two or three episodes were shot in a single week.[10] Thus the program's documentary production style, which involved generic exterior locations filmed with available light and a minimal crew, was motivated more by economics than an impulse to reproduce the minutiae of Philbrick's life.

The frugal budgets that motivated the "documentary" aesthetic of *I Led 3 Lives* undercut the specificity of the program's references to Philbrick's lived experiences. Although the show was shot in Los Angeles, Philbrick had actually lived in Boston, and his autobiography carefully details a variety of places in the city where he interacted with Communists and the FBI. None of Philbrick's recommendations about locations made it into the program. Similarly, while Philbrick envisioned *I Led 3 Lives* as a period piece situated in the political climate of World War II, the show was stripped of that context, set instead in a generic 1950s suburb. This lack of historical specificity was emblematic of this documentary melodrama's adaptation of Philbrick's experiences in general; the contradictory combination of historically grounded authority in a relatively ahistorical setting complicated the program's claims to historical truth.

I Led 3 Lives thus represents a historiographic contradiction, one in which the authenticity of its central figure is selectively invoked to legitimize a dehistoricized ideological statement. Because of the economics of production and the limitations of serial television, "fact" alone cannot authenticate the program's truth claims. Instead, the program invokes the conventions of dramatic narrative to complete that task. Indeed, the credibility of the "real" Philbrick can scarcely be distinguished from the narrative authority of the program's protagonist. *I Led 3 Lives* might thus be read as what Hayden White terms a "historical metafiction," in which "everything is presented as if it were of the same ontological order, both real and imaginary—realistically imaginary or imaginarily real, with the result that the referential function of the images of events is etiolated."[11] In other words, references to the "real" Philbrick give credence to the program's representations, but it is the principles of television narrative that ultimately affirm the truth status of the program's "historical reality." The historical metafiction of *I Led 3 Lives* is produced by conflating the "real" Philbrick with the narrative authority of his representation.

It is Philbrick's intelligibility as an individualized masculine subject that solidifies the program's status as historical drama; his authority as narrative protagonist grants him a subjectivity as a producer of historical knowledge. This codependence between "real" and narrative authority is the potential frailty of *I Led 3 Lives*' historicity, because any challenges to the protagonist within the narrative simultaneously challenge the historical agency of the "real" Philbrick. The site of struggle over the writing of history, then, is the gendered authority of the narrative's protagonist. In order for this historical metafiction to unfold on the television screen, Philbrick's encounters with America's ultimate ideological Other are thus represented as a series of gendered struggles in which he must overcome a range of monstrous Communist women and feminized Communist men in order to protect the integrity of the American family and state.

Iron-Gray Disciplinarians and Ruby Red Vixens: The Femininized Bureaucracy

At least half of *I Led 3 Lives*' 117 episodes feature powerful Communist women, and most of these women command a clan of ineffective, subservient male comrades. Virtually no episodes, however, feature even a single female FBI agent. The program pits two dramatically different bureaucracies against each other, with Comrade Herb as the intermediary between them. On the side of American virtue is the men's club of the FBI, an efficient organization of terse agents who work quietly but thoroughly, doing battle with the organization's evil twin, the Communist Party—a perversion of state power, staffed by ineffectual men and aggressive women.

The Communist women of *I Led 3 Lives* are typically portrayed as mechanistic drones. Take Comrade Alice, for example—described by Philbrick as a "squat, stocky, square-jawed functionary, a plain proletarian, and like most party women she gave an impression of drab grayness, almost the uniform of Communist femininity. She was bossy, and could tell men what to do as well as she could tell her own sex."[12] Alice, like many of the program's Communist women, is emotionless, authoritarian, and desexualized. As Joan Hawkins observed in her analysis of the Cold War propaganda film *Red Nightmare,* the lasting impact of Communism in such narratives is to disrupt essentialist categories of gender, substituting instead female characters who defy normative gender roles but who are depicted as incomplete and often unstable.[13] Often, the female comrades are clearly not American, distinguished instead by vaguely Eastern European or East German accents. They often wear severely cut suits, and their typically rigid posture mirrors the brusqueness of their voices. As one female comrade growled at Herb, "Hmmmph! You are not to ask so many questions! It is not for the good of the Party!" Communists like Alice are threatening because in their mechanistic pragmatism, they represent a female co-optation and manipulation of state power.

The program contrasts its hardline Communist women with a cast of docile, and therefore virtuous, American women. As Philbrick noted in his comments on a script, "Here again, be sure not to paint Comrade Mary as too soft a type. Anybody working at Communist Party headquarters, especially today, knows exactly what the score is. She would not be a person such as you would find working at Republican or even Socialist Party headquarters."[14] Here, a key distinction is made between loyal American women who know their place and those who are overzealous in their attempts to assume political power. These women comrades disregard traditional American centers of patriarchal authority, are vicious and cold-blooded in their dedication to their cause, and let no man stand in their way.

In fact, it is Communist men who are most likely to be undisciplined "deviationists"—those who are reluctant to follow the Party line to the letter, and who might fail to carry out their assigned missions. An episode entitled "Historical Society," for example, features a Communist woman named Jameka who runs an underground historical printing press. Here, the program's feminization of Communism merges with its principle concern over the writing of history, and Jameka is positioned as falsifying the "true" dominant histories of America's founding fathers. Jameka never trusts the men who work for her, and with good reason—her staff of obsequious male assistants ultimately fails to detect Philbrick's sabotage of a major printing project. Jameka sends Herb out to spread damaging information about Thomas Jefferson to a random mother and child walking down the street, but she decides to accompany him because she doesn't trust him to complete the assignment effectively. It is Jameka who ultimately tells little Joey and his mother about how Jefferson once stole $1,000. Later, Jameka informs Herb that the rewriting of history is a key tactic of Communist subversion. In the clipped and awkward speech typical of the program's Communist women, she advises, "by mixing up known fact with statements we want the public to accept as true, in most cases it works very well. Basic psychology."

But there is more mixing up going on here than just a series of details about a late U.S. president's life. Jameka has seized from Philbrick the power to narrate history, and she can't trust male comrades to carry out that important task. Jameka's historical account is feminized by both her gendered subjectivity and her Communist sources, and the program positions it as unreliable and

dishonest. Moreover, the historical knowledge Jameka produces is judged infe-
rior because it blurs fact and fiction (despite the irony that such a blurring is
fundamental to the program's own strategy of forming historical truths).
Jameka's challenge to conventional American history is intertwined with her
challenge to the narrative authority of Philbrick as protagonist; Philbrick stands
meekly by, mute, while Jameka takes charge. Only later, under cover of night, is
he able to counterattack. In *I Led 3 Lives,* to gain narrative authority is to gain
historical authority, and Philbrick's efforts to control historical knowledge are
figured as a gendered struggle to suppress the narrative agency of Communist
women.

While some of the show's Communist women are intellectual pragmatists,
others are highly sexualized, providing yet another means of dislocating Philbrick's narrative authority. In addition to a host of dour schoolmarms who
might easily double as bodyguards, *I Led 3 Lives* also features what producers
referred to as "beautiful Mata Hari–type commie agents."[15] This Communist
woman is threatening precisely because she turns her sexual power to sinister
ends. Severe and humorless, the "beautiful Mata Hari–type commie agent"
is portrayed as unnatural in the extreme, because she uses her beauty toward
explicitly political ends. As Hawkins might suggest, the sexualized Communist
agent is contrasted with women like Eva Philbrick, whose subservience to normative gender roles is positioned in the narrative as an expression of her essential nature and her good citizenship.

Still, the beauty of the show's Communist dominatrixes was alluring, even
to American patriots, and therein lay these women's dangerous power. The
mysterious sexuality of the impassioned Communist intrigued even the married Philbrick. A passage from his autobiography captures this intrigue: "The
alarming demonstration of Party fervor put on by this attractive young girl
lapsed into an impromptu quotation from Stalin which carried her to even
greater heights of ardor. . . . To hear her speak with such vehemence unnerved
me to the extent that when I reached home that night, I could not sleep."[16]
Philbrick makes sense of this woman by sexualizing her, and he can only understand her forceful politics as an expression of "ardor." Perhaps what kept Herb
"awake at night" was the tension between his fascination and repulsion at Communist women's sexual and political agency. Like the women of the television
series, the portrait sketched by this passage is one of a woman whose fervor is

intensely seductive, but whose sexuality is incoherent, troubled, and out of place. The mixture of elusive female sexuality and political power is simply too much for the troubled Herb to bear.

In an episode called "Deportation," Comrade Elena is an attractive Eastern European diplomat suspected of carrying damaging reports about American Communists. Mistrustful of even their own agents, Party officials send Herb to investigate her. Herb tails Elena into a lingerie boutique, and he mutters in voiceover, "Subject examined—purchased several pairs of stockings. Wears small size, has nice legs. Nothing here to interest Comrade Joe Garth. Or is there?" Elena detects Herb and eventually asks him to take her to a football game so she can learn about American culture. She then invites him to her apartment, and he has no choice but to follow since he had been given strict orders not to lose sight of her. In the elevator Herb reflects, "The things a man has to put up with leading a triple life! The things that can happen to a nice domesticated counterspy with a pretty wife and five small kids!" But once they reach her apartment, Elena ditches him and sneaks out the back door. This Communist's enigmatic sexual power is literalized when Elena slips away from Philbrick and remains uncontained.

Elena's power as a "girl diplomat" and a "beautiful Iron Curtain consular official" is manipulative and sexual. When Philbrick meets FBI Special Agent Dressler at the airport just before Elena is to be deported, he informs the agent that the Communists had been surveilling her as well:

DRESSLER: What's up? The comrades want to keep her around to run for Miss America?

HERB: Could be.

DRESSLER: She's just the girl who could do it, too. She played footsie with the Nazi bigwigs during the war, then she pulled a switch after the war and married a famous diplomat. And after his so-called suicide, she pulled another switch, now she's the comrades' number one pinup girl!

After Elena is searched by an FBI "matron," Elena taunts the male agents, "Are you convinced I'm not carrying an atomic weapon?" As far as the agents are concerned, she might as well be.

As it turns out, Elena had been concealing a valuable piece of microfilm in her lipstick. The microfilm—simultaneously historical artifact and source of counterespionage knowledge—is secretly stashed in the lipstick case, the symbol of her sexual power and seductive danger. In this scene, the threat of international espionage and the threat of the overly sexual woman are conflated—symbolically merged and embodied in the female spy's cosmetics. As Elaine Tyler May has argued, this combination of discourses on sexual, ideological, and nuclear containment conflates feminine sexuality with nationalist politics. She writes, "Subversives at home, Russian aggressors abroad, atomic energy, sexuality, the bomb, and the 'bombshell' all had to be 'harnessed for peace.'"[17] In the case of Comrade Elena, each of these discourses is articulated through the body of the sexualized Communist woman—although in this case her power cannot be fully harnessed or contained. As a result, she must be expelled from the country after an FBI agent covertly copies the information lodged in her lipstick.

The bureaucratized Communist women of *I Led 3 Lives* might be best read as a displacement of anxieties about the state of masculinity not only in the face of a potential threat from women in the workforce, but in the face of bureaucratized power in general. *I Led 3 Lives* paints women as technocratic social engineers. Philbrick, however, is just as fully implicated in the bureaucratic system as any of the Communist women. Indeed, Philbrick's anti-Communist practices rarely involve direct action. Instead, his primary task is to relay information to the FBI. Philbrick is positioned as an intermediary between two bureaucratic systems beyond his control—the Communist Party, staffed by mannish or oversexed women who issue abrupt commands and send Philbrick on errands, and the FBI, which refuses to give Philbrick any information about the cases he's working on, and instead passes his knowledge on to those who can act on it.[18] In fact, it is often difficult to determine just what it is that Philbrick does to fight Communism. Countless episodes show Herb delivering precious microfilm or paper documents to the FBI for quick copying, but we (like Philbrick) seldom learn what secrets the documents reveal. As Philbrick himself asserts, knowledge is his most effective weapon, but even that weapon often eludes him. In his struggle to assert masculine authority, Philbrick is ill equipped to fight that which he does not know—the specter of feminized Communist power.

Philbrick is faced with a troubling condition—the only source of power for him is to turn to the FBI, but this bureaucracy constantly strips him of his agency and effectiveness. He faces the difficulty, to borrow from William Whyte's *Organization Man,* of asserting his "individualism *within* organization life." In his continual deferral of authority to the FBI—the real, and invisible, source of "agency" in this narrative—Herb must learn to become an effective "organization man" and learn to, in Whyte's words, "love Big Brother."[19] But in *I Led 3 Lives* Big Brother is not so terribly different from Big Sister—the feminized Communist Party. The FBI is constructed as a benign, if constricting, social force, whereas the Communist Party threatens to undo, with violence if necessary, the stability of gendered power relations. The two are linked, though, in how each strips the masculine protagonist of his individual agency. Consequently, it is to the home that Herb ultimately retreats—to the family that depends upon his leadership, and to the secret office and darkroom where he can produce his own knowledge of his experiences. In his struggle to act as agent of his own historical narrative, Philbrick must retreat to a place of refuge in the private sphere where he can escape the prying eyes of the FBI and the Communist Party. This tension—surrounding the spy's difficulties of asserting his agency within the confines of state bureaucracies—emerges in later espionage programs as a principal point of conflict.

Communism and the American Family Ideal

In one of many episodes in which Herb's cover is nearly blown, he rushes back home to prepare yet another of his FBI reports. As he scurries down a side street looking over his shoulder, he says to himself in voiceover:

> Home, Philbrick, a man's castle. When an enemy attacks your castle, you fight—you fight with any weapon you can lay your hands on— this is your home, Philbrick, and you fight. Get to your weapon— your secret weapon. Sally said they know *everything* about you. Here's one thing they *don't* know about. A secret room in the attic of your own home. This is it, Philbrick—now *your* finger is on the trigger. Your weapon is information—get that report typed up now. This is your weapon, Philbrick—information.[20]

The home is important for several reasons: it is the local battlefield on which the global ideological struggles of Communism and democracy are staged, and it is the only place in which the "organization man" can fully exercise his agency. And more generally, it is the point at which television enters the private sphere, linking citizen-audiences to official institutions. But because the home is such a politically charged environment in this era of social containment,

Citizen Herb shares a moment with the audience in his attic office, where he is hard at work with his secret weapon: information.

Philbrick and his family are constantly at risk there as well. Philbrick's home is a place of contingent personal security always under the scrutiny of Communists and FBI agents, the site at which the counterspy, hidden in a secret chamber, generates the knowledges that enable him to produce his history.

In his autobiography Philbrick describes the secret room that became his private refuge: "The little square room [in the attic] was a household sanctuary to which I could escape. But the secret room was also a prison to which I was sentenced for long dark hours on many nights after Communist meetings." Herb, like other middle-class fathers of the 1950s, retreats to the suburban fortress of his home.[21] Even there, however, Philbrick must enclose himself in a secret attic room so that he can engage in the practice of writing history. Hidden from Communists, FBI, and family alike, Philbrick gains access to this windowless chamber through a secret door in the back of a storage closet. This place of refuge is rarely featured in the television program's narrative, but it appears in the closing credits of many episodes. As the music swells, Philbrick sits hunched over his typewriter in a dark and musty attic, giving closure to the events that have just taken place. Philbrick's narrative and historical agency merge in this diegetic space that bridges the gap between the fictional Philbrick and his "real" counterpart—as we hear Philbrick's voiceover explaining the narrative's final resolution, he invites us back again next time to witness the true experiences of the man who "really did lead three lives." Like Greaza of *Treasury Men,* the actor Richard Carlson speaks simultaneously as a fictionalization of a real figure and as a patriotic citizen.

Paralleling the prominence of the home in *I Led 3 Lives* is the show's constant assertion that the "real" Philbrick (as well as his fictional equivalent) is just another everyday family man with an upstanding social background. In his notes for the pilot episode, Philbrick imagines an FBI agent describing him as "clean as a whistle. [He] comes from a good family background, has an excellent reputation in his church and in his business, and has a long record of legitimate youth activity and work."[22] Here Philbrick bolsters his credibility through the strength of his family ties. Further, he often claimed that the one thing that enabled him to withstand nine years of Communist indoctrination was his "good family."[23] The television program worked to reinforce the importance of Philbrick's family life; his position as family patriarch invests him with credibility as a source of legitimate knowledge.

Some of the most memorable episodes of *I Led 3 Lives* are those that bring the threat of feminized Communist power into the Philbricks' home. One episode, which begins in Berlin, features Comrade Marta, another East German "Mata Hari," as she interrogates a young Communist man about his failure to recover a critical dossier:

> MARTA: You're still an American. A turncoat GI. I don't believe you. . . . Let's see you prove it.
>
> RUDY: I can't prove anything Comrade Marta, but I give you my word. As the man that brought you into the party. As your friend.
>
> MARTA: My friend!? You have the nerve to resort to such bourgeois sentiment? That proves it! You're nothing but a capitalist traitor!
>
> RUDY: (Getting more agitated, he's fighting for his life) No . . .
>
> MARTA: I've heard enough!
>
> RUDY: Please! It's like I told you. It was impossible to cross the border. I'll get the envelope for you, and I'll bring it back. I promise I'll bring it back. . . . I'll bring it ba . . .

In a burst of aggression of which a TV mom like June Cleaver or Harriet Nelson might only dream, Comrade Marta cuts short Rudy's pleas with a blast

"If I didn't know you were a loyal Party member, I'd say you were afraid of me!"

from her Luger, and he crumples to the floor, dead. When Philbrick enters the room, she looks him over with contempt: "You hope that we have no assignment for you. You would prefer to go home to your American family, to your wife. That is more important to you than Party loyalty, isn't it?" Herb protests, but as proof of her seriousness Marta orders his return to America to show the other comrades the spent shell casing from the bullet that killed Rudy. Little does Herb know that Comrade Marta will soon bring her distinctive negotiation style directly into his own living room.

Back in the States, Herb's wife, Eva, is sewing a button on Herb's jacket, a gesture he clearly appreciates: "Thanks, honey. You don't know how good it is to have a wife who sews buttons on instead of shooting them off—meaning Comrade Marta!" Later, when Marta arrives in the United States for a visit, the Party orders Philbrick and his wife to house her. After the two women meet at the Philbricks' home, Eva sits in the living room painting her fingernails. The armed and dangerous Communist operative glares at Herb's wife and snaps, "I find the charm you American women affect rather sickening. If I didn't know better I'd say you were jealous. If I didn't know you were a loyal Party member, I'd say you were afraid of me!"

After watching this exchange with dismay, Philbrick insists to himself, "You're not gonna let a girl with a little pistol try and stop you." Indeed, after ridding his family and the Western world of Comrade Marta, he ruminates, "I wonder if Eva would like to go out for dinner tonight." With a smile, Philbrick returns home to his wife, where his relief in surviving Marta's invasive presence is equaled only by his contentment in his wife's docility.

In an episode called "Child Commie," Communism infiltrates the home in the guise of a seemingly innocent ten-year-old girl. Beth, the young daughter of a leading Communist official, comes to stay with Herb and his family for a few days. Little does Herb know, however, that Beth is a Party spy who intends to expose his disloyalty: "I don't think you really care about your Party work," she tells a meek-faced Philbrick. "I don't think you really care about Communism. There's something funny about the way you act—something funny and dangerous. And by the time my father gets back, I'm going to know what it is!" Like the Communist publisher Jameka, Beth is something of a revisionist historian. She tells Herb's daughter that the American founding fathers were hypocritical cowards, and she steals some documents from the glove box of Herb's car that she believes will expose his counterspy activities. Philbrick eventually tricks her and covers his tracks, but not before she gives him a significant scare.

When she invades the Philbricks' home, Beth very nearly disrupts Herb's practice of gathering and analyzing information that can be turned against the Party. In fact, he admits to his wife that while that "junior Commissar" is in the house, he cannot risk entering the secret room where he usually prepares his reports. If the home is lost in the battle with Communism, the program seems to suggest, the counterspy will no longer have a place of refuge from which to mount his struggles over historical knowledge. Far from being an innocent child, Beth threatens Herb's agency as an historian and substitutes instead her own version of American history.

By the end of the episode, little Commie Beth has inspired more pity and contempt than fear. And it is Herb's young daughter, Connie, who delivers the moral lesson that closes the episode, ironically voicing the anxieties of a paranoid American masculine subject:

"I don't think you really care about your Party work. I don't think you really care about Communism. There's something funny about the way you act—something funny and dangerous!"

CONNIE: I just had to make sure that everything Beth Dickson told me was lies— and they sure were. . . . I didn't like her very well. I feel sorry for her.

HERB: Sorry?

CONNIE: Yes. I don't know why, but it seemed to me even though she was smiling all the time, she didn't really mean it. It seemed to me she was a sad little girl. Don't you feel sorry for her?

HERB: Yes darling, now that you mention it, I do feel sorry for her.

In this scene, Herb's daughter reiterates what the episode tells us all along— that Communism has the potential to turn otherwise charming little girls into stern disciplinarians, immune to what Elaine Tyler May has called "the cult of domesticity." In other words, Beth fails to embrace the moral and civic virtue of domestic containment. Further, her youthfulness is all the more threatening because she signals the emergence of an entire generation of Communist women for whom the cult of domesticity is not a natural fact, but rather an ideology to be questioned.

According to the program, one of the most egregious effects of Communism's permeation of domestic boundaries was that it precipitated gendered power struggles and replaced family loyalty with Party loyalty. As Philbrick insisted, "It is quite difficult for any person to move very deeply into the party unless the Comrades are certain that the husband or wife can be trusted. However, despite this 'trust,' the Communist Party still does not trust anyone; therefore it is the duty of even married couples to distrust each other. . . . Wives will turn in husbands, husbands will turn in wives, and children will betray their own parents."[24] In the program's idealized domestic family, Herb's authority is never questioned by his wife or daughters. In families "polluted" by Communism, however, women regularly contest the masculine authority of their husbands and fathers. Indeed, any feminine expression of discontent with masculine domestic authority is tainted with Communist subversion.

I Led 3 Lives is rife with families split asunder by Communism, and particularly by the fervent sentiments of wives and daughters. Permissive parenting, the program suggests, can lead to disastrous results. In an episode entitled "The Old Man," a Communist woman turns on her enfeebled and permissive father, insisting that he sacrifice himself for the cause:

> SARAH: The duty of every Communist is to be sacrificed in case of need!
> HOLMAN: But Sarah! You're my daughter! I brought you up to be loyal to the Party yes, but is there to be no loyalty, no feeling between us?
> SARAH: The party comes first, before any personal consideration!

Here, the show suggests that a Communist woman can be trusted by no one, not even her own father. Communism is constructed as an infectious force that shatters the bonds of family, weakening fathers and empowering women to seize cruel control of those around them. Sloppy parenting, the program suggests, leads to improperly socialized women who fail to embrace their own containment and who will eventually turn against their fathers.

I Led 3 Lives, like many of the suburban sitcoms with which it shared the television dial, strategically emphasized the sanctity and moral fortitude of the middle-class nuclear family. Such programs, Nina Liebman has argued, are characterized by an "omnipotence placed upon the family unit as site of both problem and solution" and "by an emphasis upon the father as the validation for a successful narrative resolution." Like programs such as *Leave It to Beaver* and *Father Knows Best*, *I Led 3 Lives* presents "idealized versions of family life, often pitted against outsider, dysfunctional units."[25] But what distinguishes

I Led 3 Lives from other programs of the period is the heightened degree to which Philbrick's family and home are threatened. Indeed, if *Father Knows Best* is an assertion of the sanctity of white American suburban life, *I Led 3 Lives* exposes just how tension-filled and anxious that construction is.

Like the Nixon-Khrushchev "kitchen debate" that displaced ideological conflict onto a discussion of the relative merits of American and Soviet washing machines and stoves, the terrain of ideological struggle in *I Led 3 Lives* is ultimately that of the idealized nuclear family. Building upon the authority of the "real" Herbert Philbrick's lived experiences, *I Led 3 Lives* constructs its historical narrative of Communism around a suburban family preserved by Philbrick's paternal authority. This precious preserve is the source of Philbrick's agency, but it is also the point at which that agency might be ruptured. The family is the site of the program's most heated skirmishes with Communism, and its patriarch must invoke the full resources of the most powerful law enforcement agency in the world to maintain its integrity.

Herbert Philbrick and the Shattered Family

The 1952 edition of Philbrick's book began with the following dedication: "To Eva, my wife: who proved that a woman can keep a secret."[26] In the pages that followed, as in the television program, Herb's family was celebrated as the source of strength that carried him through countless long nights as a counterspy. Philbrick, the man of "good New England stock," was supported tirelessly by his wife and daughters, and he led us to believe that it was ultimately for them that he acted. But not long after that first edition of *I Led 3 Lives* was released, Herb and Eva were divorced. A revised edition of Philbrick's autobiography was released in 1972, and in that version all references to Eva and his daughters were purged. Philbrick's family—the linchpin of his legitimacy in both the original book and the television series—was completely eliminated. The reader of the second edition might easily assume that Philbrick was single.

This peculiar twist has more than casual anecdotal significance. It is worth noting, not to point out the cruel ironies of history, but to bring into bold relief the dependence of the first edition of the book, and especially of the program, upon the organizing logic of Philbrick's family life. Were it not for the salient presence of the family in the tale of Philbrick's life, his story might never have had the cultural resonance it did. One is reminded of the cautionary tale of Matt Cvetic, another Communist-turned-informer from the early years of the Cold War. Cvetic's autobiography was the inspiration for the Ziv radio show *I Was a Communist for the FBI,* and had he not sold the picture rights to his story to Warner Brothers, Cvetic might easily have become the protagonist of a Ziv television series as well. But other factors might also help explain why Philbrick, and not Cvetic, became the three-lived hero. Cvetic was divorced by his wife and disowned by most of his family for his involvement in the Communist Party, and he was largely unable to recuperate his public image. Instead, he died penniless, discredited, and alone. While Cvetic never escaped the stigma of the untrustworthy informer, Philbrick, on the other hand, emerged as a heroic patriot, partly by constructing himself as a dedicated father and family man. Ziv producers then capitalized on the figure of Philbrick as a culturally sanctioned source of historical knowledge and, equally importantly, as a narrative anchor around which to build an episodic televisual account of Communism.

This anecdote also points up the disjuncture between the televisual representation of Philbrick's family and the actual lived conditions they and other American families faced. This disjuncture reveals once again how aggressively the program worked to inscribe Philbrick's complicated experiences into an episodic narrative of family life, but it also speaks volumes about the gulf between 1950s television families and the audiences that watched them. The rigidly inscribed gender norms common in 1950s popular culture texts were not so much a portrait of the time as they were symptomatic of areas of tension; programs like *I Led 3 Lives* act as what Alan Nadel calls containment narratives— popular representations that negotiate the social tensions of shifting gender identities by asserting an uncomplicated and uniform patriarchal order. The Cold War was a period of containment, certainly, in which, as Nadel writes, "the virtue of conformity—to some idea of religion, to 'middle-class values,' to distinct gender roles and rigid courtship rituals—became a form of public knowledge through the pervasive performances of and allusions to containment narratives."[27] Although such rigidly constrained narratives made persuasive appeals to conformity, they also demonstrated the distance between family audiences and the idealized proto-families that paraded before them on the small screen. As shows like *I Led 3 Lives* gave way to the more highly self-referential spy programs of the 1960s, this notion of nationalistic agency becomes increasingly impossible, and their discourses of containment slip.

On *I Led 3 Lives,* the family requires the full support of the FBI to maintain its coherence, but at least once it gets that support it is able to achieve some measure of stability. The program might, however, be read more critically as a compensatory gesture that exposes its own anxieties and points of slippage. For as Stuart Hall has argued, popular texts are marked by a double movement, a tension between containment and critique.[28] We might then consider how the idealized family unit of *I Led 3 Lives* compared to the shifting family patterns and nascent feminist movement that motivated the program's anxieties about the family in the first place. Instead of examining only the strategic ideological closure of *I Led 3 Lives,* we might read its representations of the family and Communism as a culturally productive feedback loop—a tautology that continually defers debate over these sites of anxiety by shifting their terms and displacing one onto the other.

The gendered narrative of this televisual history conflates domestic tensions over sexuality and the family with global political discourses on the Cold War, articulating anxieties about each via the representational tropes of the other. But this referential system in *I Led 3 Lives* is unstable, and the tenuous tautology of gender and Communism threatens to collapse and undo the program's strategy of containment. Critics like Nadel and Liebman have convincingly argued that containment narratives were largely, though never completely, successful in 1950s American popular culture, and that their collapse came nearly a decade later when the referential logic of Communism and gender exposed its own contradictory underpinnings. But *I Led 3 Lives,* a televisual history supported not by facts and events but by the gendered narrative authority of its protagonist, was perhaps also one of the first critical ruptures in the veneer of Cold War conformity. Thus Nadel's analysis of the 1961 political crisis of the Bay of Pigs is perhaps foreshadowed by this early 1950s television program:

> The fiasco manifested a national narrative whose singular authority depended on uncontrollable doubling, a gendered narrative whose coupling depended on unstable distinctions, a historical narrative that functioned independently of events, a form of writing that undermined the authority of its referents.[29]

Nadel argues that this media event exposed the commingling of nationalism and patriarchy, opening that dualism to popular critique. *I Led 3 Lives'* doubling of historical and narrative authority is perhaps an earlier, if less forceful, moment that similarly exposes the gendering of historical and political agency in the 1950s. Red vixens like Comrade Marta, who would rather crack a skull than a smile, may have voiced troubling tensions of which June Cleaver and Harriet Nelson dared not speak. And the weekly trials of Herb Philbrick, whose reiterations of patriarchal authority as head of the house and agent of history were constantly assaulted from within and without, may have been one of the moments on American television when the first cracks in the crumbling facade of Cold War masculinity began to show.

Certainly, though, this moment at which TV established itself as narrator of history stacked the deck in favor of the domestic father. *I Led 3 Lives* reminds us continually that the individualized American male is to be the agent of historical change and the subject of every "true" historical narrative. But counternarratives of American history lurk just at the margins of this cautionary tale. Figures like the ten-year-old Communist historian Beth are there to remind us that history itself is a terrain of infinite debate and struggle. And the strangely contorted history told by *I Led 3 Lives* reveals itself time and time again to be a battle over knowledge—over who can produce it, who has the power to act upon it, and who will contextualize it. Perhaps the show's Communist publisher, Jameka Lane, made the most insightful critique of the historiographic strategy of *I Led 3 Lives* from within its own fictive borders: "By mixing up known fact with statements we want the public to accept as true, in most cases it works very well. Basic psychology."

For a variety of reasons, the carefully constrained narrative model of *I Led 3 Lives* wouldn't survive the decade. Its precarious blend of documentarism and realist narrative, shared with shows like *The Man Called X,* brought together two ultimately irreconcilable modes of realism. While *The Man Called X* veered toward the realism available through specific references to political events and international locations, *I Led 3 Lives* ultimately depended upon the conventions of realist narrative to give legitimacy to its truth claims. Both modes would continue to influence later spy programs, but the awkward hyperbolic blend of the two that so characterized programs of the Red Scare era had begun to fray. This instability eventually contributed to the development of explicitly par-odic and comedic spy shows by the mid-1960s. In between, though, were two programs that teetered uncomfortably on the precipice—the documentarist *Behind Closed Doors* and the impossibly fantastical *World of Giants.*

3

The Irrelevant Expert and
the Incredible Shrinking Spy

This one really had me hysterical. The thought of a CIA agent hypnotizing a guy to pass on his information to him and then the London agent dehypnotizing him to find out the situation in Iraq is really beyond the scope of human imagination.... Someone must laugh you off the screen with this.... How laughable can you get?

—IRVING BRISKIN, COLUMBIA/SCREEN GEMS
EXECUTIVE, ON *BEHIND CLOSED DOORS*

In 1958 two new American spy programs entered into production. Hoping once again to capitalize on the profits to be gleaned from "real realism," NBC contracted to air *Behind Closed Doors*, a reality-based espionage drama developed and produced by Screen Gems, the Columbia Pictures short-films unit that had expanded into the burgeoning television market.[1] Like the shows that came before it, it was to be based on the files of a highly visible heroic figure—in this case, retired rear admiral Ellis Zacharias, formerly of Naval Intelligence. Meanwhile, Ziv Television added one last spy program to its catalog. *World of Giants*, which debuted in 1959 in first-run syndication, was one of Ziv's last new productions before the studio was sold to United Artists that same year.

Neither show was a commercial success. *Behind Closed Doors* made it through the 1958–59 season on the strength of its sponsorship contracts, but NBC declined to renew it after an initial twenty-six episodes. *World of Giants* was even less successful, with only thirteen produced episodes and a spotty distribution record. These orphaned programs emerged on the cusp of several crucial transformations: studio production was rapidly becoming the norm for network narrative programming; after a mid-1950s peak, the first-run syndication market was disappearing as the networks expanded both their schedules and their affiliate bases; in the waning years of the Red Scare, an increasingly powerful television industry began to diverge from the federal government and its political goals; the narrative model of "documentary melodrama" that was the product of these peculiar political relationships was becoming increasingly unwieldy in practice, and unconvincing to audiences; the simplistic treatment of the national interest central to the format was growing suspect, even to the point of parody; and, as the studios and networks began to look abroad for revenue, they realized this same jingoism would soon interfere with their global marketing goals. These transformations were ongoing from the mid-1950s well into the 1960s and can't be pinned simply to the transitional 1958–59 season. Still, these programs' awkward, contradictory, and sometimes incoherent narratives make them a fascinating portrait of an industry and a culture undergoing powerful changes.

Behind Closed Doors:
The Limits of Documentarism

Behind Closed Doors was created by Harry Ackerman, vice president of Screen Gems and already a successful television producer (he had been executive producer of *Leave It to Beaver* the previous season, and he went on to create *Gidget, Bewitched, The Flying Nun,* and other popular 1960s sitcoms). *Behind Closed Doors* was built upon the same narrative model as *The Man Called X* and *I Led 3 Lives,* using Admiral Zacharias's book as source material and Zacharias himself as an authenticating on-screen presence (the linkages among such shows were manifold; Ladislas Farago, the technical advisor for *X,* cowrote the book *Behind Closed Doors* with Zacharias, and the show employed several former Ziv directors and writers). From its inception, Ackerman sought to follow four goals in creating the new program: the show should be directly tied to issues of national security and should "show ingenuity on part of Intelligence" in carrying out real missions, but its characters should be readily intelligible and accessible (that is, they should conform to the norms of *narrative* television), and its stories should show "human interest" rather than remain "strictly documentary."[2] The tensions embedded in these goals—between officially sanctioned documentary realism and the conventions of narrative—would haunt the short-lived program. In this sense, *Behind Closed Doors'* struggle to make the transition from documentarism to fictional narrative encapsulated the broader transformations underway in television representations of spies from the mid-1950s to the mid-1960s.

By the late 1950s, Screen Gems was rapidly becoming one of the largest and most successful telefilm producers, including such programs as *Naked City,* the *Donna Reed Show, Alcoa-Goodyear Hour,* and *Father Knows Best.* The actual production of *Behind Closed Doors* was relegated to independent producer Sam Gallu, whose credentials included a popular radio adaptation of *The FBI in Peace and War* (CBS, 1944–58). This kind of production arrangement—in which a major film studio expanded into television and diversified its offerings through independent coproduction—was a common practice by the late 1950s.[3] Rather than create the programs themselves, studios like Screen Gems, Four Star, Revue, and Desilu often contracted out production to small independent producers, while the studio acted as virtual distributors, marketing the programs to networks and/or sponsors. As Christopher Anderson and Mark Alvey have shown, this arrangement often proved to be highly successful for the telefilm studios, although in the case of *Behind Closed Doors,* the mix of participants likely contributed to the undoing of the show.[4]

The interested parties who shaped the production of *Behind Closed Doors* included not only NBC, Columbia/Screen Gems, and Gallu Productions, but also advertisers and talent agencies. Rather than sell the program outright to NBC, Screen Gems secured direct sponsorship through the General Artists agency. The sponsors (ultimately Whitehall Pharmaceuticals and Liggett and Myers Tobacco) were represented by the Ted Bates and Dancer-Fitzgerald-Sample advertising agencies. Complicating things further was the program's tenuous relationship with both its official expert and the U.S. Departments of State and Defense, whose approval the producers continually sought for promotional purposes and to ensure access to military stock footage. The result was a production environment marked by divergent interests: a network, a studio, the studio's television division, an independent production company, two sponsors, three advertising agencies, two federal agencies, and a freelance official expert. The tensions among these groups often surrounded how to handle the program's blend of dramatic narrative with documentarism; each of the parties involved in the program envisioned this commingling in a different way.

Like other early spy programs, *Behind Closed Doors* began with a stamp of authority. Over a shot of the Capitol dome, the character Commander Matson announces, "This is Washington D.C.—nerve center of the Western world."

Though not directly involved in the production process, Admiral Zacharias was an important part of the publicity for *Behind Closed Doors;* the show's credibility rested on his certifying authority as an expert in international intelligence. Photographs courtesy of the family of Ellis M. Zacharias.

A close-up of a manila envelope stamped "Top Secret" fills the screen, and Matson continues, "This is where the phrase 'Top Secret' is the key to our national security—a phrase reserved for the eyes of a selected few." On a dark street, a lone figure approaches the camera, and then turns into an unmarked doorway.

"On this ordinary street lives an extraordinary man, a man who knows more about what is going on in secret today than anyone outside the government. This man is Admiral Zacharias, Deputy Director of Naval Intelligence during World War II. I work for this man. My name is Matson, Commander Matson. Tonight for the first time, we bring you an exclusive report from *Behind Closed Doors*."[5]

Typical episodes covered such topics as the development of the intercontinental ballistic missile, political assassinations, and the smuggling of top-secret documents of various types. Foreign location production was a part of the initial design, but was to be postponed until the show had developed a successful track record. Screen Gems sought to keep the show's budget at $35,000–40,000 per episode, though costs quickly crept above this figure. To supplement Zacharias's book, producers gathered materials from the State Department about foreign policy activities in such countries as the USSR, Iraq, Sudan, Ceylon, and Japan. As with other programs, documentarism was more a promotional strategy than a strict code; Ackerman explained to a writer that "while *Behind Closed*

Doors is to be presented as a semi-factual series of Intelligence cases that relate importantly to national security, we are interested in purely fictional stories, which we, of course, can then relate to some roughly comparable cases that already exist in government files." Still, the show's "semi-factual" foundations were crucial to its credibility.[6]

Almost an anthology series, the only recurring characters were the admiral, who appeared briefly in the opening and closing credits, and the fictional Commander Matson, who served as the program's narrator, sometimes engaging in brief conversations with the admiral and filling in narrative ellipses once or twice throughout the episode. In "The Photographer," for example, the protagonist is an expatriate American filmmaker who, disenchanted with his Communist handlers in Prague, turns his skills toward producing a covert documentary about the "Warsaw Riots"—likely a fictionalization of the Soviet invasion that squelched the Hungarian revolution in 1956. At the end of the episode, Commander Matson discusses the case with the admiral back in Washington, offering a commentary that seems to say as much about Hollywood of the period as it does about international relations: "We've certainly learned, Admiral, that motion picture film can be employed not only for entertainment purposes, but for vital top secret operations and counter-espionage." Though the series design called for each episode to hinge upon a U.S. agent who "sees all, knows all, and does all," the real sources of authority in the program were the admiral and the mediating figure of Matson.[7]

But while Rear Admiral Zacharias's public persona as authenticating expert was crucial to the show's truth claims, his role in the production of the show was a source of considerable internal debate. Compared to someone like Herb Philbrick, Zacharias was a bona fide spymaster and his credibility was beyond question, but his direct participation in espionage activities had largely ended with World War II. In adapting his book, the producers continually sought to relocate the espionage activities to the present, adapting stories to the context of the late 1950s, addressing such contemporary issues as the onset of nuclear proliferation and Soviet relations.[8] A paid consultant, Zacharias sought to remain at the center of the program as the key authenticating authority. Initially he was contracted simply to lend his name to the show and to appear without speaking while the fictional Commander Matson introduced each episode in voiceover. As the show developed, however, he was interested in taking over the role of "host-narrator" for double or triple his original fee. Zacharias also sought to expand the role of technical advisors—at one point recommending that a recently retired former colleague of his also be brought on the show to help develop scripts and smooth relations with the Department of the Navy.[9]

Screen Gems, however, was reluctant to embrace documentarism for a variety of reasons, related to both the cost and the narrative effectiveness of the documentary plot device. The first of these was the perceived relationship between the real admiral and the fictional Commander Matson. The top choice for the role of Matson was Bruce Gordon, a fairly well-known television character actor of the period. One of the principal sponsors of the show, Liggett and Myers, had serious drawbacks about using Gordon, who had recently appeared on several TV westerns, as well as *Perry Mason* and Screen Gems' own *Naked City*. For Liggett and Myers and their agency, Dancer-Fitzgerald-Sample, documentarism was the most important aspect of the show, and they insisted that it not be compromised. One of their negotiating team reminded Screen Gems, "I am sure everyone will remember that in our original meeting it was decided definitely that if we were to have an aide to Zacharias, he would be a complete unknown to the television audience.... It is a shame that the host selected is so well known that when people see him and he says, 'I am Admiral Zacharias' aide and have been for fifteen years,' they are going to laugh because they just saw him on *Gunsmoke* and your show *Have Gun, Will Travel*."[10] Nonetheless, Screen Gems increasingly used Matson, rather than Zacharias, to act as the on-screen narrator, though they attempted to bring in character actors who were less familiar to audiences. Initially, the program showed Matson outside the admiral's office during the opening sequence to borrow a bit of credibility from Zacharias without the cost and distraction of shooting scenes with the admiral. Even this was seen as burdensome, though, so this sequence was replaced with location footage of Matson introducing the given episode.[11]

Despite the show's assertions of authenticity, as a retired officer (even a very high-ranking one), Admiral Zacharias could not speak directly for the State Department or the Department of Defense. NBC, in particular, was deeply cautious of overstating the documentary content of *Behind Closed Doors*, and continually urged restraint. For the episode entitled "Flight to Freedom," Zacharias explained a plot in which American spies assisted in the defection of several high-ranking Soviet officials who were prepared to create a Washington-based shadow government. According to Zacharias, "Seven leading Communist officials were to defect, branding Khrushchev a tyrant and dictator, obsessed with power, and no longer guided by Marxist theories. It was tentatively arranged for American agents to land in Siberia and fly the Soviet officials out of the country. However, too many people knew about it and Malenkov, the ringleader, was arrested. . . . Malenkov, somehow, managed to commit suicide prior to his execution." NBC was deeply concerned about Soviet responses to such a claim, and insisted that the admiral "qualify his remarks by stating that these are the facts in which the most competent sources have advised us."[12] NBC's Continuity Acceptance Department advised Screen Gems:

> While recognizing in this series that the Communists are our adversaries, and in this light making them the "heavies" in our stories, it is nevertheless unwise to accuse them of crimes or complete depravity and brutality as brought out in this script. While not specifically a documentary show, the series has a strong documentary flavor, and infers that these things happened. The basic problem is that we are making very serious charges against a country with which we are engaged in a "cold war" but with which we still carry on normal diplomatic relations. . . . There is no objection to the portrayal of espionage and its by-products of stealth or violence, rather our problem lies in the portrayal of crimes against humanity and international law by the Commies. . . . I believe it would be wise through the whole series to use "Communist" wherever possible, rather than "Russian." This pits us against the leaders and the ideology rather than the Russian people.[13]

Executive producer Harry Ackerman was outraged, and vented to his associates at Screen Gems:

> To top this whole thing off, now NBC rears its ugly head. As of fifteen minutes ago, we have just received an official complaint from the network to the effect that we are injecting ourselves too much in the political scene by showing the Russians performing villainous acts against the U.S. If we must do stories about Russian espionage, apparently the NBC feeling is that we should not call a spade a spade nor a Russian a Russian, but should confine ourselves to phrases like "a certain country" or "a certain middle east group," etc. My feeling is that if we are forced to go completely in this direction, it

will be the death knell of *BCD*. We sold a series about the first time revelations of top secret stories, stories of espionage and counter-espionage activities, that shows how we have guarded the nation's security against the wiles and terrorist activities of the Russian cold enemy. If we are now forced to take out the word "Russians" and to write a large number of stories that have nothing to do with the Russians, it seems obvious to me that we will end up being a kind of cops and robbers spy chase series with no factual feeling about it whatsoever. It would also be a series in direct conflict with the kind of authentic framework we are attempting to put around it in the person of the host. I would appreciate it very much if you can arrange to contact NBC on this problem right away. I think NBC needs to be reminded about their own screen test of *BCD*.[14]

In this and other exchanges, NBC's anxiety appears to have stemmed less from domestic political concerns about unnecessarily angering the U.S. federal government, but rather international economic concerns about alienating and interfering with future markets. Just a few years later, NBC's recommended strategy of obscuring political references would prove to be highly profitable for Desilu as they marketed *Mission: Impossible* internationally, but here it was seen as a major stumbling block for a studio concerned primarily with domestic audiences.

The interests of Screen Gems thus diverged a bit from those of the network; while NBC was concerned about political responses that could incrementally erode their international relationships, Screen Gems was more intrigued by short-term profitability. Indeed, the studio saw this episode as a guaranteed hit and wanted to exploit its political fallout to attract larger domestic audiences: "We must coordinate all of our probable sources, so as not to tip it more than a day or two before air date. The most competent public relations experts have indicated . . . that such a story would be a front page news item round the world. It follows, therefore, that we can expect a sizable improvement in ratings."[15] At this moment in 1958, Screen Gems was largely interested in the immediate profits to be gleaned from domestic sales, while NBC—already beginning the international infrastructure development that would explode in the 1960s—was more concerned about long-term political relationships. By the mid-1960s, when the studios were themselves gleaning profits from international syndication, their concerns would more closely match those of the network, but in this earlier period their interests diverged.[16] The sponsors, too, were concerned about the show's international repercussions and insisted, for example, that an episode based on Vice President Nixon's 1958 run-in with an angry mob in Venezuela be handled delicately, given that their "products are widely distributed in Latin America, making it necessary that nothing be done to cause embarrassment to friendly governments."[17] Economics, rather than strictly politics, often exerted the most direct influence on the show's representations.

Behind Closed Doors was not, however, the unqualified success that Screen Gems had hoped for. The pilot, which aired on October 2, 1958, rendered disappointing ratings: 8.6/15.6 versus 19.5/35.5 for *Zane Grey* and 20.5/37.5 for *Pat Boone,* the show's direct competitors.[18] The show's Trendex ratings crept up from the pilot to the second episode, but then dropped for the third episode, prompting a flurry of exchanges among network, studio, and sponsors.[19] The awkward blend of documentarism and dramatic narrative was seen as a key factor, and as early as October Screen Gems considered renaming the show, changing the format, and/or eliminating or modifying Zacharias's role. The possible changes largely centered around moving away from the documentary-based format and toward a more conventional fictional narrative. The opening sequence of voiceover narration as Zacharias worked at his desk processing important papers was thought to be dull and inadequate. "Because all parties felt the present 'lonely street' opening was ineffectual in 'grabbing' the audience, it was agreed this be eliminated and that each program should commence with as dramatic a teaser scene as available from each respective episode."[20]

As the series struggled to reconcile documentarism with narrative, tensions among the production personnel and sponsors grew. Even as Liggett and Myers called for reinforcement of the show's connection to Zacharias, the show's alternating sponsor, Whitehall Pharmaceuticals, insisted upon more drama.[21] Richard Pinkham of the Ted Bates Advertising Company, who supervised the Whitehall account, grew increasingly frustrated:

> There seems to be a dichotomy in the thinking behind this show. *Behind Closed Doors* was sold to Whitehall as an exciting spy series full of action, ringing with authenticity and made urgent by its timeliness . . . yet I find myself in the reluctant position of having to

debate scripts with you. . . . I am as sure as I am sitting here that intellectual suspense without immediate physical jeopardy to an individual for whom the audience has generated sympathy will not produce circulation.[22]

What was at stake, for Pinkham, was the *kind* of authenticity the show generated. To him and to the sponsor he represented, the show's "authenticity" and "urgency" was generated not by documentary realism, but through the realism of classical narrative form.[23] Pinkham insisted that "there is no suspense in this close [with Zacharias]. . . . The only hope the show has is if it develops into an action melodrama series."[24]

Furthermore, Whitehall and Bates were increasingly skeptical about the ability of independent producer Sam Gallu to successfully manage this transition. Gallu preferred location shooting and natural-light photography, and wanted to relocate much of the show's production to Europe to increase the documentarist authenticity, in keeping with the show's origins in the semidocumentary cycle of early Cold War crime films.[25] This shooting style had been both successful and inexpensive for Ziv's *I Led 3 Lives* (and for the myriad other semidocumentary crime programs popular in the 1950s), but the costs of international production, coupled with Screen Gems' reluctance to surrender supervision to a producer thousands of miles away, quickly ended the practice.

The production of *Behind Closed Doors* was thus marked by a steady movement away from documentarism and toward dramatic narrative, even as some Screen Gems executives complained that such a move would "dissipate the sense of realism and authenticity the series was trying to achieve."[26] This inconsistency wasn't lost on TV critics of the period, and it caused promotional problems. Press liaison Gene Plotnik wrote to Ackerman, "A main current of reaction I've received from the press, both verbal and printed, on *Behind Closed Doors* is a sinking incredulity, which seems to be vitiating the impact and prestige of the show."[27] Plotnik had arranged for the show to be prominently featured in *Time* magazine, and he sat in on a preinterview between a *Time* editor and Zacharias:

The editor's opening gambit was "Admiral, we're curious to know why you should lend your name to a show as *fanciful* as this." We proceeded to discuss this point for the next hour and a half, during

which he was told further storylines, other experiences and findings
of Zacharias, with the repeated reassurance "These things really happen." The man from *Time* did not see how the public could be
persuaded.[28]

Thus the show was marked by deep schisms regarding how best to achieve
both public credibility and profitability. Plotnik—together with the Whitehall
Pharmaceuticals advertising representatives and the show's producer, Sam
Gallu—urged Ackerman to increase Zacharias's role in the program, bring
in additional well-known public figures to corroborate the show's claims, and
solidify the show's public-service status as a credible source of vital political
information.[29] Ackerman, the Liggett and Myers staff, and the senior Screen
Gems executives in New York insisted that such a move made the show overly
"intellectualized" and insufficiently action-oriented.[30] Furthermore, Ackerman
pinpointed the Zacharias segment that opened each episode, calling it "hokey."
He anticipated a situation in which one agency is "looking forward to the day
when we will be using Zacharias all the way through the show while at the same
time [the other] is instructing us to drop Zacharias entirely."[31] Each of the participants in these debates was seeking the same thing—realism—but through
diametrically opposite means.

Further complicating things were a series of miscommunications and dis-
agreements with federal agencies.[32] The Department of Defense (DOD) didn't
have any power to reject episodes outright or ban production (since the show
received no official endorsement), but they did insist upon reviewing scripts
before allowing location production on military bases, specific references to
military activities, or use of stock footage. This cooperation was not always easy
to secure; though Screen Gems was keen to promote *Behind Closed Doors* as
bearing the imprimatur of the federal government, the show was plagued by
communication problems with a government whose expanding bureaucracy
and generally skeptical view of the culture industries made endorsement a
chore. For example, the DOD's Office of News Services refused to cooperate in
producing an episode featuring a Regulus missile, claiming that "the story
over-simplifies the jamming possibilities of the REGULUS. It is felt that audiences might question the wisdom of the entire REGULUS program."[33]

The episode "SAC Story" prompted similar problems in securing approvals
from DOD and the Air Force. Producers had secured from the defense con-

tractor Convair Astronautics declassified stock footage of an Atlas missile exploding during a test flight. When the Air Force learned of this, however, they immediately demanded that the footage be removed. There was no direct legal claim that would have prevented Screen Gems from airing the footage, but in order to maintain their "future relationship" with the DOD, the studio felt it "urgently important to get their approval." The military contractor had released the film footage as a public service, but the Air Force apparently felt it reflected poorly on the U.S. missile program. Eventually a compromise was reached, but the incident and others like it hampered the studio's attempts to include direct documentary evidence of military and espionage activities.[34]

Because of network and sponsor concerns, Screen Gems also met with the State Department before the pilot aired to ensure that the government wouldn't disavow the show's claims. The Department's official policy regarding the show was that it wouldn't censor episodes, nor would it respond to them after airing—although they did request advance notice about programs that might question official U.S. foreign policy. The Department, did, however, have serious concerns about episodes that showed American agents operating illegally abroad, worried that they might be "fodder for the Red propaganda mill. The use of *BCD* stories as a tool for Radio Moscow is of greater concern to the State Department than any actual diplomatic objections."[35] While the State Department claimed to have no official response to fictional television programs, they raised objections to seven of the ten episodes offered them for review (two were approved without alteration, and one was felt to be outside the purview of the Eastern European division office that reviewed the scripts). Among the State Department objections:

1. re: Our scientist-escapee story. The S.D. feels the broadcasting of this story might prompt the East Germans to close the air corridor under the guise of protecting it against similar espionage by the U.S....
2. re: Our Arab-Dope Ring Outline. S.D. says such a story might infer that all Arabs are dope addicts. They point to our slim position with Nasser and say Egypt could resent inference....
3. re: Trial and attempted assassination of Tito. S.D. worried about U.S.-Yugoslav relations. Say such a story would almost certainly result in Belgrade protest to State Dept. Claim Tito is walking a slim line and hasn't full independence. Also S.D. says Tito, as a head of state, is deserving of greater respect.

4. re: Our story of SAC bases and the dope problem. Spears-Campbell pointed to previous Radio Moscow story that U.S. airmen are addicts when two were arrested in Berlin. Say that our story might give Soviet ammunition to say that here we are admitting it and trying to blame the Russians.

5. re: Our story outline on India rice market manipulations. SD touchy on India, and India would almost certainly resent it being told on television.

6. re: Our outline on sabotaging of goods for Middle-East and Asia. Our people say it might make us look bad. Also say UN is touchy on individual contributions. . . .

7. re: Our Soviet A-Bomb outline. State Department here specifically requested that such a story be withheld until after Geneva. Broadcast at this time could influence Soviets and lead to breakdown of the talks.[36]

In response to these concerns, some episodes were altered, and others were held back pending an upcoming summit with the Soviets (the summit in question didn't take place until May 1960, when it collapsed—due not to impolitic TV programs, but an incident of real American espionage, the Francis Gary Powers U2 spy-plane incident).[37] While the State Department (like the Department of Defense) claimed nonintervention in the production of the program, they made it quite clear that continued federal access would depend upon the producers' cooperation. The primary cause of federal concern was worries about how audiences in neutral countries perceived the United States. Wary of being seen as an aggressor, the State Department had begun its ideological struggle for the hearts and minds of the citizens of nonaligned countries.[38]

As part of their response to State Department concerns, Screen Gems set many *Behind Closed Doors* episodes in foreign locales. This was a way to escape some federal scrutiny, since it allowed the show to use agents who were not specifically identifiable as American. The episode "Double Jeopardy," for example, was set in London to avoid showing American agents infiltrating the Soviet embassy in Washington. Given the show's "already-shaky situation with the State Department," producers worried that a domestic location might bring unwanted federal approbation to the show's sponsors.[39] The show also actively embraced the Eisenhower era's domino theory, albeit for reasons more related to action-oriented plots than geopolitics. Episodes set in nonaligned or satellite countries were thought to be less inflammatory to both the U.S. and Soviet governments, but, more important, they could show more physical action than would be possible with the passive, overly "intellectual" confrontations between the superpowers.[40] The producers found it difficult to manage the "complex exposition" of direct spycraft between the United States and the Soviet Union, whereas violent confrontation could more easily be attributed to vaguely referenced proxy conflicts. Throughout, Screen Gems sought to "downgrade the intellectual suspense and highlight physical and active suspense."[41]

Despite the studio's efforts, the show never gained the kind of audience that would have made it profitable over the long term. Even with the decision to eliminate international production, the cost per episode was rising to over $60,000, even as ratings slumped.[42] By November 1958—barely a month into the show's on-air run—Screen Gems was struggling to save *Behind Closed Doors* and arranged hurried meetings with their sponsors. What had been conceived as a hybrid—straddling the "extremes of a documentary a la Ed Murrow's international programs, and the fiction approach as in the Foreign Intrigue programs"[43]—was now to be hastily reworked into a "purely fictional adventure melodrama spy series."[44] To reduce costs and resolve the tensions surrounding the show's documentary content, Gallu was released and production was brought back in-house for the second half of the season.[45] Furthermore, Screen Gems planned to drop both Matson and Zacharias and eliminate the show's anthology format in favor of a recurring protagonist. The show was canceled by NBC before these changes could be implemented, but one implication was clear: the awkward hybrid form known as "documentary melodrama" was waning in popularity and was giving way to fictional narrative.

World of Giants: *The Little Agent*

In 1958 Ziv Television was already among the most successful producers of reality-based espionage and crime dramas, and the company had been central to the development of the first-run syndication production model that was the precursor to 1960s studio production. That year, the company went into production on *World of Giants,* a science-fiction-tinged espionage drama. It was to be one of the studio's last projects; the syndication market was drying up and by 1959 Ziv would be sold to United Artists (atypically, the show was planned for sale to the CBS network, though the deal fell through). *World of Giants* is a transitional text not simply because it was one of the final programs of the 1950s syndicator, however. This program invokes the realist traditions of the 1950s

Life in *World of Giants* was a terrifying business; falling pencils and enraged cats were among the everyday perils faced by Mel Hunter.

Red Scare programs while simultaneously foreshadowing the self-conscious humor that marked the spy shows of the 1960s. Not quite a reverential civics lesson, but still not quite a parody, *World of Giants* is awkwardly suspended between.

World of Giants chronicles the exploits of an unlikely pair of government agents. Agents Bill Winters and Mel Hunter work for "the Bureau," a CIA-like organization responsible for both domestic and international espionage. But, as Mel tells us in an opening credit voiceover, we "are about to see one of the most closely guarded secrets and fantastic series of events ever recorded in the annals of counter-espionage. This is *my* story, the story of Mel Hunter, who lives in *your* world: a *World of Giants!*" When on a mission behind the Iron Curtain, Mel was exposed to a rocket-fuel explosion that inexplicably shrank him to six inches tall. As a result, Mel is under constant threat from his surroundings, but according to his doctors he has also been endowed with reflexes "somewhere between a hummingbird and a mongoose." The show literalizes 1950s Cold War anxieties about masculine frailty, and each episode sets about proving that even a "belittled" agent like Mel is vital to state security.

The show's connection to nuclear paranoia films wasn't just a matter of coincidence; William Alland—producer of the films *Tarantula, Creature from the Black Lagoon,* and *It Came from Outer Space*—produced several of the later episodes, and Jack Arnold, who had directed the latter two Alland productions as well as *The Incredible Shrinking Man,* directed some episodes as well. Though *World of Giants* has occasionally been cited as a British production of William Alland Productions, the show was conceived and shot entirely in Hollywood by Ziv. This confusion is understandable, likely due to the inconsistent records of Ziv in its final year and the thin distribution record, as well as to the fact that Alland was a rather high-profile producer by Ziv Television standards.[46] Though Alland's participation improved the production values (to reduce the production's use of cumbersome and expensive oversized sets, he brought in Universal Pictures' special-effects cinematographer, Stan Horsley, who instead used matte shots to represent the miniature agent), the high production costs and dubious narrative hook led to a quick termination.

The series begins not long after Mel's accident; the two agents remain together as espionage partners, with Bill becoming Mel's principal source of comfort and protection. The two are sent on a variety of missions, generally

For his efforts, Mel won the enduring thanks of his partner, Bill.

planned to take advantage of Mel's small size. Mel, however, still suffers from a sort of 1950s television version of post-traumatic stress disorder; Bill reports to the commissioner that "he has a nightmare now and again. He dreams he's back there behind the Iron Curtain where it happened. Goes through the whole experience—the missile firing, the explosion, the pain, the fantastic result, his shrinking to six inches."

The commissioner reassures the agent, telling him, "Mel is possibly the most important secret weapon this country possesses. I think he knows it, too."

Gravely, Bill agrees: "I think that's his reason for living, sir."

For a secret weapon, though, Mel is incredibly fragile. In the pilot episode, the opening credits show the tiny agent dodging human feet and falling pencils; later, he is nearly blown off a table by an office fan, and he is stalked by a housecat that we see in extreme closeup, roaring like a lion. In other episodes, a garden sprinkler is to him "a cloudburst, with the force of a hurricane." Encounters with fierce animals were a hallmark of the series, including a possum ("I couldn't talk my way past those fangs – I'd have to fight!"), a squirrel ("It looked as big and mean as a Rocky Mountain grizzly bear—judging by the look in his eye, he favored capital punishment for trespassers!"), and an angry

bee that enters the dollhouse that is his home and refuge. Although in facing these challenges Mel is serving his country and completing vital missions, the six-inch spy fights everyday objects and domesticated animals more than he does Communist spies. Given that his world is one of such constant danger, it is difficult to imagine that Mel could be of vital state importance—but this is the central conceit of the program, that the future of the nation might rest upon the actions of a fearful, shrunken agent.

In a sense, then, the show encapsulates—and exaggerates—the contradictory discourses of vulnerability and invincibility that marked the 1950s spy programs. Like Herb Philbrick, Mel is in constant danger, and his everyday environment is one of anxiety and paranoia. As Mel explains, "The risks I encountered as agent for the bureau were nothing compared to things that could happen to me in the daily job of just ordinary living." In his actions, the mundane and the fantastic collide. In "Death Trap," for example, Mel is flung from an automobile in an accident and awakes to find himself in a tangled jungle. Realizing that the "jungle" is common grass, he then plunges forward, only to encounter a gardener's brush fire. "I heard a series of explosions. . . . I thought I was back on Pork Chop Hill in Korea, but this fire was hotter than any battlefield!" The domestic landscape has literally become a battlefield, an obstacle course of the banal. As in *I Led 3 Lives,* Mel's peace of mind depends upon a secret place of refuge. While the *World of Giants* producers took care never to call it one, Mel lives in a dollhouse. Built into a secret cabinet in Bill's apartment, the dollhouse, Mel explains, is "the only place in the world where, if the pressure gets to be too much for me, I can forget I only measure six inches in my stocking feet." Twice, that inner sanctum is violated: once by a marauding bumblebee, and once by enemy agents searching for Mel. Fortunately for him, his partner is close at hand to protect him. In this way, the show exaggerates the threats of everyday life implied in shows like *I Led 3 Lives* to the point of hyperbole; control over the everyday domestic world is once again equated directly with the containment of Communism.

Given the peculiar nature of their relationship, Mel is heavily reliant on his partner. As Mel tells us, "I don't know how I'd survive without Bill." The program attempts to minimize this dependence, in part by creating situations in which the six-inch agent must overcome some obstacle to save Bill's life and complete their mission. Seldom, however, is Mel given tasks in which his size is an asset, perhaps because of the challenges of creating convincing special effects on a Ziv budget. Rather formulaically, Bill is often involved in fights with enemy agents that leave him knocked out. In these cases, it is up to Mel to get help— usually by making a phone call, tossing a message out a window, or slipping under a door. But these everyday tasks—which to Mel are Herculean—only serve to reinforce his helplessness. In one episode, Bill lies bleeding to death on the floor while it takes all Mel's strength to rotate the dial of a telephone. In another, Mel is trapped under an inverted wastepaper basket while a housecat stalks him outside. The line between heroism and impotence is dangerously thin.

Clearly, there is more than just a hint of sexual anxiety underlying Mel's feelings of inadequacy; a program about a secret agent and his six-inch partner's feelings of inadequacy invites a certain amount of playful interpretation, to be sure. Reluctant to encourage explicitly sexual readings of the pair, Ziv producers insisted that the writers not allow the dialogue to become too "coy," and they forbade any physical contact between the two agents.[47] Mel's usual form of transportation was a specially modified attaché case with a secure seat and airholes. Even in cases of emergencies, Bill never touches Mel; exposed to enemy gunfire, Bill nonetheless takes the time to lower the case to the ground, watches Mel climb in, and only then seeks shelter. An episode in which Mel has to invade a female agent's purse provoked even more editorial intervention on the part of the studio:

> Mel's proximity to a female hand, or any groping hand, the allusions and even the appearance of personal feminine things will not only make him doll-like, but will be inclined to make the audience sex-conscious, and even emasculate him. I think, also, that while we are never averse to seeing an attractive dame in our shows, his constant proximity to such a sexy dame cannot help but heighten this association.[48]

In this episode, "Teeth of the Watchdog," Bill seduces the woman while Mel crawls into the "female jungle" of her purse, wondering out loud where in this "female arsenal" an important microfilm is hidden.

While the production team was concerned about "sex-conscious" interpretations of Mel being fondled by a "groping hand," they appear to have been equally concerned with demonstrating both agents' heterosexual desire. Any possible sexual tension between the two male agents was displaced onto Miss Brown, a nurse and assistant to the agents. "Brownie," as she is called, supervises Mel's care. Bill, however, has other intentions, and repeatedly asks Brownie on dates. In one episode, he kisses her while the three of them are on an all-night stakeout, which immediately arouses Mel's jealousy. Half joking, he insists that he be "put in the middle." After a demoralizing narrow escape in another episode, Mel admits that Brownie's affections are sometimes all that sustains him in the long, lonely hours as a miniature man. "One thing about Brownie," he sighs, "when she looks at me, I never feel six inches tall."

The queerly unstable relationship of this tenuous pair of agents did more than complicate normative heterosexuality; it also invoked the specter of political subversion. Within containment culture, heteronormativity was deeply intertwined with patriotism. Not only was the idealized—and imaginary—nuclear family firmly ensconced as the appropriate cradle of development for future citizens; at the same time, gender subversion was seen as a direct political threat. Just a few years earlier the Senate had investigated homosexual employees, claiming in its report on "The Employment of Homosexuals and Other Sex Perverts in Government" that gays and lesbians might easily fall prey to the "blandishments of the foreign espionage agent." As Robert Corber writes, the period's pathologization of homosexuality "all but guaranteed that gender and nationality functioned as mutually reinforcing categories of identity. Homosexuality and lesbianism became inextricably linked to Communism in the nation's political imaginary."[49] When Bill, Brownie, and the commissioner meet to discuss Mel's fragile condition, they're in effect working to ensure the stability of his psychological state, considered at the time the foundation of normative gender identification. By extension, they're also working to ensure that Mel remains an effective national agent.

Though the narrative works diligently to remind viewers (and Mel) of his potency/agency, it continually falls short. Even to represent Mel visually in the frame with a "sexy dame" threatened to expose his vulnerability; like a miniature L. B. Jeffries in *Rear Window,* all Mel can do is watch. One episode literalizes Mel's voyeurism: In "Rainbow of Fire," Bill and Brownie are dancing in the agents' living room, practicing for a Central American trip. As Mel grows jealous once again, Bill produces a new device that will take advantage of Mel's small size. The Bureau has prepared a specially modified twin-lens camera in which Mel can ride. Rather than travel in a bulky briefcase, Mel can now be part of Bill's tourist paraphernalia, looking out through the camera's lens. As he puts it, "this is like living in a television, only I can't turn you off!" The trio is sent to Mexico, where they eventually retrieve an errant missile through Mel's effective surveillance and his ability to convince a young boy that his voice is that of a "talking burro." Unlike Hitchcock's wheelchair-bound photographer, though, Mel can scarcely hope for the possibility of sexual, and psychic, closure, and his agency is continually deflected onto Bill.

In a variety of ways, this odd 1959 show forecasts a number of the standard narrative features of 1960s spy programs: a fascination with miniaturization and the implications of nuclear-age technology; an amiable pair of agents reliant on one another for success, with veiled homoerotic overtones; a conflation of sexuality and politics, staged as erotic encounters with female agents; and an increasingly ironic treatment of the gravity of their missions. But despite the ease with which today's audiences might read *World of Giants* as comic parody, it was played straight. Mel's accident was dealt with seriously by his colleagues, and the danger he faced (from everything from Communists to houseplants) was treated with real pathos. And while the basic premise of the program was so ludicrous as to be farcical, the regular briefings by the commissioner in Washington framed the show in terms of the legitimate threats offered by America's Communist adversaries. The result is a confusing, contradictory text; the anti-Communist, civic address of the show differed very little from such "documentary melodramas" as *I Led 3 Lives* and *Behind Closed Doors,* yet *World of Giants* clearly strains the limits of believability. When in the final credits Mel turns to the camera and says, "In the meantime, be careful—the little man could be you!" one isn't sure whether to wince or laugh.

World of Giants approaches, but can't quite cross, the threshold between the state-sponsored espionage dramas of the 1950s and the spy parodies of the 1960s. As Susan Sontag wrote of camp, "The essential element is seriousness, a seriousness that fails. Of course, not all seriousness that fails can be redeemed as Camp. Only that which has the proper mixture of the exaggerated, the fantastic, the passionate, and the naïve."[50] What makes *World of Giants* so difficult to characterize is precisely this sort of earnestness—the palpable dramatic tension and the passion with which it treats the political context of the Cold War. In retrospective viewing of the program, one gets the impression that a delicate balance is nearing collapse; the precarious combination of official state politics with narratives of adventure and intrigue has reached the very limits of plausibility. Within a few short years, this tension between the agent and the state would give way, leading to increasingly referential and playful narratives. But here, there is no parody—only earnest patriotism, spoken through an impossibly fantastical narrative.

For different reasons, neither *World of Giants* nor *Behind Closed Doors* were commercially successful, and they've largely disappeared from view in most histories of the period. Still, they each offer particularly revealing glimpses into a television industry in transition. Both were created at the tail end of a period of close correspondences between narrative televisual representations and state politics; both also invoked the narrative styles of documentarism that linked spy programs of the early to mid-1950s to specific federal agencies. The economic and political dependencies that generated those narrative styles, however, were fragmenting by the end of the decade. Emerging from their first decade as powerful institutions in their own right, the television networks were likely less concerned about winning federal approval than they once had been. Sponsors—once the most powerful direct influence on many kinds of programming—were losing control, and by the late 1950s, the networks would override sponsors' time franchises if the ratings didn't hold.[51] At the same time, the telefilm studios that were flourishing as sources of programming in the new network system were reconstructing themselves to suit the new market, which was beginning to include not just domestic network sales, but international syndication as well. The influences of these various changes were sometimes contradictory, and often contentious, leading *Behind Closed Doors* producer Harry Ackerman to reflect, "I don't believe I was ever connected with a program that was so ill-starred almost from the beginning."[52]

These shifts were not just economic, but cultural and political as well. As the fervent zeal of the Red Scare dissipated by the end of the decade, the rigidly univocal narratives of the early 1950s were beginning to give way to representations that offered a more complicated portrait of the national interest. The increasing internationalism of the late 1950s and early 1960s directly influenced spy programs, which were rapidly detaching themselves from official discourses of state power. These transitional shows signaled shifts that would powerfully mark spy programs of the coming decade. Once articulated as an uncomplicated patriotic allegiance to state institutions, American nationalism and citizenship was beginning to be expressed through consumerism, travel, and class identity— principles that were, like American television itself, eminently exportable. Though neither *Behind Closed Doors* nor *World of Giants* made this transition completely, the confusion, debate, and argument that attended their production is a snapshot of an industry—and a culture—undergoing significant transformations.

Parody and the Limits of Agency

The essential element is seriousness, a seriousness that fails. Of course, not all seriousness that fails can be redeemed as Camp. Only that which has the proper mixture of the exaggerated, the fantastic, the passionate, and the naïve.

—SUSAN SONTAG, "NOTES ON CAMP"

In a real sense, then, the subject of nationalism does not exist. Conceived within this chronic duality [of self and other], the nationalist subject is doomed to demonstrate the impossibility of its own claim to subjecthood. The inner and the outer in mutual disarray, the nationalist subject marks the space of a constitutive representational debacle.

—R. RADHAKRISHNAN

In his obsequious history of the FBI (complete with a preface by J. Edgar Hoover), Frederick Collins wrote that the ideal FBI agent must "absorb the high ideals of the Bureau, [and adopt] that self-effacement or 'passion for anonymity' which is essential to the continued effectiveness of an FBI special agent."[1] This contradictory but apt phrase—"passion for anonymity"—neatly captures the tensions embedded in espionage programs. Television narrative requires individualized characters with will, desires, and, well, passions—hardly the stuff of the bureaucratic functionary. The spy is an "organization man" of the most acute sort; he must somehow be able to be an *agent* (in the sense of acting as an independent, willful subject) while sublimated to the prerogatives of the *agency*, the state bureaucracy he serves. In the documentarist spy programs of the 1950s, this tension is generally reconciled—albeit awkwardly—its contradictions elided through the closure of narrative and the authoritative stamp of the expert. But in the programs that followed, this underlying anxiety rises ever closer to the surface. To paraphrase Susan Sontag, the seriousness of the spy's patriotism fails; the premise that the spy is an autonomous representative of the statebecomes a ridiculous notion. Or, to put it another way, the television spy of the 1960s is less the *subject of* a narrative of nationalism and increasingly is *subjected to* the will of the state. The contradictory discourses that undergird the 1950s spy programs' construction of the spy as a national agent begin to unravel in the programs that followed, confounding the possibility that the spy show might unproblematically define the ideal citizen.

In many ways, the 1950s television spy narratives manifest what Daniel O'Hara calls the fascistic imagination—both by constructing an idealized masculine figure on whom rest the hopes and fears of the nation, and also by containing any expressions of cultural, racial, or gender difference within those narratives.[2] These fantasies of absolute control, though, also bore traces of their own impossibility. The harried father/undercover agent in *I Led 3 Lives* is little more than a pawn, his sense of agency a fleeting, desperate myth; the man called "X" is nameless, invisible; the putative authority figure operating "behind closed doors" (the real agent, Admiral Zacharias) is but a place-holder, insufficient to the demands of the national narrative; and Mel Hunter has simply withered away.

Part of what makes espionage narratives particularly revealing historical texts is this central tension, the possibility that the spy's status as a national subject teeters on the edge of a "representational debacle." Spy shows are more than icons of nationalistic prowess; they are also sources of intrigue and curiosity precisely because they reveal the limits of that prowess. Spy narratives' myth of agency demands an unlikely and unstable reduction of state power to the figure of the individual agent. Thus while TV espionage narratives are often overdetermined, marked by the heavy-handed and unquestioning authority of the state, they are also shot through with "multiple misrecognitions" and unstable conflations—the representational logic that reduces the national to the individual collapses into self-referentiality and parody.[3]

This collapse is the product of a number of influences, and can't be simply explained as the more or less inevitable formal and ideological devolution of a genre. It's very difficult even to characterize spy programs as a genre proper; sporadic and inconsistent, these programs appeared in fits and spurts that were more closely linked to shifting cultural and political conditions than to a linear process of refinement, revision, and decay. The film genre criticism that emerged in the 1970s and 1980s—influenced by a blend of structuralist anthropology and Marxist cultural criticism—took as its principal object the iconic genres of classical Hollywood cinema. Tom Schatz, for example, has argued that genres move from an early period of experimentation through classicism, refinement, and finally a baroque stage of stylized self-reflexivity.[4] Such a model is perhaps best suited to relatively clearly defined genres like the musical and the western, both products of a vertically integrated, efficient studio system. It is a bit harder to affix such a model to television in general—given its complicated economic foundations and hybrid textual forms—and to a format as emergent and shifting as espionage.[5] Instead, Rick Altman's recent critique of film-genre criticism seems doubly important to television. In order to understand how generic patterns operate in this medium, the text has to be understood as but one part of a complex set of determinants that include audiences, industries, and cultures.[6] The flourishing of parodic, self-referential spy programs in the United States beginning in 1964 is the product not just of generic self-referentiality, but rather of multiple transformations: industrial, textual, cultural.

The early 1960s saw the reorientation of the U.S. television industry around studio production. As production values of prime-time television programming began to more closely match those of film—particularly with the coming of color mid-decade—the comparatively crude semidocumentary style became an aesthetic anachronism. Furthermore, the new studios creating these programs saw their markets not simply as a single buyer (the national television network), but rather a burgeoning international market within which ideologically pedantic programming could be an impediment to sales. This international market was augmented by an exploding ancillary merchandising market that made outlandish gadgetry highly profitable; product tie-ins were generating tens of millions in sales, and they weren't simply being directed at children. Licensing issues aside, it's hard to imagine a large market for a J. Edgar Hoover doll—but a *Man from U.N.C.L.E.* gun-shaped cigarette lighter, board game, or comic book generated not just free publicity, but free profits.[7]

These transformations within the television industry were enmeshed in a culture emerging from the reactionary excesses of the Red Scare, which had militantly policed the boundaries of the nation and its ideal citizens. A growing incredulity toward political institutions and practices—prompted by such events as the Bay of Pigs scandal, the civil rights movement and its uneasy relationship to legislative politics and governmental agencies, the escalating and increasingly incomprehensible conflict in Vietnam, the assassinations of progressive leaders across American society—made the neat ideological package that was the 1950s spy drama an untenable proposition. The containment culture within which the federal agent represented an ideal citizen was fraying, as well. Betty Friedan gave a public voice in 1963 to the frustrations of women constrained by its narratives of family and home, and an emergent youth culture that was itself intertwined with the rise of television and other commercial media began to assert its cultural and political power.[8]

The cumulative effect of these influences is anything but linear, and it would be simplistic to suggest that the parodic programs that surged to popularity in the mid-1960s somehow inoculated the figure of the spy, vitiating the ability of that figure to speak for and about the nation. Nationalism wasn't rendered obsolete. Still, these programs opened up a space for debate about just what the "national" might mean in a shifting cultural climate. This moment of convergences—televisual and otherwise—exposed the inconsistencies in these programs' representations, particularly their tight conflation of the nation, the state, and the agent. These shows increasingly detached from the state, even mocking the official political discourses of anti-Communism and civic nationalism. Instead, the national interest was represented as participation in a global economy. What was once represented as duty began to be recrafted as privilege and pleasure.

Parody is a fiendish narrative form to make sense of; its pleasures, seemingly of the text, are of necessity contextual, evanescent, temporary. It is both within and outside the seductive pull of narrative, between interpellation and refusal, between ideology and skepticism. It's tempting to embrace parody as an inherently critical mode of narrative, and, further, to assume that to enjoy parody is to critique all that is conventional in its object of ridicule. By doing so we might read such shows as *Get Smart* and *The Man from U.N.C.L.E.* as pointed satire, mocking all that preceded them in uncomplicated glee. Such parodies seem an ideal form for audience-centered critics, eager to find the moments of rupture that perforate the text's normative ideals. But parody is not of the text; it is not a self-contained vessel, laden with social criticism. Instead, parody offers a "producerly text"—a porous narrative, rent with gaps into which audience members might (or might not) write themselves and their particularities.[9]

Parody is best understood not as a textual object, or outcome, but as a process. As Dan Harries argues in *Film Parody*, it operates as a discursive mode—a process of citing, revising, and commenting on its referent in such a way as to recontextualize its meanings, truth claims, and authority. Parody is thus of necessity both performative and intertextual; it "creates a sort of heightened 'intertextual dialogism' and demonstrates the importance of examining not only the textual qualities of a text based on another but also the contextual factors involved, including the viewer's previous experience with texts." Linda Hutcheon similarly characterizes parody as a "historiographical meta-fiction" in order to draw attention to the ways in which parody necessarily requires a look backward, even as it rejects or critiques the past. Its principal object is not history (or perhaps more specifically, the past), but is rather historiography, for its referent is the already-said—parody comments on and revises existing narratives of the past in order to reframe our relationship to them.[10]

In his discussion of British serial drama, John Caughie argues that certain kinds of TV spectatorship might be productively understood as an almost-Brechtian state of ironic reflection. "Rather than the abstract figure of the interpellated subject, ideologically seduced in the narrative, which seems to dog film theory," he writes, "art television seems to imply a viewer conceived to be intelligent, and possibly critical, 'reading' an author conceived to be intentional, and possibly creative." For Caughie, TV's continual interruptions, extratextual references, star system, and immersion in everyday culture work against the "relentless goal-oriented narratives which Bordwell, Staiger, and Thompson discuss in *The Classical Hollywood Cinema;* the 'everydayness' of space works against the fantasmatic identification with the narrative space which one experiences in the cinema."[11] This state of distracted viewing may be particularly characteristic of parodic narratives, which invite the viewer to look beyond and through the text, finding pleasure in its conceits. Parody requires a split spectator who oscillates continually between immersion and detachment:

> By "irony" I am trying to describe forms of relaxed detachment by which the viewer may be intellectually or emotionally engaged; or better still may be intellectually *and* emotionally engaged. These forms of detachment are by no means to be confused with distanciation, subversion, resistance, or political progressiveness, though some or all of these may be in play. Irony carries no guarantees of value, but it may be the condition in which values are put in play, and in which the viewer exercises her creativity.[12]

Caughie offers not an either/or, but a both/and; the emotional, interpellating pull of realist narrative is intertwined with ironic—and possibly intellectualized or politicized—skepticism.

The politics of this sort of spectatorship—which Caughie compares to Alan Wilde's "suspensive irony"—are deeply uncertain, since its playful acceptance of incongruity and absurdity threatens to slide ever closer toward political nihilism.[13] This mode of irony embraces the uncertainty that so disturbs some Marxist critics. Fredric Jameson, for example, argues that the "blank parody" of pastiche simply cites other texts in an endlessly manneristic, blind mimicry that has become a "neutral practice . . . without the satirical impulse, without laughter, without that still latent feeling that there exists something *normal* compared to which what is being imitated is rather comic."[14] Without a clear social referent, blank parody is, for Jameson, stripped of history, with the nihilist effacement of politics that accompanies this amnesia. For Jameson, parody must have a clear object of ridicule for it to have political salience. Otherwise, it slips into the endless play of surface references that he decries as characteristic of late capitalist culture. Though parody offers opportunities to see through and around the text in something akin to the "political unconscious," its referent is not simply social reality, but other representations, other histories; the hermeneutic loop refuses to close.

Caughie instead suggests that the politics of such representations reside not in the relationship between narrative and the social (that is, between representation and the real), but in the performance that mediates between the two. For Caughie, televisual spectatorship is not characterized by our uniform surrender to the identificatory pull of classical narrative, but rather by our "pleasure in detail, our engagement held not by the drive of narrative but by the observation of everyday manners and the ornamental."[15] Caughie's mode of spectatorship is intensely intertextual, referential to our broader experience of the medium. In this way, we might reconsider spy programs' relatively speedy transformation from documentarism to the embrace of artifice as symptomatic not just of political and cultural changes tied to the erosion of containment culture and resistance to the excesses of the political right, but also to the changing status of television narrative itself. The spy parodies of the mid-1960s required an audience literate in, and thus capable of skepticism toward, televisual narrative form.

Accompanying these programs' shift—from documentarist official discourses of national truths to their own parodic inversion—is a transformation in the mechanisms that bind these representations to the broader social sphere. The 1950s programs are, for the most part, antiperformance. Their flat, almost deadpan delivery, low production values, use of lesser-known actors, absence of stars, and continual reinforcement of the authority of the designated expert link them to discourses of public service and patriotism. But what emerges in the shows of the mid-1960s is something entirely different—an embrace of performance, of artifice, of stardom and its plastic pleasures. These programs' humor—and their political potential—resides in the glance, the aside, the intertextual moment that offer pleasures outside those of the always and already closed ideological world of the diegesis.

Agents and Acronyms: The Man from U.N.C.L.E.

From 1959 to 1963 very few spy programs reached the American airwaves. The Red Scare programs continued in second-run syndication, and a few shows dealt occasionally with international espionage themes, but the resurgence of spy programs didn't really begin until 1964. NBC aired a short-lived 1963 program called *Espionage*, for example, but it failed to capture much attention. A British-produced anthology drama, it most often dealt with historical incidents such as spy plots during World War II and IRA uprisings in the early twentieth century. In September 1964, however, *The Man from U.N.C.L.E.* premiered as the first significant American spy program of the decade. Eventually becoming a highly self-referential parody—of both itself and other spy shows—the first season of *The Man from U.N.C.L.E.* begins where *World of Giants* left off. In its earliest episodes, *U.N.C.L.E.* borrows heavily from the narrative conventions of the 1950s American spy shows—direct address to the American citizen, claims of "official" government sponsorship, and a reduction of geopolitics to gendered struggles over the individual agent's autonomy. Despite its increasingly comic tone, the show continues a basic inquiry common to all of the U.S. spy shows: a concern over the limits and possibilities of masculine agency within a bureaucratic system.

In part, of course, the show was a direct attempt to capitalize on the popularity of the new James Bond films. The Bond novels were already widely popular,

Illya, Solo, and Waverly, the men from U.N.C.L.E.

with some 30 million copies already sold worldwide throughout the 1950s and early 1960s. When *Dr. No* was released in 1962, American TV producers quickly moved to produce a derivative television program. Television producer Norman Felton, known for his dramatic television work on *Studio One*, *Dr. Kildare*, and

The Eleventh Hour, began work on developing a pilot. After reading Ian Fleming's travel book *Thrilling Cities,* the producer flew to New York and London for meetings with the author. Fleming wasn't interested in the television concept, but helped with the development of the lead character, Napoleon Solo, whose name was to be the original title of the series.[16] Fleming's involvement— and particularly the fact that a character in Fleming's novel *Goldfinger* was also named Solo—led to a series of legal battles between the producers of the Bond films and MGM-Arena, the studio developing the television program. The case narrowly avoided a court decision when, at Fleming's urging, MGM changed the show's title to *The Man from U.N.C.L.E.*

As a result, *U.N.C.L.E.* was the American spy show most directly associated with the Bond films. And indeed, the program's association with Fleming was an important point of promotion for MGM, and it helped build NBC's interest in the show as well. Napoleon Solo's suave demeanor certainly referenced Bond, as did the show's witty double-entendre dialogue and the playful sexuality of its agents. Another clear parallel is that *U.N.C.L.E.*'s enemy agency, T.H.R.U.S.H., is borrowed from Bond's archenemy, SPECTRE. But these quasi-governmental organizations also mark one of the most important points of departure of the U.S. spy programs from the British model of Bond films. Even as SPECTRE became a more understated part of the Bond diegesis, American spy television staged its conflicts as bureaucratic struggles between such organizations. In *The Man from U.N.C.L.E.,* conflict with T.H.R.U.S.H. is an organizing principle, shaping the show's central narrative preoccupation with the place of the agent within a state hierarchy.

This preoccupation marked one of the most significant points of departure between the American spy programs and the British variants. Like Bennett and Woollacott in *Bond and Beyond,* Toby Miller reads British espionage narratives as symptomatic of an overall decline in British geopolitical power in the aftermath of the two world wars. As a result, the figure of the secret agent becomes an important rallying point around whom British audiences could redeem "Britishness" as a vital national identity. Like the Bond films, the British spy television exports *(The Avengers, Danger Man/Secret Agent),* are about Britain in decline. The British spy programs, unlike their American counterparts, were much less concerned with forging links to official state agencies. As Miller writes, "For most of *The Avengers'* classic years, government is in off-screen space, kept from us . . . by Steed. He is the conduit who alone holds ideological and organizational keys to precisely what is being avenged." It was only after the program was explicitly marketed for sale in the United States that *The Avengers* began to explicate the institutional hierarchy within which the agents worked. In 1968 the program added the character of Mother, the spymaster modeled after Bond's superior "M" and Waverly of U.N.C.L.E.[17]

In contrast, the world of the American spy is a maze of acronyms. Nowhere is this more the case than in the parodic programs *The Man from U.N.C.L.E.* and *Get Smart.* The official agencies of the FBI, the CIA, and the KGB are supplanted by fictional ones: U.N.C.L.E., T.H.R.U.S.H., KAOS, CONTROL. In different ways, each of these shows extends the preoccupation of the 1950s spy programs with the anxiety of the agent operating within an institutional hierarchy. Where Herb Philbrick faced the organization man's challenge of finding a sense of individual identity within organization life, the agents of *U.N.C.L.E.* and *Smart* draw their authority from agencies unknown, and increasingly irrelevant, to most Americans' daily lives. Of course, this is all part of the fun; in the shows of the 1960s, the palpable tension surrounding earlier spies' crises of authority has given way, revealing that authority to be largely a façade. Unlike Britain, the United States was not weakened in the aftermath of World War II; it was strengthened. Throughout the early 1960s, the United States was in political and cultural ascension, with a robust economy and political power to match. Whereas James Bond—particularly in the novels and early films— redeemed the possibility of a virile British nationalism, the problematic of the American spy shows became much more a matter of how a government agent might retain some sense of individuality working within the bureaucratic machine of a growing empire.

Like the earlier spy programs, *U.N.C.L.E.* was promoted by NBC as one of "international intrigue" and "spine-tingling danger."[18] "This secret organization," NBC told viewers, "headquartered in New York, faces problems of enormous scope. It battles international crime or anything which may affect large masses of people or nations or a dangerous local situation somewhere . . . anywhere. Its principal enemy is T.H.R.U.S.H., ruthless, powerful, evil worldwide group for hire." In a significant departure from earlier programs, the United Network Command for Law and Enforcement was not a specifically American institution. Beneath a façade of a Manhattan nonprofit foundation lay "a maze of corridors and suites containing brisk, alert young personnel of many races, creeds, colors and national origins as well as complex masses of modern machinery for business and communications," according to an NBC press release.[19] U.N.C.L.E. was the United Nations, recrafted as a spy agency.

In keeping with the show's global reach (as well as with the détente that characterized U.S.-Soviet relations post-1962) Solo's partner was an enigmatic young Russian named Illya Kuryakin. Some episodes hinted that Illya might have been a double-agent, but this possibility didn't provoke conflict within the *U.N.C.L.E.* hierarchy. According to Felton, the spies in *U.N.C.L.E.* were "small, intelligent, unique, not particularly muscular... fans seemed to go for heroes of all nationalities. That's why the show was so successful both here and overseas. We offered a new type of hero."[20] This "new type of hero" stood as much for the cosmopolitan pleasures to be gleaned from international travel as it did for any particular government. The shadow enemy of this show is abstract and diffuse; as Solo put it, "T.H.R.U.S.H. might be a man. Or a woman. T.H.R.U.S.H. is the head of a secret international organization. Very powerful, very wealthy. T.H.R.U.S.H. has no allegiance to any country nor to any ideal. It will embark upon any undertaking which T.H.R.U.S.H. may decide is in its own interest." Like the American spy shows that were to follow it, *The Man from U.N.C.L.E.* often explored the dangers of international criminal movements without national allegiances. Rather than dealing with a clearly defined Soviet superpower, U.N.C.L.E.'s agents must confront splinter political movements and rogue multinational corporations; rather than pursue specific national interests, its energies are directed toward maintaining the flow of the global economy.

In the opening credits of the program, Solo and Illya arrive at the U.N.C.L.E. headquarters in New York, clearly meant to imply a UN special espionage division. Entering the headquarters through a secret entrance at the rear of a tailor's shop, Solo and Illya pass through several security checkpoints and dark hallways, eventually arriving at a central communications room where they meet their chief, Alexander Waverly. Turning to the camera in a direct address reminiscent of early spy shows, Solo tells us, "My name is Napoleon Solo. I'm an enforcement agent in Section Two here. That's operations and enforcement." Next, Illya similarly addresses to the viewer. "I am Illya Kuryakin, also an enforcement agent. Like my friend Napoleon, I go and I do... whatever I am told by my chief." Finally, the chief (played by Leo G. Carroll, who had in 1959 played the tweedy spymaster in Alfred Hitchcock's *North by Northwest,* a role clearly modeled on the real CIA chief Allen Dulles) turns to the camera, "Oh, yes. Alexander Waverly, Number One, Section One, in charge of this, our New York headquarters. It's from here that I send these young men on their various missions." This standardized intro (used only in the first season) is clearly fictional, but it allows the lead characters to speak to the audience in the authoritative voices of civic leaders, reproducing the documentarist address of the semidocumentary programs from which *U.N.C.L.E.* emerged.

In the same vein, each episode featured a statement in the credits: "We wish to thank the United Network Command for Law and Enforcement, without whose assistance this program would not be possible." The same stylistic cues that were for 1950s programs evidence of their unabashed patriotism are here invoked ironically. Still, the show generated some confusion, and the United Nations was swamped with calls from fans looking to enlist; the director of the UN General Services Division told the Associated Press that one would-be spy "was so intent on becoming a secret agent that we finally suggested that he get in touch with Interpol. I don't know what they told him."[21]

The tie-in promotions associated with the show encouraged this ambiguity. In addition to a host of novels, comic books, and toys that quickly hit the U.S. market, MGM released a tell-all "nonfiction" espionage book based on the "real" techniques of U.N.C.L.E. agents. Much in the style of books like *Behind Closed Doors* and *The FBI in Peace and War,* the *ABCs of Espionage* (1966) purported to offer a glimpse of the secret work of real secret agents. "All telephones are assumed to be tapped and all conversations must be conducted in code," the book began:

> Buildings with two or three exits must be used for assignations. All agents must master Judo, Karate, Aikido. All agents must be able to fit explosives into lighters, pens, matchboxes; prepare poisoned food and drinks; reduce documents to stamp-size microdots; learn the use of death-gas firearms. [These] ABCs of Espionage apply to the man from U.N.C.L.E. They also apply to the man from NKVD, OSS, CIA, the Deuxieme Bureau, and MI5. Here are the facts about how the world's great spies are trained in the deadly job of espionage— from the USA to the USSR.[22]

But in this particular case, these "facts," were corroborated not only by former spies, but by the fictional characters of *U.N.C.L.E.*: "Fantastic? It's all true. Here's the book that introduces you to the world's master spies, from Richard Sroge to Mademoiselle Germaine; here's where you'll discover that what Napoleon Solo and Illya Kuryakin do on TV is only what the real spies do—everyday, everywhere!" *The ABCs of Espionage* then goes on to describe a variety of espionage missions and training practices, all told in a similar breathless style. The agents the book discussed were real, including a number of World War II operatives whose cases had already been revealed in public. But notably, the book begins with an introduction by Illya and Solo—the fictional U.N.C.L.E. agents—who tell readers, "We present herewith an ABC of espionage—based on U.N.C.L.E. files. When you read these facts—and they are all *true facts*, not fiction—you will be studying details that are also recorded in the files of the CIA, MI5, and Deuxième Bureau."[23]

Thus despite the fact that *The Man from U.N.C.L.E.* made no direct claims to the kind of authoritative authenticity of the early 1950s programs, it nonetheless appropriated important aspects of their documentarist mode of narrative address. This authoritative address was prominent in the first season, though by the third season it was largely replaced by outlandish plots and self-conscious camp humor that in its embrace of popular culture, Pop Art, and political skepticism increasingly called authoritative nationalism into question. First among the spy programs of the 1960s, *The Man from U.N.C.L.E.* gradually supplanted explicit politics with consumerism. In the program, the nation-state was increasingly an object of nostalgia, ridicule, or both; what remained unquestioned was the flow of global capital that made their jet-set adventures possible.

When *U.N.C.L.E.* premiered, critics were simply confused by the program. A *Variety* reviewer wrote, "There is something wholly inadequate about MGM-TV's *The Man from U.N.C.L.E.* . . . The fact that you couldn't tell whether they were playing it for satire or for real made it all the more damning."[24] The show initially failed to find an audience, and it was only after the Christmas 1964 release of the third Bond film, *Goldfinger,* that audiences discovered it. Teetering on the edge of cancellation, the show became popular during the second half of the season and continued on the air for another three years. In part, the show's growing popularity was attributed to youth audiences—and particularly college students—who were becoming increasingly critical of the interventionist policies of the federal government. The show's young costar, David McCallum (Illya) was thought to draw the "college crowd, what Vaughn calls the 'hippies.'" Capturing his fans' ambivalence, McCallum told reporters, "There's a certain H. G. Wells prophecy about the show. It makes you say to yourself, 'Oh boy, I'm laughing, but maybe it's true.'"[25]

Even more important to the show's connection to left politics was Robert Vaughn. Son of a "loud-mouth liberal" radio actor who would likely have been blacklisted had he not suffered a fatal heart attack before appearing before the Committee, Vaughn was among the most politically active performers of the decade.[26] He had little contact with his father growing up, but was raised by staunchly Democratic relatives in Minnesota. Remaining in the family business (his mother was an actress), Vaughn relocated to Los Angeles in the mid-1950s to continue college and enter the film industry. His political clout expanded alongside his career, and he eventually became chairman of the California Democratic Party speakers' bureau. He spoke regularly around the country and helped found and led Dissenting Democrats, a national group critical of President Johnson's ongoing commitment to the Vietnam War. Though he insisted that he wasn't yet prepared to enter electoral politics himself, he was rumored to be interested in running for either the U.S. Senate or governor of California; when he appeared alongside Robert Kennedy and Martin Luther King, *TV Guide* called him "the other Bobby in politics."[27]

While working on *U.N.C.L.E.*, Vaughn continued his education, entering a doctoral program in communication at the University of Southern California. His dissertation, completed not long after *U.N.C.L.E.* was canceled, remains one of the definitive accounts of HUAC and the Hollywood blacklist. It was published in 1972 as the book *Only Victims* (with a foreword by Senator George McGovern), and has remained in print since.[28] The combination of his celebrity, education, and political commitments not only made him a preeminent public spokesperson of the antiwar movement, but also tied the movement to *The Man from U.N.C.L.E.* He spoke out regularly about the "national paranoia about anti-Communism," telling reporters, "I am totally involved in, and critical of, the Administration's foreign policy in Southeast Asia. The world is on the brink of atomic disaster. I consider this war madness."[29]

Friendly with Robert Kennedy, Vaughn once flew to Washington to spend the weekend with the senator and his family. After meeting with several senators and escorting fifteen-year-old Kathleen Kennedy to a dance, he spent the weekend discussing politics and American culture with the senator and Arthur Schlesinger Jr.[30] *Saturday Evening Post* described him as having a special bond with the late President Kennedy:

> There is a large American flag in one corner of Robert Vaughn's spacious office, and . . . on top of the desk, a replica of the one used by President Kennedy, rests a portrait inscribed by the late President. Also displayed are the *Public Papers,* in three volumes, that contain every word JFK ever spoke for the record. Vaughn signs all his own letters with the initials RFV. President Kennedy was assassinated on Robert Vaughn's birthday, and after a visit to the Kennedy grave, the actor admits he wept sporadically for several hours. As amateur Freudians might say, television's *Man From U.N.C.L.E.* quite visibly identifies with the martyred President.[31]

The *Post* article went so far as to suggest that his ideal wife would be a woman like Jacqueline Kennedy. When *The Man from U.N.C.L.E.* was canceled in 1968, the actor seemed poised for a political campaign, but reportedly "lost heart for the battle" when his friend and political role model Robert Kennedy was assassinated in June of that year.[32]

Vaughn was skeptical about the political and cultural worth of popular culture and became increasingly concerned about playing Napoleon Solo, a character he called "marginally psychotic." He reportedly kept two pictures of himself on his dressing-room wall. One showed him as Hamlet, performing for free in a Pasadena Playhouse stage performance, and it was labeled "ART." That photo hung next to one of Vaughn on the set of *U.N.C.L.E.,* labeled simply "COMMERCE." When *U.N.C.L.E.* was canceled, he expressed relief, claiming that "the violence in the show made me physically sick and, later, after what happened, I could not have continued to do it."[33]

Though Vaughn may have been reluctant to acknowledge it at the time, he was a principal symbol of a changing cultural climate in which art, commerce, and politics increasingly overlapped. His ideals led him to see the three purely separated from one another; he sought to dedicate himself, after his television career, to a life of public political service. But the cultural reach and lasting significance of *U.N.C.L.E.* lay not in its purely commercial appeal, nor in its status as high art, nor as a forum for explicit political commentary. Instead, the program was at various moments all of the above; serious issues of American foreign policy and official politics coexisted alongside the ironic pleasures of popular culture. *U.N.C.L.E.*, the show's young fans knew, was Pop.

Although Vaughn treated the late president as "pure" political martyr, the spectacle of the Kennedy administration (and even Kennedy's own admitted fascination with spy fiction) had itself become one of the most prominent symbols of the new sensibilities of Pop Art.[34] The art critic Mario Amaya declared in 1965,

> We have taken for granted a whole new set of signs, symbols, emblems and imagery, which has settled into our subconscious as a commonly shared visual experience.... As hideous, vulgar, repulsive, and cheap as some of them may appear, these commercial artifacts constitute a new potent means of visual communication.... The new art relies for visual and emotional impact on widely accepted trivia of the commonplace world, as seen and understood through movies, television, comic strips, newspapers, girlie magazines, "glossies," high fashion, "High Camp," car styling, billboards and other advertising. Rather than value art exclusively as something separate and distinct from life, these young artists have begun to see it as something inspired by the ready-made, fresh from the assembly line, as it enters everyday reality.[35]

Espionage programs, after *U.N.C.L.E.*, were central to this new Pop aesthetic.[36] Not only were the sets of these shows decorated with icons of Pop Art, the narratives themselves increasingly reflected Pop themes. Indeed, these programs increasingly explored the play of surfaces and fixated upon consumer goods and everyday objects—pet dogs, birdseed, typewriter cases, packages of pudding, ice cream trucks, a bottle of liqueur, suitcases, and candy... all are at once seductive and dangerous. In one *U.N.C.L.E.* episode, a package of candy sent to the daughter of a Yugoslavian scientist releases a gas that induces a paralyzing fear in its victim, Illya. A treatment for another episode proposed that "a dog turns into a four-footed weapon of terror... [and] Solo discovers that in various cities of the world animals have been trained to kill." Spy shows, in their

blend of the everyday and the urgently political, embrace the uncertain pleasures and terrors of modern life. As Toby Miller points out, "espionage has always
been part of pop."[37]

Though *The Man from U.N.C.L.E.* was a highly visible Pop icon, the movement exploded in early 1966 when the TV adaptation of *Batman* premiered on
ABC as a mid-season replacement. The show was created by William Dozier—
like Felton, famous for his work in the "golden age" of live television drama, lion-
ized for its transcendence of crass consumerism. *Batman* directly targeted the
same audience as *The Man from U.N.C.L.E.*, in hopes that it would catch on
with "young and old swingers alike."[38] *Batman*'s connections to the Pop movement were an important part of ABC's promotional strategy, which staged a
number of public events to reinforce the connection.[39] *Daily Variety* joked that
a promotional event featuring creator Bob Kane's artwork at the Guggenheim
might "stimulate some fresh dazzling quotes from pop-art high priest Andy
Warhol, who might be stimulated to attempt a nine-hour flick of the Batman
torso."[40] Blending high and low—and ignoring the middle—*Batman* was a
nearly overnight sensation.

By April, any hesitations Dozier might have felt about being associated with
such an unapologetically commercial program were likely ameliorated by his
unexpected new status as cultural authority; he appeared with Marshall McLuhan,
encyclopedia publisher William Jovanovich, and anthropologist Dell Hymes at
the Annenberg School in a public discussion entitled "From Gutenberg to Bat
man." In a self-promoting gesture that would likely have made Robert Vaughn
cringe, lead actor Adam West embraced his celebrity, pronouncing, "*Batman*
will be considered pop culture in the time continuum of our society. Talking in
art terms, I guess you could say that I am painting a new fresco. If you twist
my arm, I'll say that I'm the pops of film pop culture."[41] *Life* columnist Shana
Alexander devoted her "Feminine Eye" column to the new show, writing,

> The dynamic duo in their baggy underwear, the faint pot belly on
> Batman, the enormous size of the "boy," Robin, produce in me a
> small quiet joy.... By the time *Batman* was over, I had decided that
> it pleasantly parodied its own commercials, its own TV trailers, all
> other TV adventure series, all the old B movies—in short, tele-
> vision itself. Three cheers![42]

Batman turned inward upon its own representational history in a way reminiscent of *U.N.C.L.E.*'s ironic appropriations of the narrative conventions of Red Scare spy dramas. In anticipation of the television show's premiere, the 1940s *Batman* "B" serials were rereleased in theaters in December 1965, attracting an audience of college students who appreciated them as "Super Camp." The films had been created in two fifteen-episode packages in 1943 and 1949 and were hastily produced with minimal costumes and sets. Their forthright patriotism was as crude as the sets—the Dynamic Duo faced such threats as Fifth Columnists and "slanty-eyed Japs" in the earlier films, and a creeping Red menace in the 1949 sequence.[43] To 1960s audiences, however, the films were purely comic: "Those ears of his. They're hysterical. And those leotards he wears. There's a hole in the knee."[44] *Batman* premiered on television to audiences literate in, and critical of, the show's own intertextual history. As Lynn Spigel and Henry Jenkins write, "It reread mass culture through irony. Its appeal was based on laughing at the empty ideals of outworn texts and faded stars" in a way that offered an opportunity to critique cultural norms that just a few years earlier had been considered beyond reach.[45]

As the Pop movement filtered through television in 1966, its disruption of traditional hierarchies of cultural value and its embrace of ambiguity and the double entendre began to attract attention through a variety of sectors of American society. *Batman* was featured on the cover of *Life,* and *Newsweek* splashed a Lichtenstein-inspired comic across its cover, declaring, "POP! It's What's Happening . . . in Art, Fashion, Entertainment, Business."[46] Though the show was derided by some cultural conservatives and child psychologists, it was part of a broader transformation that was simultaneously cultural, economic, and political. Not a critique of normative culture from the margins, the show was broadly accessible and targeted at the mainstream; and its politics were entirely dependent upon the audience.[47] In what was inadvertently one of the most camp moments associated with the program, apparently the only ones not in on the joke were the Soviets. *Pravda* wrote that Batman was "the representative of the broad mass of American billionaires," that he brainwashed soldiers into becoming "willing murderers in the Vietnam jungle," and that Batman "kills his enemies beautifully, effectively and with taste, so that shoulderblades crack loudly and scalps break like cantaloupes."[48]

The overnight success of *Batman* in the winter of 1966 prompted NBC and MGM to reinvent *The Man from U.N.C.L.E.* The network wanted to capitalize on the Pop movement, and *U.N.C.L.E.* was the Bat's clearest competition. By the beginning of the show's third season in the fall of 1966, *U.N.C.L.E.* fully embraced the heightened intertextuality, consumerism, and slapstick comedy of Pop. The show's connections to the movement were sometimes overt; an episode about a deadly "hiccup gas" directly referenced the movement in its title, "The Pop Art Affair," and some episodes were scripted by *Batman* writers. The show began to embrace celebrity as well; in "The Hot Number Affair," for example, the popular duo Sonny and Cher guest-starred. The episode features Sonny and Cher music as in the background, "The Beat Goes On," "I Got You Babe," and other songs are freely interspersed with the *U.N.C.L.E.* theme. Set "somewhere in Greenwich Village," the episode opens with the death of a fabric designer at the hands of T.H.R.U.S.H. thugs. Apparently, he had designed a swatch of fabric for them that contained a secretly coded T.H.R.U.S.H. report, and once his work was done, he was executed. Chief Waverly sends Illya and Solo on a mission to recover the dress, telling them, "If we can find and decode that dress, we can deal T.H.R.U.S.H. a devastating blow." Thus the episode literalizes the period's growing attention to fashion, style, and pop culture; the dress is not simply the symbol of a T.H.R.U.S.H. conspiracy, it is the object of pursuit itself.

Working from an ad in a fashion magazine, Solo and Illya trace the dress to a pair of struggling garment dealers, known simply as Harry and Harry, and the agents pose as buyers. Meanwhile, Sonny and Cher work for the dealers— Sonny's character, Jerry, is a cutter and apprentice designer, while Cher, as Ramona, is their top model. Jerry had designed the dress in the photograph, made from the T.H.R.U.S.H. fabric, and now both T.H.R.U.S.H. and U.N.C.L.E. are desperately trying to recover it. Jerry, we quickly learn, is head over heels in love with Ramona, but she won't give him the time of day, regularly forgetting his name and calling him Gary instead.

The episode is marked by often-comic confusions, not only over the whereabouts of the dress, but over the identities of the characters involved. Harry and Harry are Armenian (Parkaginian and Sighn), but are heavily stereotyped as Jewish merchants. Just in case their accents and liberal sprinklings of Yiddish expressions and syntax aren't enough, the primary set piece in the shop is a stage used for fashion shows and product demonstrations. Behind the stage rests a large backlit screen, unmistakably patterned in six-pointed stars. Similarly exaggerated (and played for laughs) is Illya's cover character, that of a Japanese fashion buyer. Harry and Harry are skeptical at first, but are convinced by Illya's prolific bows and heavily accented speech that he will help them break into the Asian fashion market with the dress, their new "hot number." It is difficult to pin down just what is distinctly "national" at all in such instances; such moments reduce the national to the interplay of crude stereotypes in a mad scramble to the international market.

The U.N.C.L.E. agents cross paths with T.H.R.U.S.H. several times throughout the episode, as all are searching for the dress. It is nowhere to be found, since Ramona is unsure where she left it. After several chase sequences—punctuated by Illya and Solo unsuccessfully trying to convince the garment dealers that they are legitimate government agents—the dress finally turns up at Ramona's apartment in a package from a dry cleaning shop. Ecstatic, Harry and Harry rush home, elated at their success at recovering the dress, which has prompted calls from fashion buyers across the country. T.H.R.U.S.H., of course, arrives immediately behind them and prepares to torture them to turn over the dress. Bound on a table in their cutting room, one Harry says to the other, "Harry, like shish-kabob we're going." The final showdown is a slapstick brawl in the cutting room, set to a kazoo version of a Sonny and Cher song on the soundtrack, as Ramona watches and laughs. The U.N.C.L.E. agents are victorious, and the dress is recovered.

In the episode's final scene, Harry and Harry still don't recognize that they've been involved in what could easily have become an international incident, and they proposition the U.N.C.L.E. team to join them. Waverly arrives on the scene, declaring, "Well, it appears T.H.R.U.S.H. has been stymied after all once again, gentlemen. We've sent samples of the coded dress to U.N.C.L.E. offices throughout the world."

Eagerly, one of the dealers jumps in, "Did they like the samples?"

"As a matter of fact," Waverly says, "we've just received reports from our headquarters in Copenhagen and New Delhi. They're being besieged with buyers."

The second Harry is tremendously excited, crowing, "Beautiful, beautiful! Mr. Waverly, you'd have a great future in the dress business, and we could use a good outside man!"

The convoluted episode ends with Ramona finally turning her attentions to Jerry only after Solo has told her that the bumbling designer is actually one of U.N.C.L.E.'s must valuable operatives.

The episode thus fully melds the ostensible political crisis over the T.H.R.U.S.H. code (the consequences of which are never explained in detail) with a farce over the dealers' atavism. Blind to all else, Harry and Harry are desperate to save their business and turn Jerry's design toward a healthy profit. The U.N.C.L.E. agents are seen as irritants who have complicated their lives, and their recovery of the precious dress is only useful for its economic value. Much of the pleasure of viewing the episode, though, counts upon the viewer's familiarity with the star personae of Sonny and Cher. Cher's character is dismissive and aloof, while Sonny plays a forlorn suitor, desperate to win her attentions. It is difficult to read the episode as anything but an outright parody, for it suggests that the agents' intervention is not only unappreciated, it is largely irrelevant compared to the more immediate demands of commerce and the pleasures of fashion.

Another episode from the campy third season turns inward upon television itself, making a mockery of the domestic sitcom and the characters that inhabit it, while also inviting the kind of gender-bending queer readings that by 1966 even the mainstream press recognized as a central to Pop and camp.[49] "The Suburbia Affair" opens in an idyllic suburban neighborhood, filled with uniform rows of single-family homes. "Peaceful Haven Estates" is a growing community, we learn, and Illya and Solo pose as a pair of bachelors in search of the perfect home. They are greeted by a beaming real estate agent who calls the neighborhood "an adventure in serenity . . . perfect for two bachelors." The neighborhood's serenity is short-lived of course; U.N.C.L.E. and T.H.R.U.S.H. are both converging on the area in search of an elusive scientist who has discovered a process for creating antimatter.

Before the agents even have a chance to unpack, this storybook containment world begins to collapse around them. When the neighborhood milkman arrives with a complimentary sample, Illya sends him away. "No," he tells him. "We don't drink milk."

The milkman is dismayed; "You don't drink milk?" he asks. "Everybody drinks milk—it's the American beverage!"

The curt Russian simply replies, "Thank you, no."

Solo, eager to fit in, tells Illya not to be "unpatriotic" and takes the sample. The milkman, of course, is a T.H.R.U.S.H. agent, and the milk is the first of several bombs that explode in the kitchen. Fortunately, no one is hurt, and Solo quips, "I'm glad we didn't take the cottage cheese."

The episode continually plays upon the agents' awkward presence in the family suburb. The two quickly divide the housekeeping duties; Illya insists upon doing the cooking, while Solo is to do the housework. The two prove to be incompetent homemakers; the once-spotless house is wracked by explosions that Solo can't keep up with, and Illya's plan to make dinner for the pair is forever delayed by disaster. The episode continues to pun on the perceived tranquility of the suburb, turning it into a literal war zone, with enemy agents posing as milkmen, bakers, schoolteachers, and pharmacists.

The lead T.H.R.U.S.H. agent in the town is a stern matron named Mrs. Witherspoon, who resembles nothing so much as one of the schoolmarmish Communists of *I Led 3 Lives*. A fierce leader, she rules by intimidating her male associates. When the milkman fails to execute the U.N.C.L.E. agents, she looms over him, "So far, I haven't had to discipline you, but there's always a first time!" When another of her subordinates fails to complete an assigned task, she threatens to administer a spanking.

The episode collapses into a farce on mistaken identity; both U.N.C.L.E. and T.H.R.U.S.H. become convinced that the town's witless real estate agent is the missing Dr. Rutter. In a comic chase scene, Illya and a pair of T.H.R.U.S.H. operatives simultaneously converge on him, all disguised as ice-cream men. As the real estate agent makes a presentation to a pair of prospective buyers in a trailer on a construction site, Illya approaches in his ice-cream truck, locks them in, and hitches up the trailer. At about the same time, the T.H.R.U.S.H. team arrives—similarly disguised in an identical ice-cream truck—and a wild chase ensues. As the real estate agent and the prospective suburbanites bounce around in the trailer, Illya attempts to evade capture by careening wildly through the town's streets. The T.H.R.U.S.H. agents follow in hot pursuit, and the entire scene is set to the music emanating from the trucks' tinkling music. Thus as in programs like *I Led 3 Lives* and *World of Giants*, the everyday domestic world is fraught with tensions and threats. Here, however, the possibility that the geopolitical missions of international secret agents would lead them to a sleepy suburb is a source of farcical humor. But the episode's humor doesn't come simply from the slapstick antics of ice-cream truck chases; the episode instead references earlier spy dramas, even as it perforates the stability of the suburban landscapes of the domestic sitcom.

While the references to suburban sitcoms of the 1950s are a bit oblique, the episode's other references to film and television become overt. Mrs. Witherspoon supervises the proceedings from the living room of the house that is T.H.R.U.S.H.'s hideout. Through closed-circuit hidden cameras, she is able to monitor her agents' activities on the screen of a large console television in her living room. The T.H.R.U.S.H. ice-cream men, after a shootout that involves automatic gunfire and bombs, manage to capture Illya and the hapless real estate agent, taking them into a secret underground bunker beneath the T.H.R.U.S.H. safe house. When Solo arrives and blasts his way through the front door, a neighbor sees him and calls the police, telling them, "He put something on the door, and boom! Just like in the spy movies!"

Just as the police arrive, Solo finds his way down into the secret T.H.R.U.S.H. hideout. The slapstick tone continues, and the police watch the proceedings on the living-room television. As Illya and Solo fight it out with the T.H.R.U.S.H. agents, the police think they're watching a rerun of an old spy movie. Settling in to watch, the police laugh, "These movie fights—they always look so fake!"

Meanwhile, Mrs. Witherspoon has captured the real Dr. Rutter, played by musician and comic Victor Borge. He has kept the antimatter formula secret by converting it to a musical code and memorizing it. In order to stop T.H.R.U.S.H. from torturing his friends and neighbors, Rutter reluctantly reveals the formula by playing it on a piano as a punchcard computer verifies its scientific feasibility. At precisely the moment he is finished, Mrs. Witherspoon triumphantly declares, "I'm master of the world!"

Shortly thereafter, Illya and Solo then break in, rescue the doctor, and subdue the T.H.R.U.S.H. agents. The gender-bending continues in the denouement, in which Illya insists that he be allowed to finish the dinner he had planned to make. To celebrate their last night in the suburbs, he tells Solo petulantly, "I'm going to make a soufflé."

Particularly during this third season, *U.N.C.L.E.*'s most outlandish comic moments are often also moments of Pop-related gender subversion. Moe Meyer has argued that though camp was quickly appropriated by the mainstream in the mid-1960s, it nonetheless privileged queer textual reading strategies that confounded heterosexual gender norms.[50] The dialogue in such episodes as "The Suburbia Affair" openly encouraged queer interpretations of the Solo/Illya couple, and mocked the gendering of domestic relations that so characterized the suburban family sitcom.[51] Though the program is more convincingly interpreted as an opportunistic appropriation of Pop Art—and the queer subcultures that were central to it—than as an intentionally radical transformation of prime-time television, it is still particularly noteworthy given the discursive legacy of American spy programs.[52] Just a few years earlier, the spy was unerringly, even militantly, a heterosexual patriarch; any hint of gender instability in these shows was a marker of Communist subversion. Within such a context, *The Man from U.N.C.L.E.*'s gender play is profoundly political, inasmuch as it consciously foregrounds the arbitrarily constructed nature of social norms that were in the early Cold War invested with such cultural weight.[53]

The same season *The Man from U.N.C.L.E.* swerved headlong into camp, MGM developed and aired *The Girl from U.N.C.L.E.* When NBC and MGM executives met with Felton in the weeks following *Batman*'s January 1966 premiere, they urged the producer to develop a spinoff that might compete with *Batman*'s twice-weekly juggernaut. The character April Dancer was introduced in "The Moonglow Affair" in February 1966, and preparations quickly began for a fall premiere of what was originally to have been titled *The Lady from U.N.C.L.E.* (The pilot featured former Miss America Mary Ann Mobley in the title role, but she was replaced in the series by Stefanie Powers.) NBC was likely seeking to compete with ABC, which had a virtual monopoly on the teen girl market; ABC had not only aired the teen sitcoms *Gidget*, *The Patty Duke Show*, and *Tammy*—as well as the female detective program *Honey West*—the previous year, but had also picked up the British spy series *The Avengers* for its first appearance on network television for the 1966–67 season (the show had aired in syndication in some U.S. cities since the early 1960s).[54]

Given the period's shifting representations of women and girls—as well as the increasingly parodic tone of spy programs, once so predominated by a bifurcation between masculine action and feminine passivity or sexualized subterfuge—*The Girl from U.N.C.L.E.* might have been a truly groundbreaking show. Following on the heels of *Honey West* (a character Julie D'Acci notes was described in the press as "'Jane Bond,' 'Jane Blonde,' 'James Bond in skirts,' and the 'Woman from A.U.N.T.'"), it seems that the moment was ripe for a female character who might transcend the conventional confines available to women on American television.[55] As D'Acci and Moya Luckett have each shown, while the "single girl" programs of the mid-1960s imposed considerable limits on their protagonists' cultural and sexual mobility, such shows as *The Avengers* and (to a lesser degree) *Honey West* weren't simply reactionary, and instead "dismantled traditional binaries of sexual difference, producing new models of gender that permitted greater equality" and "focused on active female bodies to show a greater continuity between women and public space."[56]

Despite—or perhaps, ironically, because of—her place as title character, April Dancer was far more constrained than even other women in leading roles of the mid-1960s. Instead, she often seemed little more than one of the many distractions in an already convoluted narrative. Felton was reportedly lukewarm about NBC's request that he develop the new show, and he suggested instead that he produce two hours per week of a show titled simply *U.N.C.L.E.,* which would feature each of the agents in rotation. When that plan was vetoed, Felton suggested a shorter half-hour spinoff, "because to have a girl as the principal running character will make it more difficult to hold up in the hour form."[57] Giving in, he eventually paired April with agent Mark Slate and made her his trainee (April was originally to have been just seventeen years old, but in the eventual version she was twenty-four). April's usual task was to conduct surveillance, while Slate and other U.N.C.L.E. agents carried out the physical work of fighting with T.H.R.U.S.H. agents. April's principal contribution to one typical episode was to stand by while Napoleon Solo unraveled the sweater off her body in order to make an emergency rope; in other episodes it was not uncommon for her to be dunked in water, nearly raped by enemy agents, or otherwise reduced to a passive spectacle.

As with *The Man from U.N.C.L.E.,* though, some of the show's most interesting moments of gender subversion involve masculine sexuality; when in "The Kooky Spook Affair" Slate comments that an enemy agent was "quite good looking," his boss Waverly quickly snaps, "All right, keep it professional." "The Mother Muffin Affair" pushed even farther, featuring the aging horror

Boris Karloff as "Mother Muffin" in *The Girl from U.N.C.L.E.*

actor Boris Karloff in drag as Mother Muffin, leader of a band of assassins. It's difficult to assess whether the episode is queerly subversive, homophobic, or both; the scenes between Mother Muffin and her minions are often intensely sexualized, including the simulated fellatio of an assault rifle. But even in this period when representations of spies diverged from the narrowly defined allegiance to the state that marked earlier programs, an autonomous female spy was apparently unimaginable.

Still, the willingness with which both *U.N.C.L.E.* programs eschewed rigid nationalist narratives and instead embraced irony, parody, and even sharp social satire marked a powerful transformation in TV representations of American spies. These shows didn't abandon nationalism per se, but they were symptomatic of a representational sea change. In the *U.N.C.L.E.* programs, the national is difficult to pin down; rather than reproduce earlier programs' rigid linkage of self, nation, and state, they increasingly detached from the state and embraced instead a newly emergent model of national identity that replaced stern patriotism with commercialism, essentialist norms of gender and sexuality with camp play, and absolutist national boundaries with global mobility.

Get Smart: *The Spy Sitcom*

MAXWELL SMART: Agent 56 reports everything's normal in South America.
CHIEF: How normal?
SMART: Two revolutions and one assassination.
CHIEF: Perfect week.

"If any one series ever owed its life to *The Man from U.N.C.L.E.*," wrote one fan historian, "it was that ultimate parody of spy mania, *Get Smart*."[58] And indeed, *Smart* was by far the most explicitly comic programs of the spy cycle of the 1960s, adopting the parodic tone of *U.N.C.L.E.* and often turning it toward explicitly satirical ends. Created by Mel Brooks and Buck Henry, and produced by Leonard Stern, the show took American media culture itself as its principal frame of reference. Some historians have noted *Smart* as marking a generational change in television production; the program's writers were among the first to develop their careers entirely working within the new medium, rather than radio or film. Unlike the sitcoms of the 1950s and early 1960s, *Get Smart* offered a hero who "ditched cozy hearth and humble home for a bachelor flat with a booby trapped fireplace. Where *The Andy Griffith Show* based plots on finding mason jars for Aunt Bee and putting up pickles, *Get Smart*'s writers relished the ramifications of stashing those pickles and jars in fallout shelters, or using the ingredients of a salami sandwich to propel a rocket to the moon."[59]

Like *U.N.C.L.E.*, *Get Smart* was developed by a producer with roots in socially relevant drama. A former vice president of programming at ABC, Dan Melnick had cofounded Talent Associates with David Susskind, his partner in producing *East Side/West Side*, a critically acclaimed drama about New York social workers. *Smart*, however, was conceived as a social satire. Melnick approached ABC in 1964 with his proposal to develop a spy spoof that lampooned James Bond films and spy television programs, and the network agreed to fund the pilot. When presented with the Brooks/Henry pilot script, however, the network balked, with one executive reportedly complaining that the story about a bumbling federal agent's attempt to deflect an enemy attack on the Statue of Liberty was "dirty and un-American." ABC rescinded their offer, and *Smart* (like many of the decade's popular spy programs) eventually aired on NBC; the program premiered in September 1965 alongside *I Spy* and ran for five seasons. The show was a quick success, praised by *Time* for daring to be "healthily sick while the competition is all sickeningly healthy."[60]

Maxwell Smart, Agent 86, was everything Napoleon Solo was not. Clumsy, physically weak, and painfully dense, Smart is CONTROL's finest operative—twice winner of the CONTROL "Spy of the Year" award. Regularly captured, tortured, and misled, Smart is utterly inept. Nonetheless, he is the nation's best and last defense against foreign aggression. Smart is a deeply committed agent, fiercely loyal to his country, and anxious to thwart the aims of KAOS, the shadow criminal organization that threatens to disrupt the American way of life. The character was an amalgam, based partly on Brooks's and Henry's original series concept, and partly on a stand-up comedy routine that Don Adams had popularized in the 1950s. In his act Adams had developed a character of a wisecracking detective, a loose parody of the William Powell *Thin Man* films. Adams went on to appear on *The Danny Thomas Show* and its spinoff *The Bill Dana Show*, where he further developed the character as "Glick," a hotel private detective. When *Get Smart* premiered, it was assumed by some to be a spinoff.[61] Something of the second-rate hotel detective remained, for Smart was constantly finding himself in over his head.

Where *The Man from U.N.C.L.E.* skirted the boundaries between comedy and drama, *Get Smart* reveled in absurdist humor. Like *U.N.C.L.E.*, the pilot episode of *Get Smart* begins with an authoritative voiceover, evoking the documentarist spy thrillers of the 1950s. Against the backdrop of the U.S. Capitol—virtually the same shot that opened *Behind Closed Doors* and *The Man Called X*, among others—the narrator intones, "This is Washington, DC. Somewhere in this city is the headquarters of a top secret organization known as CONTROL. Its business is counter-espionage." We then cut to a concert hall, as a symphony orchestra is performing before an audience in formal evening wear. "This is Symphony Hall," the narrator continues. "Somewhere in this audience is one of CONTROL's top employees. A man who lives a life of danger and intrigue." Suddenly, a shrilly ringing phone disturbs the pastoral moment in the concert hall. The audience members glance around, startled, as the camera zooms in on Smart. "A man," the narrator informs us, "carefully trained never to disclose the fact that he is a secret agent." Of course, the ringing is coming from somewhere on Smart's body, and he leaps to his feet, dashing out of the hall. The ringing is coming from his shoe, which he answers only after forcing his way into the

Agent 86 takes an important call.

lobby, down a hall, and into a broom closet. Smart, we quickly learn, is anything but subtle.

Gimmicks like the impossibly absurd shoe phone were the hallmarks of *Get Smart*. When discussing secret missions with his boss, the Chief, Smart insists that they use the "Cone of Silence," a Plexiglas bubble that descends over the

Chief's desk to shield them from eavesdroppers. The cone, however, makes it impossible for those inside to hear one another, forcing them to bellow at the top of their lungs to be heard, which broadcast the conversation widely to anyone in earshot. Other devices in Smart's arsenal included the "inflato-coat," with mock arms to facilitate escape when captured and tied up; an "inflato-girl," used as Max's date while conducting surveillance on Lovers' Lane; the "Professor Peter Peckinpah all-purpose antipersonnel Mini-Mauser pocket pistol"; the "magna-lamp," a light table designed to illuminate sensitive documents that incinerated them instead; and a vast array of telephones embedded in combs, belt buckles, neckties, automobile steering wheels, and balloons. The technological wonders that were the Cold War spy's everyday tools were, in *Get Smart*, ridiculously ineffective.

The show quickly became popular, with Agent 86's stock phrases and strident delivery finding their way into widespread popular use. One of Smart's tactics, when under threat by KAOS agents, was to blurt out "would you believe . . ." followed by an unbelievable threat. In the pilot episode, he is held at gunpoint by Mr. Big, played by the dwarf actor Michael Dunn, who later that year became a recurring character on *Wild Wild West*. "At this moment," Max crows, "seven Coast Guard Cutters are converging on us. Would you believe it?" Mr. Big is unimpressed. "Hmm," Max replies, "would you believe six?" Mr. Big remains unconvinced. "How about two New York cops in a rowboat?" is Max's final offer. This "Would you believe?" line quickly became a standard fixture of television and radio ads. Impressionists mimed Don Adams nasal tone, as in the following spot for a New York radio station: "Hi, this is Maxwell, and the Smart thing to do is tune in to the seacoast's powerpacked hit machine, where every night Bob Prince will give away ten thousand dollars. Would you believe seven thousand five hundred dollars? Would you believe a salt and pepper shaker in the shape of an orange?" Another of Smart's catch phrases was, "Sorry about that, Chief," blurted out whenever Max made a blunder. According to historian Donna McCrohan, "When a urine bag broke aboard the Gemini 7 mission, NASA ground control commiserated with a 'Sorry about that, Chief.'"[62]

Maxwell Smart's partner was Agent 99, played by Barbara Feldon, who had recently achieved fame as a Revlon model. The program was Feldon's first starring role, after having taken smaller roles in several other Talent Associates programs as well as a guest role on *The Man from U.N.C.L.E.* The most capable spy working for CONTROL, 99 regularly extricated Max from difficult situations, all the while insisting that he was the real superagent. Preceding *The Girl from U.N.C.L.E.* by a year, Feldon was the first female lead on an American spy show. The fact that *Smart* was played strictly for comedy—together with Feldon's glamorous persona—likely broadened the range of the show's gender representations. As with *The Girl from U.N.C.L.E., Get Smart* doesn't offer a female agent as an alternative to a conventional masculine protagonist so much as it destabilizes the gendered discourses that underlie the masculine agent's authority. Feldon was also the show's link to the Pop Art world; owner of a prominent Pop gallery in New York, Feldon was painted by Andy Warhol for a *TV Guide* cover in 1966.[63] One of the running gags on *Get Smart* was that the urbane, sophisticated 99 struggled with her unrequited love for her clumsy partner. Eventually, she wins his heart, and the pair is married during the fourth season, which precipitates the show's steady movement toward more conventional sitcoms before its cancellation the next year.

Much of the show's humor is centered around the notion that CONTROL is just another top-heavy, impossibly complex government bureaucracy. Everything in CONTROL must be done by the book, and Max would be the last one to violate official procedures. Max is thus the most unlikely of secret agents; in his dogmatic adherence to regulations, he is the antithesis of a James Bond or Napoleon Solo. While those fictional spies were constantly at odds with the institutional hierarchy, Max is perfectly at home there. Demanding the Cone of Silence, Max gives the Chief a lesson in appropriate procedure:

> MAX: Well, Chief, rule 13 says that if . . .
> CHIEF: Max, why do you always have to live by the rules?
> MAX: Because rule 27 says that you must always live by the book!
> CHIEF: Someday I'll learn . . .
> MAX: Well, it's all right there in the book, Chief. All you have to do is look.

Each time he enters the Chief's office, Max dutifully punches a time clock, just another bean counter ready for his next mission. *Get Smart* took the CIA's own claim that its agents were anonymous bureaucrats to its most absurd extreme.

While *U.N.C.L.E.* intentionally obscured the show's references to the U.S. government, *Get Smart* reveled in them. The opening credit sequence of some episodes featured establishing shots of various federal buildings and monuments in Washington, D.C., and story lines about federal agencies were reportedly culled from newspaper headlines. When in 1966 FBI agents threatened to strike over a contract dispute about their pension fund, Buck Henry and Leonard Stern seized upon the event for a future script.[64] Among the show's running gags were phone calls from the president to the Chief's office. The only character who believed that the president was actually on the line was the Chief himself; other agents put the call on hold or simply told him to call back later. In an episode entitled "The Little Black Book," Max's old Army buddy Sid—played by Don Rickles—stumbles onto a case but refuses to believe that CONTROL is a legitimate spy agency. In order to prove that the case is a matter of vital national security, Max convinces the Chief to call the president in the middle of the night. Sid seizes the phone and apparently carries on a conversation with Lady Bird Johnson. "Yeah, sure," he laughs, "and I'm *Sidney*-bird."

Like any other state agency, CONTROL constantly faces budget cuts that threaten its operations, and Max often gets into trouble for wasting precious resources. In "Shipment to Beirut," for example, he attends a fashion show in search of a dress made of coded "micro-thread" that contains the plans for a "supersonic bomb." (This episode may have inspired the similar plot in *U.N.C.L.E.*'s "Hot Number Affair.") Max is repeatedly fooled by KAOS into thinking he's found the correct dress, so he buys several. None of them actually contain the plans, however, and Max is scolded by the chief for wasting thousands of dollars of taxpayers' money. To make matters worse, Max orders an "M4 complete mobilization raid" on the dress boutique, which depletes the CONTROL operating budget. In several episodes, the Chief is kidnapped by KAOS and held for ransom. Ransom money is apparently in quite short supply, however, and Max and 99 are stumped as to how to raise the necessary cash:

MAX: Where are we going to get that kind of money?

99: Couldn't we ask the government for help?

MAX: (exasperated) We're a top-secret organization. Not even the State Department knows about us! We just can't go running to them every time we have a problem!

99: Then what about Congress, Max? They could put through a special appropriation.

MAX: How long would that take?

99: Three months.

MAX: How about if it's an emergency?

99: Four months.

With resignation, the agents coordinate a "Help Our Chief Fund," complete with a raffle and prizes. Desperate, Max calls President Johnson for help, and the chief executive offers to contribute twelve dollars. In other episodes, a number of agents, including Agent 99, are laid off; in another, CONTROL is forced to lease their Cone of Silence to the CIA to raise money.

TV Spies and the CIA

[The malaise of the CIA] is part of a larger, more ominous trend, whose earmarks are a grotesque diffusion of responsibility, an accelerating dehumanization of the entire profession of intelligence, an enormous propensity for error, and the ever-growing phenomenon of a suffocating bureaucracy.

—PATRICK GARVEY, FORMER CIA AGENT

Get Smart was one of the few programs on American television of the 1960s that dealt with growing resistance to Vietnam in even the most oblique form. While a few military programs were on the air—including shows like *Rat Patrol, Combat,* and *Hogan's Heroes*—these all were set during World War II. And as film historians Linda Dittmar and Gene Michaud have noted, Vietnam was nearly invisible in American movie theaters, as well; *The Green Berets* (1968) was the only major Hollywood film set in Vietnam during the 1960s.[65] While *Get Smart* didn't explicitly mention Vietnam, the show's regular lampooning of the ineptitude of the federal government was more than simply slapstick comedy—it was an important point within American popular culture that gave voice to the antiwar movement. Most often, this was expressed in critiques of the CIA.

While other programs on the U.S. networks during the 1960s—including *The Man from U.N.C.L.E., I Spy,* and *Mission: Impossible*—avoided referring to actual federal agencies, CONTROL was engaged in an ongoing rivalry with the CIA. In "Temporarily Out of CONTROL," Max and the Chief are to be called up for active duty in the Navy and are unable to use their official status to obtain a waiver from service. The Chief explains that "CONTROL is such a super-secret agency even the Army and Navy don't know we exist."

Max is unwilling to accept such an explanation, complaining, "I still don't think it's fair. After all, they never draft the CIA."

The Chief, who understands the discrepancy, tells Max, "That's because the CIA isn't a secret organization. It's supposed to be, but it's not." The episode's direct references to the CIA, together with a plot line about the draft and the possibility of being sent unwillingly to war, made it rare among fictional programming of the era.

More significant, though, was how *Get Smart* became increasingly aligned with the domestic antiwar movement. Without the extensive production budgets of other spy shows of the era, and given its half-hour sitcom format, nearly all *Get Smart* episodes were set domestically. Thus while shows like *I Spy* and *Mission: Impossible* broke new ground through international location production and themes of international intrigue and travel, *Get Smart's* typical plot scenarios involved counterespionage on the homefront. The rise of *Get Smart's* popularity closely paralleled the growing criticism of both the Vietnam War in general, and the role of the CIA in particular. Just as the 1950s saw an increased visibility surrounding the work of the FBI, by the mid-1960s the secretive CIA was exposed to public display and critique.

By the mid-1960s, the luster surrounding America's "real" covert operatives was quickly wearing off. The process began with the botched invasion of Cuba at the Bay of Pigs in 1961, which was acknowledged to be a CIA-directed operation. The incident led to the resignation of Director Allen Dulles, a holdover from the Eisenhower administration who had been largely credited with developing the agency into an effective international espionage unit. In the aftermath of the Bay of Pigs, the agency became the subject of journalistic accounts and personal memoirs. In 1966, the *New York Times* ran a multipart investigative report on the CIA, discussing the agency's attempts to provoke a Burmese proxy war against China and its operations in Formosa (Taiwan), Congo, Laos, and Cuba.[66] At the same time, personal accounts of former spies began to be published both in the United States and abroad. These were confessional first-person tales of intrigue, similar in style to the books that were widely popular in the United States during the 1950s. These, however, were deeply critical of the United States.

Books critical of the CIA began to be published in English in countries around the world, including such titles as *I Was a CIA Agent in India,* published and distributed by the Communist Party of India. The author, John Smith, was a CIA agent who later defected to the Soviet Union. "Nevertheless," he wrote, "I still love the American people and I cannot become reconciled to the brain-washing which they are subjected to and which may eventually end in disaster for the land of my birth. I hope my autobiography will open the eyes of my readers to the great danger threatening the peace—the activities of the United States Central Intelligence Agency abroad."[67] These books were published as anticolonial critiques of American policy, but they were distributed in the United States as well.

By the end of the decade, critics were charging that the agency was "an insufferable bureaucratic morass with little or no central direction, sorely needing drastic change." The agency, far from being an icon of American valor, was reported to be damaging to its agents, who were described as "beaten to a moral pulp by their profession" and reduced to "little more than vegetables."[68] At the head of this "bureaucratic morass" was a series of directors, who each retired under questionable circumstances. The CIA director at the time of *Get Smart*'s premiere, Admiral William Raborn, was considered to be particularly inept. The *Saturday Evening Post* reported in 1967 that Raborn was

> a greenhorn at the spy game; he was insensitive to the professional pride of his staffers, inept at dealing in nuances, so unlettered in international politics, indeed, that he could not pronounce or even remember the names of some foreign capitals and chiefs of state. . . . At one staff conference, a well-placed source said, the Admiral interrupted his briefing officers to ask the meaning of the word "oligarchy." "Jesus," one sputtered afterward, "if he doesn't know what an oligarchy is, how can he handle about two thirds of the countries we deal with?"[69]

The bumbling Admiral Raborn was directly incorporated into *Get Smart* as Admiral Harold Harmon Hargrade, the director of CONTROL and the Chief's boss. He is a doddering old man who lives on prune juice and apparently thinks that Herbert Hoover is still president. The admiral's favorite hobbies, we learn, are burying old war buddies and napping. Played by William Schallert, the admiral is a regularly appearing supporting character, often called in during moments of crisis. He appears from a trapdoor beneath the chief's desk, and not only is he unaware of the intricacies of his agents' missions, he is incapable of carrying on a conversation. He drifts off to sleep, spontaneously falls over, or forgets his name regularly. Like his namesake, the admiral is but a figurehead, detached from the everyday operations of the agency.

During *Get Smart*'s second season, the CIA became embroiled in one of the largest public fiascos in its twenty-year history, one of direct relevance to *Get Smart*'s college audiences. The CIA had been secretly funding the National Student Association (NSA), an association of university student governments from across the country, giving the student group at least $3 million from 1952 to 1967. The NSA students were flown around the world as representatives to various international student congresses, while other members were supported as "resident representatives" in a number of countries. The CIA had been providing 80 percent of the NSA budget, including a free headquarters building in Washington, D.C.[70] The story was originally broken by the New Left journal *Ramparts* and was quickly taken up by the mainstream press, including the *New York Times, Newsweek,* and *Time. Newsweek* reported,

> The disclosure tarred the nation's biggest student organization as having been, for fourteen years, a CIA instrument overseas—and inflicted on the agency itself its most damaging scandal since the Bay of Pigs. . . . What [the CIA] bought was, principally, a credible public counterpoise to the Communists in world student affairs—plus some discreetly private intelligence reports on rising young political leaders abroad. The story thus conjured up particularly unlovely visions of the CIA's cloak-and-dagger pros seducing NSA's apple-cheeked amateurs into a corps of junior G-men known privately, around the agency, as "the kiddies."[71]

The revelation of the CIA's involvement with the "kiddies" provoked a widespread public debate over the agency's practices. Students for a Democratic Society (SDS) began a pamphlet campaign to raise public awareness, including a reprint of a *Village Voice* article written by Todd Gitlin and Bob Ross, "The CIA at College: Into Twilight and Back." They wrote, "Scratch an NSA man overseas, and he's likely as not to be a file-keeping, Washington-reporting spy for the CIA. In this way, the covert operation turned NSA into a tool which the CIA bought in installments, and kept in good running condition."[72]

The National Student Association had branches on 300 campuses nation-wide, and despite the CIA's involvement, it had a leftist reputation, passing resolutions condemning HUAC and the Vietnam War. "CIA agents, however," according to *Newsweek*, "not only influenced but penetrated virtually every NSA program abroad. And it favored certain handpicked, overseas representatives with secret stipends beyond their NSA pay, in exchange for reports on student politics considerably more detailed than the ones they sent the association."[73]

The CIA's actions were defended in other press accounts, however. *U.S. News and World Report* maintained that the agency was a last line of defense against "Red" aggressions. The magazine printed a sympathetic report, quoting a CIA agent's claim that "Now that the CIA cover has been blown... it will take a long time before any U.S. organization or group can regain the effectiveness that the National Student Association had. These students were not instructed how to act, except in a very few cases."[74] Nonetheless, critics called for a radical reappraisal of U.S. foreign policy. Senator and future presidential candidate Eugene McCarthy was one of the first to learn of the story, and he used the incident as a rallying cry to rein in the agency's hidden power (in another intertextual turn, one of McCarthy's most visible supporters was Robert Vaughn, whose day job was that of TV spy Napoleon Solo).[75] The scandal led to a presidential commission, headed by Undersecretary of State Nick Katzenbach, to reevaluate the CIA's role in covertly funding some 100 organizations, from political advocacy groups to labor unions.[76]

The scandal helped fuel growing critiques of the CIA. Further reports emerged, examining how the agency had attempted to use Fulbright scholars as espionage liaisons.[77] The CIA increasingly began to be seen as far more than just an international information-gathering arm of the government. As another SDS pamphlet wrote, "The elementary canons of democracy were sacrificed to the CIA's need for secrecy and the government's need to bolster its foreign policy aims. It is not too much to say that the CIA, which has repeatedly trampled on the principle of self-determination abroad, has denied that principle at home as well."[78] A cartoon that ran in newspapers and magazines across the country captured this sentiment aptly. It shows a slouching, bearded, and sandaled young man walking across a college campus. In the background, two young co-eds stand watching him, and one says to the other, "Oh, is he CIA? I thought he was FBI."[79]

With an episode entitled "The Groovy Guru," *Get Smart* brought this controversy to fictional television. The Groovy Guru, a popular radio disc jockey, is numbing the minds of America's college students with his trance-like music. The episode begins with Max undercover as a young hippie, complete with a wig, bell-bottom jeans, and beads. He accepts a package from a young woman he believes to be a CONTROL agent, but it turns out be a bomb, intended to sabotage CONTROL headquarters. Max and the Chief take this as a warning sign that the Guru must be stopped immediately. When Max and 99 investigate, they discover a fiendish plot: through the music of a popular band, The Sacred Cows, the Guru is sending out subliminal messages to his young fans. "Thrill, thrill, thrill," the Cows sing, "kill, kill, kill. Make a big scene...knock off the dean." Needless to say, Max and 99 subvert the Groovy Guru's plan, narrowly averting disaster. In part, the episode is a critique of late 1960s youth culture, portraying the Guru's young followers as dupes of a malevolent political manipulator. But while the episode treats youth movements as a subversive threat, it does so with an air of ironic detachment, and the anachronistic Smart is the real outsider here. Set against a context when political violence on college campuses was an immediate reality, this espionage sitcom was among the most topical and explicitly political of fictional television programs.

The episode bore more than a passing resemblance to an episode of ABC's *The Mod Squad*, which had premiered in the fall of 1968. In "The Guru," the Squad goes undercover to investigate the bombing of a radical student newspaper named *The Guru*. The episode begins sympathetically to the students and their concerns, and the Squad is sent in not to disrupt but to protect the paper. As the episode progresses, however, it becomes clear that the paper's own editor committed the crime himself in order to provoke a controversy and generate public sympathy. Tensions rise between the supporters of the paper and the various representatives of the establishment (most notably the "fuzz" who intervene when a protest turns violent). When the editor is murdered in his apartment, the Squad begins to suspect Daphne, a likeable but apparently misguided young woman who was the editor's oft-ignored girlfriend. Eventually it is revealed that Daphne's "two-button straight-laced" older brother was the murderer, but the episode's most trenchant criticism is really leveled at the students; whether criminal and manipulative (like Rick, the editor) or simply misguided and naïve like Daphne and her friends, the youth counterculture is portrayed as morally and spiritually adrift, desperate to restore stability to their lives. Through such representations, Aniko Bodroghkozy writes, the show "achieved a reputation for dealing sympathetically with the issues and perspectives of concern to the nation's rebellious young but did so in a manner that did not seem calculated to unduly ruffle establishment feathers."[80]

The most compelling implications of the parodic spy programs of the 1960s, though, may have less to do with their mechanisms of narrative closure than with their energetic and chaotic disruptions. Read only as narrative, episodes like "The Groovy Guru" generally resolved neatly, deftly containing whatever threat to the social order had emerged. In these programs, though, narrative is often secondary; their humor is farcical, disruptive, and intertextual. Rather than privilege narrative, these shows offer what John Tulloch calls a "comedy of formal disruption (which 'aware of language,' disorders and recombines it)."[81] In them, self-aware formal play—with narrative conventions, with star personae, with celebrity, with authoritative state institutions, with television itself—continually deflects our attention away from the flow of narrative, and toward intertexts of various sorts: the actor who played U.N.C.L.E.'s master spy was a prominent political activist deeply critical of the federal government's foreign policy; on *Get Smart* Agent 99's enduring affections for the pathetically ineffectual Maxwell Smart were made all the more absurd by actress Barbara Feldon's cosmopolitan glamour; when Michigan State students protested the university's $25-million covert CIA program, they sang a mocking song to the tune of Johnny Rivers's theme from *Secret Agent*.

At the same time, though, these programs can't be uniformly characterized as satirical social criticism. Though it generates critical opportunities, parody has a constructive, rather than simply deconstructive, relationship to the object of ridicule. It continually canonizes that which it mocks.[82] Looking at the root "para," Linda Hutcheon suggests that parody is as much "beside" the original text as it is in opposition.[83] Parody's potential lies not in its ability to shatter dominant norms, but to encourage us to rethink our relationships to them. The parodic spy programs didn't completely detach the spy from nationalism, though they did rather forcefully disarticulate the spy from the state. These shows rested upon a discursive legacy—inherited from the zealous anti-Communist programs of the 1950s—that was shot through with contradictions. The Red Scare's central conceit that the spy protagonist might convincingly and comprehensively embody the prerogatives of the state had become increasingly untenable. Shows like *Get Smart* and *The Man from U.N.C.L.E.* were part of a general cultural reevaluation that changed the relationships between the figure of the spy, the state agencies he ostensibly served, and the nation of which he was a citizen.

Other programs of the period reinvigorated espionage as a forum for the exploration of questions of citizenship and nationalism, but it was the parodies that most clearly exposed the inconsistencies and instabilities surrounding these issues in mid-1960s America. They bespeak a culture at odds with itself, one in which the legitimacy of the state's authority over, and ability to speak for, the nation was undergoing popular scrutiny. Ernest Gellner described nationalism as that force which binds the political to the cultural; it is "primarily a political principle, which holds that the political and national unit should be congruent."[84] For a variety of reasons, the turbulent conflicts of the mid-1960s confounded the neat equation of the nation with the state, and espionage programs (parodies and otherwise) were important sites for reimagining this relationship.

I Spy and *Mission: Impossible,* both of which were produced either contemporaneously to or after *The Man from U.N.C.L.E.* and *Get Smart,* actively worked to reconstruct an American citizen-subject within the changing cultural climate of the mid- to late 1960s. Neither of these shows portrayed the ideal national agent with quite the reductive singularity of the 1950s spy dramas, but they were no less concerned with negotiating dominant definitions of citizenship. *Mission: Impossible* dispenses with the notion of individual agency, instead constructing agents who operate as a highly technologized anonymous team. *I Spy,* on the other hand, engaged with ongoing cultural struggles surrounding the civil rights movement, carving out a space for a new black subject within dominant conceptions of the nation-state. The parodic programs *The Man from U.N.C.L.E.* and *Get Smart* didn't evacuate espionage of its ability to speak of and about citizenship, nor did they dilute the workings of nationalism within these texts. Instead, they contributed to a generalized reopening of cultural conversations about the linkages of state power to popular culture. At stake was the reinvention of "the national" itself.

5

I Spy a Colorblind Nation
African Americans and the Citizen-Subject

Everything I do is history. . . . They sell my seats for $250, project me on Telstar, and I keep my promises because nobody can whup me. . . . I am a very intelligent boxer, you know, and people don't ask me about my muscles. They ask me about Zanzibar and Panama and Cuba, and I tell them what I think.

—MUHAMMAD ALI, AFTER WINNING THE WORLD HEAVYWEIGHT
BOXING TITLE AND JOINING THE NATION OF ISLAM

In the cover photograph of his 1964 Blue Note album *Speak No Evil*, jazz saxophonist Wayne Shorter confronts the camera from behind a veil of bamboo. In the soft-focus foreground, an anonymous Asian woman gazes across the frame, aloof to (or unaware of) Shorter's presence. In the image, the musician has slipped the bounds of the North American continent, caught in a trans-Pacific tangle. The album's title, *Speak No Evil*, is superimposed by the scarlet smear of a woman's lip print, literally sealing Shorter's secret voyage with a kiss. In the liner notes to the album, Shorter reflects, "I'm getting more stimuli from things outside of myself. Before, I was concerned with myself, with my ethnic roots, and so forth. But now, and especially from here on, I'm trying to fan out, to concern myself with the universe instead of just my own corner of it."[1] In such cuts as "Witch Hunt," "Dance Cadaverous," and the title track "Speak No Evil," the music on the album similarly speaks to the seductions, pleasures, and dangers of travel. The implications of Shorter's international journey, however, are ambiguous. Shorter and the woman look past one another, deflecting what might otherwise be an Orientalist gaze onto her exoticized body. As increasing numbers of African American men in the mid-1960s were being drafted and sent to Southeast Asia, Shorter represents a different possibility for black American travel. Literally standing behind a "bamboo curtain," he has slipped beyond American cultural reach. Particularly in the context of the civil rights struggles taking place in the United States, Shorter symbolizes an increasingly interconnected black diaspora—one formed around allegiances both political and cultural.

In 1964 a number of highly visible black Americans were "fanning out," concerning themselves with "the universe," instead of just their "own corner of it." For a brief moment in the mid-1960s, black internationalism reached a point of high cultural visibility; Malcolm X and Stokely Carmichael made trenchant critiques of American racism while traveling in Europe and Africa, a number of black leaders actively promoted connections between African Americans and the newly independent nations of Africa, and the past experiences of earlier black American voyagers such as W. E. B. Du Bois and Josephine Baker were revived as symbols of cultural and political mobility. The mid-1960s were a particularly potent period when the possibility of an internationally derived African American political sensibility achieved unprecedented attention within popular culture. As the civil rights movement achieved a degree of legal sanction with the passage of the Civil Rights and Voting Rights Acts in 1964 and 1965, the movement was quickly written into a normative national history of what Manning Marable has called liberal integrationism.[2] International black activism, on the other hand, represented a radical departure from the nostalgic American idealism ascribed to the civil rights movement by mainstream American society. The period was thus marked by highly visible, public, and contentious debates over the international and social mobility of African American citizens. This tension was manifest in a number of sites of popular culture during the period, and succinctly encapsulated by the mid-1960s television program *I Spy*.

Like earlier espionage programs, *I Spy* (1965–68, NBC) is centrally concerned with questions of nationalism, agency, and the relationship between the self and the state. For the Red Scare programs, the central narrative project is to establish a singular voice of historical continuity and citizenship; these shows posit a unitary (and white and masculinist) figure as an ideal citizen whose actions are closely linked to institutions of state power and emerge along an unbroken historical timeline of patriotism and service. In *I Spy*, a variety of cultural and political transformations—most notably the civil rights movement—complicate the ideological determinacy of such a citizen-agent. Amid a context of African Americans forging identities informed by non-U.S.-centric nationalisms, the show links African American agency to what are perceived to be the founding principles of the American nation state; the national is founded on the historical.

While the tongue-in-cheek humor of shows like *Get Smart* and *The Man from U.N.C.L.E.* contributed enormously to the popularization of the espionage cycle in the 1960s, some spy programs remained responsive to "serious" social issues of the period. *I Spy,* in particular, represents something of a turn toward relevance.[3] The show did not avoid humor, but unlike the sharp parody of *Get Smart* and *U.N.C.L.E.,* the mild comedy of *I Spy* cemented the relationship of the agents and anchored them in familiar American cultural contexts. Spy dramas' central narrative prerogative was to preserve the integrity of the United States, which required that they be responsive to a shifting international and national political climate. The reductive binary logic of the Red Scare programs, though, could not sufficiently accommodate the challenges posed by the turmoil in Southeast Asia or the activism of African Americans fighting segregation. As the United States began to extend its political and cultural reach internationally, American "internal" race relations and "external" foreign policy were beginning to converge, with destabilizing consequences. The program that most directly engaged the period's converging discourses of race and nationalism was *I Spy.* At stake was the constitution of a new black American citizen; amid uncertainties about the place of African American and pan-African political movements in the new "global village," *I Spy* anchored black citizenship in normative American discourses of freedom and rights. At precisely the moment when increasing numbers of African Americans were crafting nation-based identities that had little to do with the United States, the show reoriented questions of American national identity around discourses of economic class mobility.

The civil rights movement manifested not just a domestic but a global crisis for the U.S. government. When President Eisenhower sent federal troops to enforce desegregation in Little Rock, he explained in a television address that this intervention was essential to U.S. foreign policy, which increasingly needed pro-American coverage in the international press.[4] And when Birmingham, Alabama, police commissioner Bull Connor unleashed his attack dogs and turned firehoses on black marchers in 1961, the entire world watched in disgust. The *London Daily Herald* reacted, "Racial intolerance in the South is a grave handicap to America's foreign policy, particularly as liberty is the keyword of that policy." *Paese* in Italy was even more direct in its editorial critique:

"Kennedy's future will perhaps be decided in the U.S. and not in Cuba, Laos, or summit meetings, because if the racists have a free hand they will rob of its value any 'democratic' policy America may pursue in the world."[5]

Some of the most critical responses to U.S. racism came not from the capitals of Europe, but from the developing world. As Johnson's head of the U.S. Information Agency, African American diplomat and journalist Carl Rowan admitted, "We have paid a harsh price throughout the world in recent years for the outbreaks of racial conflict in our country. There are remote areas of the world where 'Little Rock' and 'Selma' are more familiar names than Chicago or Washington DC."[6] To be sure, the editorial pages of many African and Asian newspapers were filled with condemnations of American racism. The *Ethiopian Herald* wrote, "It is no use telling us that the incidents occurred only in Alabama and not elsewhere in the U.S. . . . It is quite understandable that Africans feel that any segregation against the (American) Negro is simultaneously segregation against Africans."[7] American racial conflict destabilized the U.S. government's efforts to maintain its political influence in the rapidly decolonizing Third World.

At the same time, outspoken African Americans like Angela Davis and Stokely Carmichael found that their travel to North and West Africa, as well as to European universities, gave them important opportunities to vocalize their critiques of American racism. During the 1950s, the U.S. State Department had restricted the travel of Josephine Baker and Paul Robeson, accusing them of Communist subversion and warning them that "they considered the treatment of Afro-Americans a 'family affair' unfit for discussion abroad."[8] In 1956 HUAC launched an investigation of Robeson and Arthur Miller to determine whether to seize their passports; while Miller's hearing was "notable for its air of sober amiability," Robeson's quickly became a show trial, with the Committee eager to pillory the black performer for using the international stage as a political platform.[9]

By the decolonization period of the mid-1960s, both the international circulation of media images of civil rights violence and pan-Africanist critiques by black intellectuals like Robeson constituted major obstacles to U.S. efforts to expand its anti-Soviet "spheres of influence." In the context of this potential disruptive travel, *I Spy* offered a more palliative treatment of the globally mobile African American. A warning shot across the bow of international black activism, the show treated diasporic African critiques of American racism as tantamount to treason. Within the program, Bill Cosby's character Alexander Scott is figured as a key Cold War emissary, and his most important missions are those in which he blunts the political reach of pan-Africanism.

In this way, the program is deeply resonant of more generalized tensions within American popular culture surrounding the historical foundations of African American political activism. Particularly after the initial political successes of the Civil Rights Act and Voting Rights Act, mainstream discourses increasingly described African American political consciousness as emerging out of treasured American values of freedom and equality. At the same time, a growing pan-Africanist movement situated black agency outside the foundational mythology of the American nation-state. In *The Black Atlantic,* Paul Gilroy writes,

> [T]he acquisition of roots became an urgent issue only when diaspora blacks sought to construct a political agenda in which the ideal of rootedness was identified as a prerequisite for the forms of cultural integrity that could guarantee the nationhood and statehood to which they aspired. The need to locate cultural or ethnic roots and then to use the idea of being in touch with them as a means to refigure the cartography of dispersal and exile is perhaps best understood as a simple and direct response to the varieties of racism which have denied the historical character of black experience and the integrity of black cultures.[10]

This figuring of a "historical character of black experience" whose origins lay symbolically and physically outside the United States was unacceptable to much of white America, perhaps most powerfully symbolized by the charges of Communist subversion leveled at civil rights activists who dared link domestic and global race relations. As Plummer has argued, popular discourses on civil rights often "divorce it from its roots in a sophisticated understanding of the global arena and a general critique of imperialism."[11]

When *I Spy* reached American airwaves in 1965, it emerged not only at a point of prominent visibility for U.S. race relations, but also at a moment of uncertainty over how civil rights activism would be encoded in American history. The program interweaves the civil rights movement, African American social mobility, and international politics; *I Spy* offers a new kind of national agent, one who adopts an emerging civil rights sensibility and yet remains loyal to the state. Produced at a time when black activists were accused of Communist subversion, *I Spy* performs a subtle act of incorporation. In the show, *failure* to support civil rights is portrayed as far more dangerous and subversive than any act of civil rights protest itself. As a result, the program hollows out a space for a new black subject, one whose historical relationship to the foundational principles of the American nation-state is strengthened, not weakened. Primary among the responsibilities of the traveling black American, the show suggests, is to demonstrate to the world that the civil rights movement is not fundamentally a critique of mainstream American culture, but is rather its fullest, most patriotic expression.

Bill Cosby, Nostalgic Patriotism, and the Formation of the Civil Rights Subject

The first network drama to star an African American actor, *I Spy* featured Bill Cosby and Robert Culp as globe-trotting American spies Alexander Scott ("Scotty") and Kelly Robinson. Nearly every episode was filmed internationally, leading critics to call it an "exotic extravaganza," and a "chop suey of Fu Manchu, James Bond, and the Rover Boys Abroad."[12] Most of the first season's episodes were shot in Asia, with subsequent production in Central and South America, Europe, and North Africa. Produced by Desilu/Paramount for NBC from 1965 to 1968, *I Spy* was a heavily promoted tour of the exotic corners of the world. While other espionage shows on the air at the time originated overseas, *I Spy* was unique in its use of international location production as an ongoing stylistic and narrative element. *I Spy* introduced a model black citizen to the world; it offers an opportunity to consider not only how American television responded to the civil rights movement, but also how it did so within an explicitly international context.

I Spy's unprecedented representation of a racially integrated pair of agents was crafted so as to minimize the threat to white American sensitivities. Although Kelly and Scotty were professional equals, their cover identities were as a white tennis star and his trainer. More important, Culp's character, Kelly, was flirtatious and sexually promiscuous, and women of all races eagerly succumbed to his charms, while Scotty seldom was allowed such dalliances. As both black and white critics of the show noticed, Scotty never engaged in suggestive behavior with white women, and only occasionally did he get involved with women of color. This televisual celibacy wasn't lost on audiences, and one black comic derided the show, saying, "Man, this cat can't get a chick anywhere! In Acapulco he can't get a chick, in *Egypt* he can't get a chick, in *China* he can't get a chick!"[13] Rather than pursue romantic liaisons, Scotty was an amiable companion, striking up friendships with the many children that the pair often enlisted as junior spies and local tour guides. A model agent and model American citizen, Scotty did little to disrupt the white social order.

In this way, *I Spy* is not dissimilar from other adventure films and programs that feature an integrated pair of male "buddies." Like the *Lethal Weapon* films of the 1980s and 1990s and the TV series *Miami Vice*, *I Spy* constructs a pair whose friendship apparently supersedes any racial inequality. As Robyn Wiegman writes, such pairings become "a mechanism through which the history of racism among men is revised and denied." Furthermore, as Wiegman observes, these buddy pairs rely upon an explicitly gendered treatment of the politics of race. In such narratives, normative heterosexual masculinity is the prequalification for recognition of the black male as an "equal" member of the pair. These representations defy "the legacy of emasculation that attends black male representation," suggesting that the proof of equality is that the black character is recognized as having sexual desire. Through the sharing of desire, interracial buddy pairs appear to demonstrate that the black man has achieved full equality. As Wiegman writes, "The claim to sexual difference—to be a 'man' or a 'woman'—works to define and invoke a social subjectivity (and hence psychic interiority) previously denied the slave. . . . The slave's rhetorical claim to enfranchisement can thus be read as hinging, in part, on sexual difference."[14]

But in *I Spy* Scotty's sexual agency is particularly limited. Forbidden from expressing any interest in white women, even his liaisons with women of color seldom go beyond casual flirtation. Furthermore, Scotty is Kelly's sidekick, reveling in his white partner's sexual escapades and covering for Kelly when those escapades interfere with their official work. While Kelly's flirtations and flings are incidental to the pair's missions, on the few occasions when Scotty does get romantically involved, it is because his liaison is central to the narrative; in a few episodes, Scotty "rescues" black women and encourages their repatriation.

Scotty's sexuality is constrained by its political utility. Unlike Kelly, whose white privilege allows him to temporarily set aside his official missions for sexual escapades, Scotty is always an agent of the state.

The increased visibility of black Americans on American television in 1965 led *Newsweek* to declare, "As any steady viewer can deduce, this is the Summer of the Negro or, as some black cynics have dubbed it, 'the race race.'"[15] That year, ABC produced a six-episode series called "Time for Americans," featuring such prominent black performers as Lena Horne and Harry Belafonte, and NET aired a nine-part "History of the Negro People."[16] But while these TV documentaries attempted to rewrite the place of African Americans in U.S. history, blacks were still largely invisible in dramatic programming.[17] Though *I Spy* marked a significant milestone, its producers and stars insisted the show wasn't about race. The show's creator and executive producer, Sheldon Leonard, proclaimed, "I will not force upon viewers a consciousness of social problems."[18] Leonard was adamant that the program not scratch too deeply the veneer of racial egalitarianism between the lead characters. Keenly aware of the economic imperatives of commercial television, Leonard wanted to ensure that the program would be widely accepted. He told an interviewer,

> I must give the sponsor what he thought he bought—a show to lure, to attract people to the television set long enough to retain his message. . . . I want the audience's attention. I want everybody. I even want the bad guys. . . . I will not make a conscious effort to exclude the Ku Klux Klan from among my viewers. I will not compromise an ounce of my principle to retain them, but I will not go out of my way to drive them away from my sponsor's product. My obligation to the sponsor includes refraining from an overt action that will deprive him of the sales advantages that the purchase of my program is supposed to assure.[19]

Costar Robert Culp—who also wrote some of the program's episodes that comment most directly on issues of race—gave a more politicized explanation of the show's assimilationist liberalism; he declared that the show's silence about racial conflict was "doing more than 100 marches. We're showing what it could be like if there had been no hate."[20]

Whether this ambitious claim was accurate, the show suppressed the political importance of racial difference in nearly every episode, insisting—despite compelling evidence to the contrary—that racial conflict in 1960s America was a relic of the receding past. Set against the Birmingham and Selma marches, the Goodman-Schwerner-Chaney murders, the assassinations of numerous black leaders, and the Watts riots, *I Spy* constructed a kind of idealized "pax Americana" in which race was secondary to national interests abroad. Agents Kelly and Scotty were Americans first, the program told us, and racial difference was inconsequential in the face of the important political threats to U.S. global supremacy.

In this way, the Cosby character in *I Spy* was an early prototype for what Herman Gray has called the "civil rights subject," a narrowly defined African American subjectivity inscribed within a progress narrative of equal rights and gradual assimilation. As Gray writes, this subject is made "an exemplar of citizenship and responsibility—success, mobility, hard work, sacrifice, individualism," and it "works to reinforce and reaffirm the openness and equality of contemporary American society."[21] As it became clear that African Americans would maintain a higher degree of political and social mobility than that afforded them in the 1950s, popular cultural discourses linked black political activism to an American progress narrative of individual rights. The civil rights subject, according to Gray, is a particularly palatable trope of African American identity because it largely conforms to dominant norms of individual autonomy and liberal pluralism formulated by a white political elite. As a call to conscience that ultimately reinforced ideologies of individualism and rights, the civil rights subject denied the structural inequalities and institutionalized racism within American society. American racial conflicts, the civil rights subject asserted, could be solved by American solutions. International political developments of the 1960s, however—and particularly the strong political and cultural connections being forged between African Americans and decolonizing Africans—threatened to disrupt the equation of black American political activism with core American principles.

The mid-1960s was a crucial period when the civil rights subject coalesced as a coherent set of discourses that differed from more radical expressions of black American identity politics. As its most prominent symbol, Martin Luther King Jr. has come to be understood as articulating a political sensibility that was founded upon key principles of the American nation. In his intellectual history of the civil rights and black power movements, Richard King argues that conventional historical approaches to the civil rights movement "assume that it can best be understood from within the institutional and conceptual confines of post-war liberal pluralism with its emphasis upon the pursuit of interests and defense of political and legal rights as the *raison d'etre* of politics."[22] And indeed, the formation of the civil rights subject is a cultural response to a fundamentally historical problem; given the disruptive political transformations wrought by the civil rights movement, the central problematic for dominant white culture became one of historical continuity, of how to enclose the political activism and turbulence of the mid-1960s within dominant historical conceptions of the American nation-state.

Political liberalism and assimilationism were not, however, the only possible means of understanding black political expression of the 1960s. Potentially more radical was the possibility that "the political culture set in motion by the civil rights movement fell outside the hegemony of the 'liberal tradition.'" By the mid-1960s, casting Martin Luther King Jr. as a liberal American traditionalist was more acceptable to mainstream white Americans than the radical critiques of the Nation of Islam, Student Nonviolent Coordinating Committee (SNCC), and the Black Power movement. The preferred version of King that has been sacralized within American popular culture is that of a genius who used "the American political tradition—the civic culture defined by the Declaration of Independence and the Bill of Rights—against itself." Certainly, King drew upon foundational American principles and documents, in part by quoting liberally from them in his public speeches. But the reduction of King to an American patriot overlooks the radicalism within the civil rights movement that questioned the possibility that American racism could be solved by "democratic" American principles. Indeed, by 1965 King himself was beginning to link African Americans to African and Southeast Asian independence struggles, proclaiming that "[o]ur heritage is Africa. We should never seek to break the ties nor should the Africans."[23]

Organizations like SNCC actively began to encourage connections between American blacks and Africans in the mid-1960s. Starting in 1964 SNCC members and leaders made visits to Ghana and Zambia, as well as to Japan, Vietnam, and Cuba, and visited the United Nations in support of Palestinian autonomy. The group began to be heavily influenced by the Marxist pan-Africanism of Algerian revolutionary Frantz Fanon, and the slogan "black power" was first used by SNCC leader Stokely Carmichael in June 1966. Black Power was more threatening to the white establishment than the liberal pluralism of the Southern Christian Leadership Conference, not only because it was more open to revolutionary action, but also because it viewed black liberation as completely outside the purview of white American society. As SNCC leader Julius Lester said, "It simply means the white man no longer exists.... He is simply to be ignored, because the time has come for the black man to control the things which affect his life.... For so long the black man lived his life in reaction to whites. Now he will live it only within the framework of his blackness."[24] The period from 1964 to 1966 was a crucial period in the elaboration of the civil rights subject, because it was a period in which popular discourses worked to polarize the distinctions between black liberalism and what was deemed to be the treasonous, separatist black nationalism associated with SNCC, Malcolm X, and the Nation of Islam. Historically, these competing definitions of black political subjectivity have come to be seen as mutually exclusive—a testament to the effectiveness of the civil rights subject as an organizing trope that constrains definitions of "appropriate" black political activism.

Since the beginning of his career, Bill Cosby has been a focal point for these debates over racial assimilation. In the mid-1960s, Cosby admitted his sympathies for black activism, but he was reluctant to make explicit political statements. Cosby avoided ethnic humor in his standup comedy routines and instead told nostalgic tales of his childhood, earning him the label of the "color-blind comic" and "an electronic Mark Twain." *Newsweek* noted that "as Cosby's humor is devoid of race, so too is his public image. He doesn't speak out on racial matters." Prefiguring the mainstream popular reception of *The Cosby Show* in the 1980s, the *National Review* proudly commented that "Cosby's great achievement is that he has succeeded in Just Being A Guy—on television."[25] By "just being a guy," Cosby seemed to show that the social inequities that led to the civil rights movement were largely cured, and that race need no longer be a matter of ongoing public concern. As Sut Jhally and Justin Lewis and others have argued at length, Cosby has since the 1960s been a polysemic public figure, one who can operate simultaneously as a progressive black role model and a symbol for white audiences of the completion—and ultimate irrelevance—of the civil rights movement.[26]

In the mid-1960s Cosby stood out from other black performers because of his reticence about racial conflict. Comedian Dick Gregory, for example, pointedly

Scotty and Kelly, at work and play.

discussed race in his act, and he was famous for telling white audiences, "You know, things always work themselves out. I can't go to Mississippi, and you can't go to the Congo." The *Chicago Defender* called Gregory a "serious" comic, writing that "the casual approach of his act portrays him as an 'observer' of racial problems. But off the stage he is a militant campaigner for equal rights." Gregory helped raise money for Mississippi food programs, and he posted a $25,000 reward that helped lead to the arrest of suspects in the infamous Chaney, Schwerner, and Goodman murders during the 1964 Mississippi Freedom Summer.[27]

In contrast, Cosby was credited with taking a "different approach to comedy." "Originally, he used racial material, but weary of being likened to Nipsey Russell, Redd Foxx or Dick Gregory, he decided not to allude to 'the problem,' as he puts it, on stage." Cosby consequently enjoyed wider mainstream success, with frequent visits to *The Tonight Show* and Groucho Marx's variety hour. "There is no great difference between an American Negro and white Americans," Cosby insisted. "When I do my piece on street football, I have one guy run behind the black Chevy to catch the ball. I send another one in my living room to receive a pass. I tell another to run take the bus and have the driver leave the

door open so I can fake a pass. . . . Many of the white men out there laughing in the audience have had the same experience."[28]

Cosby's easy accessibility to white audiences fit neatly into the work of Sheldon Leonard, *I Spy*'s executive producer. The successful producer of such "wholesome" American comedies as *The Andy Griffith Show, The Danny Thomas Show, The Dick Van Dyke Show,* and *Gomer Pyle, USMC,* Leonard had built a career around nostalgic comedies of American life. *I Spy,* with its international settings and multiracial cast, seemed to diverge from Leonard's standard formula.

But read alongside Leonard's other programs, an unbroken timeline begins to emerge. While *Andy Griffith* and *Gomer Pyle* evoke a naïve America, innocent of racial conflict and nostalgically located in some sort of Rockwellian past, *I Spy* leapfrogs forward—beyond bus boycotts and firehoses—to form a utopian American myth custom-tailored for the tumultuous civil-rights years. "An absence of a statement was the idea," Culp claimed. "We did it with such success that finally people forgot he was black and I was white."[29] What *I Spy* shares with Leonard's rural sitcoms is a faith that in the founding mythology of the American nation-state lay the solutions to any and all social, political, or cultural ills. By exploiting the figure of Cosby as a post–civil rights all-American "guy" and erasing the legacy of racial injustice, *I Spy* imagined an integrated nation that was fully compatible with a simplified notion of America's past.[30]

One episode, entitled "A Few Miles West of Nowhere," offers a rare explicit treatment of civil rights, mapping racial tension onto a conflict between states' rights and federalism. In it, Scotty and Kelly are sent to a rural southern U.S. town, where a group of locals are resisting the planned development of a federally built nuclear power plant. Another government agent has already been killed by a secretive militia group, and Scotty and Kelly are attempting to investigate. Scotty meets a young girl at the local store, and he invites her to share an ice cream with him. In the context of mid-1960s U.S. society, the two are a potentially inflammatory pair—a blonde white girl sharing a single ice-cream cone with the black agent under the southern sun. Their friendly chat is disrupted, however, by the arrival of the girl's immense but dim-witted uncle "Tiny," played by Richard Kiel (who went on to play the character "Jaws" in Bond films of the 1970s). Tiny seizes the ice cream, mashes the cone into Scotty's chest, and bellows, "I want him out of here!" When Scotty and Kelly refuse to leave, a gang of Tiny's friends shows up, taunting the agents and attacking their car with a chain. The source of the conflict is unmistakable; by speaking to the white girl, the black agent has overstepped his bounds in this small southern town, and Tiny's gang is prepared to drive him out or kill him.

Tiny, we learn, is under the influence of Clay, the forceful leader of the gang. After several violent encounters with locals who try to run them out of town, Kelly and Scotty spy on a meeting of the local militia where leaders are explaining a plan to thwart the completion of the federal nuclear power project. The reconnaissance mission fails, however, and the agents are driven away by a violent mob throwing rocks. Later, Scotty and Kelly discover a vast cache of machine guns, bazookas, and other firearms. Preparing for war against "those men in Washington who are selling out the country," the militia fears that the atomic plant will be a military installation.

The episode portrays the militia group's xenophobia, thinly veiled racism, and crude anti-Communism as threats to national security and authority. The conflict thus parallels the state/federal conflicts that marked civil rights conflicts over segregation. Like Governor George Wallace, who attempted to block the federal enforcement of desegregation at the doors of the University of Alabama, the militia leader Clay accuses the U.S. government of being controlled by Communist social engineers, with the African American agent Scotty as its chosen representative. "So far since the war," Clay tells his supporters, "the Commies have taken over 17 countries, and only 1 by force." The militia forces Scotty to fight Tiny, who soundly beats him. Their fight is interrupted by a well-timed minor disaster, however, when Tiny's young niece falls down a well. After a violent confrontation with Clay that precipitates the militia leader's death, Scotty helps to save the little girl and wins the group's respect.

Explicitly portraying southern segregationism and anti-federalism as threatening to U.S. economic and political interests, the episode suggests that the embrace of the civil rights movement was crucial to continued American prowess. The episode's antiruralism is also centrally a class conflict; the redneck militia's refusal to accept the nuclear program signals their antagonism toward the class mobility enabled by professionalism, globalism, and technology. Their rural working-class ignorance is constructed as a key impediment to the professional and technological utopianism represented by both the nuclear plant and Scotty himself. Scotty's success story is as much one of class as it is of race; his social progress is a product of his participation in a newly emergent kind of American identity—one rooted in "timeless" American principles but which also looks ahead to a global, professional future.

Black Americans Abroad: I Spy *and 1960s Internationalism*

Despite a few such domestic episodes, however, *I Spy* more often dealt with international conflicts and settings. Beyond modeling a post–civil rights America, the program asserted the viability of a post–civil rights world and inscribed a place for black Americans within it. Largely shot and set abroad, the show intermingled American citizenship, racial pluralism, and global mobility. While the transnational politics of Black Power was a source of considerable anxiety for the U.S. government, *I Spy* offered instead a "safe" version of African American mobility that was recoded as national service and leisure travel. One of the privileges granted by the successful "completion" of the civil rights movement, the show suggests, is that African Americans could become middle-class citizens and international tourists.[31]

I Spy was an implicit, and occasionally explicit, vehicle for the promotion of tourism. NBC promoted *I Spy*'s international locations, and the episodes themselves typically opened with panoramic vistas of international cities such as Athens, Venice, Hong Kong, Tokyo, and Paris. After the first few episodes, tourism boards from all around the world solicited the producers to set an episode in their countries.[32] Distributor Desilu's vice president of promotion encouraged these liaisons with tourist boards, explaining to the show's producers that "one of the things we will be playing up are the exotic locales of some of the stories."[33] NBC lent the assistance of their international news bureaus, and various government agencies were consulted for each location. Episodes set in Hong Kong, for example, include stock footage from NBC, and preproduction plans were approved by the Hong Kong Ministry of Tourism. As a result, *I Spy* was rich in outdoor locations, with important rendezvous and climatic chase scenes playing out against the backdrop of national monuments, picturesque vistas, and lively urban street scenes. *I Spy* thus recoded the black agent's social mobility in the United States through international travel and intrigue.

I Spy's treatment of foreign locations as an exotic playground was also influenced by pragmatic decisions related to the demands of international production. The production team would often shoot five to ten episodes at a time in a given country, which required the approval and support of local officials. Mexican censors, for example, objected to a 1967 episode entitled "The Name of the Game," in which President Johnson was to be the target of an assassination plot. The censors would not "tolerate that throughout the world ignorant people could think of Mexico as a country where . . . assassination plots against foreign [leaders] are allowed, [particularly] in the case of President Johnson who is identified by name."[34] In response, producers quickly changed the script to accommodate the censors' concerns.[35] Similarly, a nine-episode Greek production trip was nearly scuttled by censorship conflicts and political instabilities. Leon Chooluck warned Sheldon Leonard,

> I also wish to remind everyone involved that there are certain words and descriptions which could effect the approval or disapproval of a shooting script. I quote from . . . the description of a Greek area which states, tavernas, tenements, and "stinking alleys." It is very true that these alleys may be stinking to us, but to the Minister of Education and Tourism, or the Minister of Cinematography or any other persons including the United States Embassy or Public Relations officer, these descriptions are detrimental to our purpose. . . . One of these days we are going to be turned down on a script.[36]

The Greek production schedule, nearly scuttled by the 1967 military coup, was saved only by a frenzy of negotiations with the Greek government.[37] With location expenses sometimes accounting for half of *I Spy*'s already high budget of over $200,000 per episode, producers sought to maintain cordial relations with host countries. Even so, international production aroused local sensitivities in many cases. "Don't go into Morocco ever again," Friedkin told Leonard, because "one of its citizens is going to see to it that they declare war on Three F" (Leonard's production company).[38] *I Spy*'s producers had to appease multiple audiences—not only white and black Americans and network censors, but also foreign officials who might revoke their production privileges.

Travel and tourism offered an effective promotional device—likely motivated by an effort to produce a novel television program, and enabled by improved international transportation, national film production boards, and the international news divisions of NBC—and it also provides the ongoing narrative problematic of the series. International travel is both the lure and source of conflict within the program. For example, in "Bridge of Spies," an Italian tour guide who specializes in arranging accommodations for American tourists is secretly using her clients to deliver surveillance devices. Similarly, in the episode entitled "Lisa," Soviets use an innocent Greek girl coming to the United States as a mail-order bride as bait to locate an infiltrator in their midst. In other episodes, Kelly and Scotty act as bodyguards to important international visitors to the United States or investigate when Americans or Soviets have gone abroad and turned against their native countries.[39]

In one episode, entitled "Always Say Goodbye," Kelly and Scotty are sent to Japan to curb the sexual appetites of a womanizing American diplomat. A U.S. ambassador named Winthrop is in Tokyo for a critical gold conference, at which the Japanese are expected to announce plans to convert a large sum of currency to gold with detrimental effects to the U.S. economy. Winthrop has a reputation as a woman-chaser, and Kelly and Scotty are supposed to keep him out of the nightclubs and away from the showgirls so he can negotiate a successful deal with the moralistic Japanese. They plan to divert Winthrop's energies into an appreciation for jazz clubs, but their scheme is complicated when a rival Japanese political faction pays off a "flower girl" named Akira to seduce the ambassador.

Winthrop slips away from the agents, and Kelly and Scotty follow him to a strip club where a Japanese woman dressed as Marilyn Monroe is strewing her clothes on Winthrop in the front row. He writes her a note, stuffs it in her glove with a wad of money, and hands it back. The agents barely manage to get Winthrop out of the club before arousing suspicion with the Japanese, and Kelly masquerades as a diplomat the next morning to cover for Winthrop's hangover. As the Japanese officials remind him, honor and respectfulness will be the key to a successful conference. Once Winthrop recovers, however, he is back on the prowl again. Confronted by Scotty, Winthrop denies everything, insisting that he wanted simply to find his old flame, Aliska, a cabaret singer whom he knew in the past.

The episode concludes by defending the intentions of the Western traveler at play in an exotic and sexually permissive Orient. After Winthrop explains himself, Kelly and Scotty agree to help the diplomat find his friend. The agents find her home and take Winthrop there, where they are shocked to discover Takata, the leader of the Japanese negotiation team, in her bedroom. By helping Takata escape before a raid upon the house by his political enemies, they win his gratitude and ensure a successful negotiation of the gold transfer deal. Thus while the episode (like many others of the program) generally implies that the non-white world is a sexual playground for American travelers, it ultimately deflects its sexualization of the Orient back onto the Japanese, representing the country as a libidinous zone of indiscretion and immorality, against which the American traveler must be continually vigilant. In this way, the episode converts the domestic Red Scare discourses of the 1950s to an anxiety over the spread of Communism in Asia. Indeed, as U.S.-Soviet relations thawed after the first Soviet test-ban treaty in 1963, growing tensions in Asia led to more open hostilities with China. Not only was the Vietnam conflict escalating, but the Chinese had become a nuclear power in late 1964.

When not covering for the indiscretions of American tourists and political leaders, Kelly and Scotty often must contend with international travelers with less clearly defined national identities. Unlike programs like *Mission: Impossible,* which places its agents in conflict with the agents of distinct (albeit fictitious) nations, the crises in a number of *I Spy* episodes are provoked by autonomous villains with ambiguous national allegiances. In some cases these villains are expatriate Americans. In "Crusade to Limbo," for example, a number of American intellectuals, writers, and actors are preparing to join a revolutionary movement in Latin America. In the program, the dangerous antithesis to American nationalism is not socialism, or even Communism, but ambivalence or nonalliance. *I Spy* evinces more than a bit of nostalgia for the early period of the Cold War, when national alliances could be more easily understood and mapped out. What is often most threatening in the program is the prospect that the United States might face enemies who have little use for "nation" as an organizing political and cultural principle.

In the most acute conflicts of the series, the political implications of transnational mobility take on an explicitly racial tone. In particular, a number of episodes feature either internationally mobile African Americans, or diasporic Africans who seek to undermine the authority of the American state. In "Tonia," for example, guest star Leslie Uggams plays an African American woman living in Rome and organizing an anti-American activist organization. And in "Trial by Treehouse," the racial politics of international mobility lead to an attempted terrorist attack on the United States. In the episode, a Jamaican radical named Prince Edward Prince is the leader of a subversive faction composed of black American jazz fans, Afro-Caribbean revolutionaries, and dissatisfied working-class white Americans.

Prince, we learn, is both a dangerous radical and the host of a popular radio show entitled "Coffee, Croissants, and Classics." Prince's radio show is mostly a front, however, and his real mission is to sabotage a hydroelectric generator at a Southern California dam. By doing so, he hopes to create an embarrassing public relations fiasco for the U.S. government that will undermine American efforts to relocate industries abroad. Prince skillfully exploits class tensions in the United States, persuading a paranoid white factory worker to shuttle secret documents to Venezuela.

The program portrays Prince as an exploitative dilettante, driving around in a vintage Rolls Royce chauffeured by an assistant he calls Iago. As if to make his deviance complete, the program implies that Prince is homosexual in a scene in which he kisses Iago and declares, "boys want to play mommy and daddy," referring to his and Iago's patronage of the revolutionary movement. Prince's ambiguous sexuality, ostentation, and terrorist activities all operate together to exclude the possibility that he might be considered a citizen of any sort— American or otherwise. Prince's animosity stems from a childhood of poverty and deeply rooted class envy in Jamaica, but the episode more directly references Robert F. Williams, a prominent African American activist of the period. An advocate of armed resistance and author of *Negroes with Guns,* Williams was under intense FBI scrutiny and emigrated to Cuba in 1961. Once there, he created Radio Free Dixie, a political and cultural radio program that was broadcast into the United States via Radio Havana. An important influence on SNCC and the Black Panthers, Williams has since been largely overlooked, but for at least some audiences in the mid-1960s, the reference was likely unmistakable.[40]

In contrast to Prince's meddling deviance, the agency assigns Scotty to pose as the live-in boyfriend of a single black mother. Struggling to raise a young son alone, Sheila welcomes Scotty in as a surrogate father. In the course of his mission, Scotty grows close to both Sheila and her son, and it is only with difficulty that he leaves them at the end of the mission. Unlike Prince, Sheila clearly declares her intentions to raise her son to be an honest patriotic American, and she largely conforms to the norms of the civil rights subject. Sheila and Prince have responded in radically different ways to a common economic condition. While Prince has become a manipulative and nationless outcast whose affectations and feigned class superiority reveal a bitter contempt for the United States, Sheila is reminded by Scotty of the virtues of American citizenship. Determined to work hard and raise her son honestly, Sheila is rewarded with the support of the U.S. government.

When abroad, Scotty is as often a cultural diplomat as a spy. The program continually asserts that in a new colorblind American society, there is no incongruity between Scotty's race and his national identity; the two fit seamlessly. In the episode entitled "Incident at Tsien Cha," for example, Scotty builds a rapport with a young Chinese boy named Li-Ho. The boy is fascinated with American westerns, and he parades around in a hat and gunbelt. When Li-Ho sees Scotty, he draws his gun and advances on him, puzzled by his dark skin. Scotty, however, doesn't play the role of the Indian that Li-Ho expected of him. "No gunfight, mister?" the boy asks, and he reaches up to Scotty's face in wonder.

"No, it doesn't rub off," Scotty assures him. "That's not warpaint." Later, joking with Kelly at a village celebration, he tells his partner, "They made me a living legend," as he rubs his face, saying "it doesn't rub off!"

What the young Chinese boy hadn't understood was the revised racial logic of the program; he erroneously assumed that racial difference was synonymous with national difference, and as a cowboy, he had cast Scotty in the role of an antagonistic Indian. But unlike the binary racial system of Li-Ho's beloved westerns, Scotty is a fully vested agent of the state. He thus delivers to Li-Ho an important lesson about racial difference and its relationship to national identity: race does not supersede nationalism—instead, it is sublimated to it.

Although they are relatively few, the episodes that pit Scotty against other African Americans are crucial to the racial logics of the program; in them, Scotty's post–civil rights subjectivity is most clearly elaborated. "The Loser" and "So Long Patrick Henry," for example, comment directly on the political volatility of African American migrancy. In them, Scotty's successful mobility as an international spy is contrasted with embittered black Americans whose travels have led to personal and political failure. "The Loser" is set in familiar terrain for the show—a Hong Kong jazz club where Chinese taxi dancers entertain American businessmen and tourists. The club is a front, however, for an opium den, and the episode quickly becomes an object lesson in the dangers associated with exotic desire. Guest star Eartha Kitt plays Angel, an American nightclub singer and junkie who is a virtual slave to Ramon, the Latin American smuggler who runs the operation.

After escaping from capture by the drug ring, Scotty returns in hopes of saving Angel. Several times throughout the episode, she has the opportunity to go away with him, but he is unable to convince her to leave. Her face twisted in a grimace, she begs Ramon, "It's been a long time. . . . I need it now." Scotty is torn, upset that he can't do more for Angel, explaining to Kelly that "[s]he's nothing but a dumb, funky loser. . . . I come from a long line of losers. Whenever I see one, it hurts." The implication, of course, is that while there may have been "losers" in Scotty's past, he has firmly moved beyond any such problems. Nonetheless, his social conscience forces him to help.

After a fierce fight, Scotty once again comes to Angel's aid. To his dismay, she chooses Ramon and his ready supply of heroin, saying, "There's someone who needs me. I know he knocks me around a little bit, but I know what's happening with him. I know where I stand. Not like you—some kind of weird old boy scout." At that, the "weird old boy scout" turns to go, disappointed but satisfied that he did his best. As he leaves, Angel gets the last word, "So long hot shot. Sorry to have caused you so much trouble, but . . . don't get killed on the way out." For his efforts, Scotty only earns her derision. This episode reinforces one of the most enduring tropes of the civil rights subject—that the "loser" is a failure by choice. Because this incident plays out in a global forum, the conflict is particularly acute. The episode contrasts two conflicting modes of African American transnational mobility. While Scotty's patriotic progress narrative takes him abroad as an agent of the state, Angel's travel leaves her morally adrift, victim to the manipulations of a multiethnic, multinational band of gangsters with no allegiances other than the draw of money.

"Our Black Kissinger" or "Ill-Will Ambassador"? Muhammad Ali and the Black Civil Subject

> He's practically turned the title over to the Black Muslims. . . . Harm has been done to the Negroes' cause and the way the rest of the world regards it by the one who calls himself Muhammad Ali.
>
> —BOXER FLOYD PATTERSON

The pilot episode of the ostensibly "colorblind" *I Spy* unmistakably charted the show's treatment of the politics of racial identity. "So Long Patrick Henry" features a prominent African American Olympic champion who defects to Communist China. Even more overt than the show's fictionalization of Robert F. Williams, the episode was a direct commentary on the most prominent African American athlete of the 1960s—Muhammad Ali, known until February 1964 as Cassius Clay. It brought black internationalism to the forefront, providing an instructive lesson regarding the implied diplomatic responsibility of prominent African Americans. This episode inserted the series directly into ongoing conflicts over "appropriate" models of black American citizenship.

Returning from the Rome Olympics in 1960 as an eighteen-year-old Olympic champion, Clay advanced quickly through the professional ranks. Hailed initially as a national hero, Clay developed a reputation as a "big-mouthed braggart" whose battles against his opponents began not in the ring, but in the press conference. By early 1964 Clay was poised to challenge the reigning heavyweight champion, Sonny Liston. Before that historic fight, Clay was looked on by many as an irritating but colorful figure. The boxer became famous for his rhymes, and for his ability to predict in which round he would win a given fight. Often, he would make such claims as, "I said he'd fall in eight to prove I'm great." Usually he was right.[41]

The arc of Ali's early career not only corresponded with the growth and influence of the Nation of Islam; Ali was also one of the first international media figures. The 1964 Clay-Liston fight was one of the first closed-circuit television events, and his subsequent fights were broadcast via satellite. Before the Liston fight, sportswriters from around the country "tossed questions at Liston and Clay in Miami Beach over a three-way hookup." Clay was eager and self-conscious about the camera, asking, "Which camera am I on?" so he could gaze directly at the viewer. Although only a little over 8,000 spectators watched the fight live in Miami, hundreds of thousands watched it via 371 Theater Network Television connections nationwide.[42]

Rumors about Clay's religion began to circulate before the fight. The match was nearly canceled after Clay voiced his respect for Malcolm X to reporters in New York. Threatened with a cancellation, Clay agreed to sidestep questions about his religious affiliation. The underdog, he went on to win in a knockout that captured headlines worldwide.

Two days after his victory, Clay announced at a press conference that for some time he had been a practicing Muslim, and that he would take the name Cassius X. (A few days later, he officially changed his name to Muhammad Ali.) At his side was Malcolm X, who declared, "Clay is the finest Negro athlete I have ever known, the man who will mean more to his people than any athlete before him. He is more than Jackie Robinson was, because Robinson is the white man's hero. But Cassius is the black man's hero."[43] After this pronouncement,

Shortly after winning the professional heavyweight boxing championship in February 1964, Muhammad Ali told the world, "Islam is a religion and there are 750 million people all over the world who believe in it, and I am one of them." His subsequent appearances before television cameras with Malcolm X and Elijah Muhammad made him a polarizing figure in the racial politics of 1960s America.

Life magazine called the boxer "a man-child taken in by the Muslims," claiming he had been seduced by the persuasive Malcolm X who "soon had his 22-year-old friend glibly talking Muslim doctrine." It was widely assumed that Ali had been duped by the Nation of Islam, and that the "Muslim at his ear" wouldn't allow him to appear in public without an escort.[44]

Literally overnight, the boxer went from national hero to pariah. *Sports Illustrated* reported,

> When he came along he was America's sweetheart, the guy who was going to kick sand back in the bully's face. . . . It took Cassius and a bunch of shaved-headed, agate-eyed types one year to turn Liston into the most popular public favorite since St. George. They gave Cassius the part of the marshal in *High Noon,* and he wanted to be the guy in the black hat. He's the kind of guy who could get people rooting against the doctors in an epidemic.[45]

Ali quickly became a focal point for public debates over integration and civil rights. Consistent with the teachings of the Nation of Islam, he told reporters, "I don't wanta marry no white woman, don't wanta break down no school doors where I'm not wanted."[46] Far from earning the respect of whites, of course, this statement only inflamed his critics. Like the Nation of Islam and Malcolm X, Ali was dismissed as a racist by the white press; the integrationism of the civil rights movement was turned against him in an effort to contain his exuberant criticism. The U.S. Boxing Commission threatened to revoke Ali's title because of his religious beliefs, and Congress threatened to investigate the promoters who organized the fight, citing financing improprieties.[47] Amid these controversies, though, Ali reveled in his notoriety and global visibility.

After the fight, Ali made clear that he aspired to be more than just another American boxing champion. He traveled to New York, where he visited the UN and announced an upcoming world tour and pilgrimage to Mecca, with Malcolm X as his traveling companion.[48] With the announcement of these plans, the press coverage surrounding Ali only increased. He told one reporter, "I am a very intelligent boxer, you know, and people don't ask me about my muscles the way they would ask Liston or Patterson. They ask me about Zanzibar and Panama and Cuba, and I tell them what I think."[49] The more Ali said what he thought, however, the more actively he was criticized for his potentially un-American behavior. *Sports Illustrated,* for example, insisted that while there was no place for any discussion of race or religion in the sporting world, Ali's planned trip to Mecca was "tragicomic nonsense" and "what can only be an ill-will tour of Africa and Asia."[50]

When Ali went to Africa a few months later, he was followed by a crowd of American journalists.[51] Reporting that he had "gone native," magazines and newspapers printed full-page photo essays of his trip, including several shots of him in African clothing. *Ebony* provided some of the most complete coverage of the trip, reporting, "It was mutual love at first sight. Muhammad Ali (alias Cassius Clay) loved Africa and Africa loved him." On the trip, he visited Senegal, Ghana, Nigeria, Egypt, and Liberia. He was received by the Ghanan president Nkrumah, as well as by President Nasser of Egypt. To the chagrin of his American critics, Ali's popularity internationally continued to grow, even as he became a more outspoken critic of U.S. foreign policy. His subsequent fights were simulcast on the Early Bird satellite, making him one of the first global media figures. He traveled the world on boxing tours, quickly dispatching his opponents, causing some consternation for promoters who paid large advance fees for the satellite time. "I'm giving all the countries the chance," Ali said, "Canada...Germany...the Middle East." Keenly aware of his own political status, when he went to Zaire a decade later for the "Rumble in the Jungle" with George Foreman, Ali proclaimed himself "the Black Kissinger."[52]

Ebony compared Ali to Jack Johnson, the heavyweight champion from 1908 to 1915 who outraged white audiences when he

> flaunted a succession of white wives and mistresses before the world.... Jack Johnson was hated by whites not only because he became the first Negro to hold the title (touching off the first big search for a "white hope"), but because he refused to abide by the taboos with which the white populace of the time circumscribed the kind of life a Negro in America was supposed to live.[53]

But rather than prompt a search for the next "great white hope" who would put the unruly black boxer in his place, another black boxer—one much more palatable to white boxing fans—came forward to take on the task. The same month that *I Spy* premiered with its episode about a controversial black athlete, Ali was challenged by Floyd Patterson, an aging former champion, who called Ali a disgrace to his race.

The Ali-Patterson fight was even more heavily promoted than Ali's earlier bouts; sportswriters called it a "religious war."[54] In October 1965, Floyd Patterson wrote a prominent article in *Sports Illustrated* that began dramatically with a full-page handwritten note that read, "*I love boxing.* The image of a Black Muslim as the world heavyweight champion disgraces the sport and the nation. Therefore, CASSIUS CLAY MUST BE BEATEN." Because "The Black Muslims [are] a menace to the United States and a menace to the Negro race . . . [they] must be removed from boxing. There is only one way to do the job. That is to take the championship away from Cassius Clay. This I hope to do."[55]

In retaliation, Ali began calling Patterson the "Black White Hope." He prepared one of his signature poems, declaring, "I am going to put Floyd flat on his back—so that he will start thinking black."[56]

The stage was thus set for a showdown between two conflicting models of black American identity; the Muslim Ali, who claimed to have little use for the civil rights movement, versus Patterson, who vowed to support the movement by contributing his winnings to the NAACP. In a global event carried by AT&T's Early Bird satellite, Patterson was badly beaten, but in his physical defeat Patterson was credited in the mainstream press with winning a moral victory for having brought something "back to boxing that has seemed to be missing of late, particularly in the heavyweight division: a sense of high valor."[57]

The fight between Ali and Patterson, then, was far more than a physical contest. For like the contrasts drawn between the black leaders Malcolm X and Martin Luther King Jr., these boxers stood in for a much broader uncertainty over "appropriate" models of black leadership in 1960s America. Like Malcolm X, Ali was threatening because he refused to identify himself with the integrationist ideals of the civil rights movement. In retrospect, the public outcries of 1964 and 1965 surrounding Ali's conversion marked a significant turning point in American racial politics at which civil rights became encoded as continuous with the American political tradition, and alternative models of black political expression were marked as insurgent. Ali himself only grew in notoriety; when he was called up for the draft in February 1966, he refused to enlist, insisting,

"I ain't got no quarrel with the Viet Cong." His career in the United States nearly destroyed, Ali's title was stripped, and he was banned from fighting in the United States for three years.

Ali, of course, wasn't swayed by his critics. The boxer, however, didn't have to defend himself before the compelling arguments of secret agent and model citizen Alexander Scott. The pilot episode of *I Spy* imagines precisely such a historic confrontation. The episode begins with NBC stock footage of the 1964 Tokyo Olympics, followed by champion Elroy Brown's triumphant medal ceremony.[58] Brown disrupts the patriotic fervor of the moment, however, with an impromptu news conference on the steps of a Chinese plane. At precisely the moment when Ali would have reminded his audience that he was "the greatest," Brown flashes a smile and declares, "I'm here cause I'm the best! I worked like a slave, if you pardon the expression, to get that way. After much soul searching, I've decided I will not return to the United States, but will make my new home, from this day forward, with my new friends in the People's Republic of China."

The episode then returns to the present, a year later. U.S. intelligence has revealed that Brown might be dissatisfied in China, and Scotty and Kelly are dispatched to persuade him to return home. Already a volatile political situation, the stakes are raised further when we learn that Brown is en route to Hong Kong to help the Chinese organize a new international sporting event—the "Afro-Asian Olympic Games." The Chinese were hoping to establish a foothold in Africa, and the hero Elroy Brown, together with his fiancée, Princess Amara of Mali, was to be their principal propaganda weapon. Aware of Brown's importance as a political symbol, Scotty enters a battle of wits with Brown over the responsibility of African Americans to their nation.

All the evidence suggests that Elroy Brown is a thoroughly contemptible character. He mocks Scotty, calling him Patrick Henry, the revolutionary American orator who asked, "Is life so dear or peace so sweet as to be purchased at the price of chains and slavery?" Scotty, Elroy thinks, is a fool to be willing to die for a racist country. Not only is Brown portrayed as a selfish traitor who defected in exchange for a quarter-million-dollar ransom, he's a racist bigot, as well. To Scotty's dismay, he says of Africa, "It's a nice country. It'd make a nice zoo." Next, he turns on his Chinese escorts, saying, "They're all right, you just gotta step on 'em once in a while and let 'em know which end of the bus they belong in, know what I mean? Don't pay any attention to Charlie Chan here. You give him a fortune cookie, he goes away happy."

The episode's contrast between Brown and Scotty couldn't be more complete. While Scotty is polite and respectful, Brown is crass and rude. While Scotty is a loyal patriot, he proudly boasts, "I'm the first bonus baby of the Cold War. That's my politics, sweetheart." A Rhodes scholar, fluent in seven languages, Scotty tells Kelly that "with a little luck and less talent, [Brown] could have gone to the gas chamber." In short, while Scotty reaped the benefits of the American meritocracy through discipline and hard work, Brown is a sell-out—offering his loyalty to the highest bidder.

Princess Amara is embarrassed and dismayed by her fiancé's belligerence. Educated in China, she nonetheless agrees with Scotty and attempts to sway Elroy's mind. Amara (played by Cicely Tyson, who won an Emmy for her performance) is something of a stand-in for Muhammad Ali's first wife, Sonji. In early 1965, Sonji separated from Ali after his African tour, apparently because she refused to convert to Islam. Although the marriage ended in divorce, Sonji told reporters, "They've stolen my man's mind. I love him. I'll never give him up, because he loves me."[59] In the *I Spy* episode, Princess Amara is instrumental to Scotty's plan to repatriate Elroy. She encourages her fiancé to listen to Scotty, telling Elroy that if he wants to be a great king like her father, he must "learn to bend."

The episode includes what would turn out to be the most emotional confrontation of the series. After courting Elroy for several days under the watchful eyes of the Chinese, Scotty grows frustrated and challenges him:

> Go on to Switzerland. Collect your money. Ten, twenty years from now, you'll be sitting in some villa on the side of the hill watching the sun set, drinking martinis. Got the whole thing licked. And back home, a lot of poor dummies, not as smart as you are, are eating their hearts out trying to make the law of the land stick. Holding the world together with one hand and trying to clean their own house with the other. Yeah, something no other country's ever done before, ever, in the history of the world. Go ahead, Elroy, go on to Switzerland! You don't need that kind of grief! . . . The whole world's trying to keep bloody fools like you from selling themselves back into slavery, but you did it anyway. You gotta laugh at that. No deals, Elroy. You get your citizenship and a plane ticket home. After that, you're on your own.

This speech, which marked a turning point in the struggle for Elroy's allegiances, was hailed within the television industry as one of the most memorable moments of the 1965–66 season. When the National Academy of Television Arts and Sciences published a retrospective book about the Emmy awards, they asked Sheldon Leonard for a script excerpt from the show that would demonstrate that "television is not all the bowl of pap its critics like to think it is. . . . It [should be] a speech that says something, that is 'educational' without being pedantic."[60] As a sample, they showed Leonard an excerpt lifted from a stern lecture delivered by Jack Webb in *Dragnet*. To represent *I Spy*, Leonard sent them this speech.

The program also won an NAACP Image Award in 1967, the first year they were awarded.[61] Cosby was regularly praised for his work on the show, and he won the Best Actor Emmy three years in a row. Furthermore, Eartha Kitt won an Emmy for her performance in "The Loser." While other espionage programs on the air at the time were criticized for their violent content, *I Spy* was praised for offering valuable lessons in American citizenship.

In the episode, the Chinese agents grow suspicious, however, and they turn on Elroy. They inject Elroy and Amara with typhus and prepare to deliver a proxy speech from Brown to the assembled African delegates. The lead Chinese agent gloats, "I will deliver your excellent speech. The Afro-Asian Olympics will be a reality by the end of the day. By the end of the year, China will be firmly entrenched in Africa, helped by means of these Games."

To further prevent Elroy from attempting to intervene, the Chinese whisk Amara off to a waiting plane that will take her back to Beijing. At the last moment, Scotty and Kelly stop the plane from taking off, rescue Amara, and return to the hotel where the sick Elroy waits. Now fully aware of the Chinese deception, Elroy insists on speaking before the conference to denounce their plan. Scotty (conveniently fluent in Swahili) translates for Elroy, who tells the gathered African officials that the Chinese are "fakes" who bought him off to speak in favor of the Games. "The Afro-Asian Games would be great," he tells them, "but they'll poison it for you. Have your games, but you do it. You do it yourselves. I'll help you if I can. Right now, I just want to go home."

The episode demonstrates that the political and cultural influence of black Americans upon African political sensibilities is unmistakable. For while *I Spy* tended to suppress civil rights political struggles, it nonetheless placed African

Americans at the heart of U.S. Cold War politics. By the mid-1960s, American race relations were playing out on a global stage; racial discrimination and violence were watched closely by audiences around the world, and the United States began to enlist prominent African Americans as international representatives to demonstrate the progress being made in all sectors of American society. Like Dizzy Gillespie, who was sent by the State Department on a musical goodwill tour of Africa, Bill Cosby and *I Spy* were important figures of public diplomacy. Motivated by a fear that all of Africa might fall like so many political dominoes, the United States scrambled to recontextualize black political mobility. Sympathetic to that mission, *I Spy* offered the world a traveling black hero who was a tourist, not a critic; an emissary of a colorblind nation, not a political exile; a patriot, not a "loser."

Agents or Technocrats
Mission: Impossible and the International Other

Intelligence seems to be a virility symbol for many Americans—
one that immediately equates the profession with such allegedly
masculine ventures as murder, coup-plotting, intrigue, and a dash
of illicit love making. Their minds somehow entangle the violence
of pro football, the screen antics of James Bond, and lingering
World War II memories of parachuting behind enemy lines with an
exaggerated sense of "duty, honor, country.".... The saddest aspect
of this attitude is that it is based on myth.... A career in intelligence is dull. Bureaucracy, conformity, and paper mill are more
meaningful power phrases to an intelligence professional than coup
d'etat, clandestine operations, or even "spy."

— PATRICK GARVEY, FORMER CIA AGENT

[The CIA agent] has more in common with IBM's 360 than Ian
Fleming's 007.

— TIME, 1966

By the mid-1960s, American espionage programs had largely abandoned reality-
based narratives, favoring dramatic realism over the documentary variety. Sometimes, the failures are as telling as the commercial triumphs; screenwriter Jay
Dratler spent several unsuccessful years developing a series called *OSS: Of Spies
and Stratagems* that evoked the documentarist style of the 1950s. The premise
had been attempted before; the similarly titled semidocumentary *OSS* aired on
ABC during the 1957–58 season, though its demise was even swifter than that of
Behind Closed Doors, which it closely resembled. Dratler had hoped to take
advantage of newly released additional files from Bill Donovan, the wartime
chief of the Office of Strategic Services (OSS), the forerunner to the CIA. The
program was to be based on recently released stories from World War II, focusing
on the activities of the OSS in Europe. To supplement Donovan's files, Dratler
prepared an annotated list of 106 possible biographies and histories of wartime

espionage that could be used as possible sources.[1] The show was to be centered on a professor—described as a "Lionel Barrymore–Charles Coburn–Jimmy Stewart–Einstein" type—who is recruited to head the National Defense Research Committee, which developed ruses and technologies for the OSS. Based on the real Stanley Lovell (who had written a book of the same title), the professor developed such weapons as the "Firefly," a time-released gasoline bomb; the "Casey Jones," a light-activated explosive designed to disable trains as they passed through tunnels; the first truly silent and flashless handgun (based on a weapon first demonstrated to President Roosevelt in the Oval Office during the war); a "high explosive which looked like ordinary wheat flour called Aunt Jemima"; the "Beano, the baseball which, when thrown, armed itself"; and an "ultra-violet ray signal, which could only be seen at great distances by people who had had cataracts removed."[2]

First proposed as a Jimmy Stewart vehicle, the cast was to include a team of specialists whose cultural backgrounds helped them to conduct underground operations: Josef Wyscinsky, a Polish American former college football star; François Perrault, a French race car driver seeking revenge for the death of his family at the hands of the Nazis; Johnny Casanova, an Italian American "driven almost to the point of exhaustion trying to live up to his name—but what a way to go," and Hiroshe Takasuma, a Japanese American expert in Asian languages and sleight-of-hand. The show was intended to be strictly documentarist. "We will be dealing with the truth—with the facts," Dratler wrote. "This will be blunt and factual about the underground warfare in which the United States engaged as tutor, commissary, liaison, supplier, inventor, comrade—this will be the equivalent of a *Dragnet* about the war."[3] Though Dratler was a successful writer, with an Academy Award and extensive experience writing TV espionage narratives for *Burke's Law* and *I Spy* (at one point *I Spy* producer Sheldon Leonard was attached to the project), the show was never produced.

It is difficult to assess precisely why, though the show's points of convergence—and divergence—from other espionage programs of the period are telling. Most notable are the comparisons between *OSS* and *Mission: Impossible*—the most successful of American spy dramas of the Cold War. *OSS*'s close connection to the U.S. military was likely at odds with public sensibilities regarding covert military action in the mid-1960s. Furthermore, the show's attempt to be a "*Dragnet* about the war" resurrected an anachronistic narrative style that had increasingly become subject to critique and parody. Nonetheless, certain characteristics of the *OSS* series design would prove extremely success-ful for *Mission: Impossible*—in particular the combination of a multicultural cast with an emphasis on the use of sophisticated technology. For reasons related to efforts to attract both domestic and international audiences, *Mission: Impossible* adamantly avoided the political and historical specificity of the 1950s semi-documentary, but substituted instead a kind of cultural and technological real-ism, enhanced by employing a research firm to verify the show's representations of intricate technologies and foreign cultures.

With a rhythmic theme song and a similarly syncopated visual style, *Mission: Impossible* quickly became U.S. television's most successful foray into the spy cycle of the 1960s. Although it was predated by such programs as *The Man From U.N.C.L.E., Get Smart,* and *I Spy,* as well as by several James Bond films, *Mission: Impossible* was the most enduring American spy program, running from 1966 to 1973. Acting as America's foreign agents during a tumultuous period of decolonization and the Vietnam War, the Impossible Missions Force (IMF) used a variety of technological and psychological devices to commit espi-onage for the United States. Whereas most spy programs and films of the 1960s featured agents whose authority was legitimated by governments or quasi-governmental institutions, the IMF was composed of anonymous soldiers of fortune. As the self-destructing tape reminded Phelps at the beginning of each episode, "Should you or any of your IM Force be caught or killed, the secretary will disavow any knowledge of your actions." Thus the IMF was simultane-ously positioned as a legitimate unit that maintained the integrity of the Amer-ican nation, and as an illegal expeditionary force that subverted the sovereignty of local governments and blatantly violated international law. A group of well-funded techno-mercenaries, the IMF meddled in the affairs of Second and Third World countries—and got away with it—on a regular basis. Rather than intervene by physical force, the IMF used treachery, masquerade, and disguise to protect U.S. interests abroad.

Most espionage programs of the Cold War reduce the national to the figure of an individual agent. In the programs of the 1950s, the spy's agency is explic-itly gendered, gleaning authority from civic community relationships and the institution of the family. In *I Spy,* the national ideal is crafted around the "civil

rights subject" through exclusionary discourses on race and international mobility. Bill Cosby's character, Scotty, is able to become an agent—both figuratively
as an autonomous individual capable of independent action, and literally as a
spokesperson for the state—because he largely conforms to the ideological
rules by which a black man in 1960s America could be recognized as a U.S. citizen. The notion of a rational, willed individual is generally at the center of
these conventional television narratives. As Susan Jeffords has observed, in
highly masculinist and nationalistic genres, the protagonist often is imbued
with a heroic self-determination, capable of willful action while others around
him are helpless and inert. The *Rambo* films she discusses, for example, rewrite
the perceived U.S. failure in Vietnam through the Stallone character who refuses
to surrender in the face of overwhelming odds. Such representations often reso-
nate widely within popular culture and contribute to a particularly jingoistic
form of national identification. In the early 1980s Ronald Reagan was called
"Ronbo" (sometimes nostalgically, sometimes critically and ironically), precisely because he promised to reinvigorate the notion of a virile American hero
capable of forceful, willful action.[4]

But what to make of a television program that defies these generic conventions of individual self-determination and action? *Mission: Impossible* marked a
significant departure in its representations of American national prowess. An
ensemble program with no back story or serialized narrative elements, its agents
had no personal histories and were nearly devoid of individual personality.
Lacking many of the defining characteristics of conventional generic protagonists, they were technocrats rather than heroes; or, perhaps more accurately,
they were heroes *because* they were technocrats. Alexander Scott of *I Spy* and
Herb Philbrick of *I Led 3 Lives* become idealized figures of nationalist identification precisely because of their self-determination and individualism. Similarly, much of the popularity of the James Bond character rests upon his ability
single-handedly to embody the desires and goals of the British nation-state. But
the agents of *Mission: Impossible* were all ego and no id—automatons, stripped
of desire, they exist only as functionaries, acting at the behest of a nameless,
faceless recorded message. Even while in the parodic spy shows of the mid-1960s
discourses of the ideal national subject crumbled, *I Spy* reinvigorated that ideal
by crafting it around a specific set of social concerns about civil rights. *Mission:*

Impossible, on the other hand, represents perhaps the final breakdown of the spy ideal. By evacuating its agents of individual identity, they become pure expressions of state power.

Mission: Impossible was also television's most direct fictionalization of the CIA's claim that its ideal agents must possess a "passion for anonymity." In a notable departure from the conventions of narrative television, the show was promoted not primarily through its characters, but through its precision of technique. *Mission: Impossible* was intended to be a marvel of accuracy—everything from psychological manipulations and the design of weapons and explosives to the representation of international cultures was carefully researched. The result was that *Mission* extended spy programs' realist conventions to their most reductive end; rather than skirt the basic tension between bureaucratic documentarism and the narrative emphasis upon the individual spy's heroic agency, the show obliterated the notion that the spy was anything but a mechanism of state power, substituting technological realism for narrative protagonists.

Furthermore, the show inverted the dialectic logic of self and Other. Within most spy programs, the agent is marked as most profoundly "American" when he acts as an individual; his service to the state and his patriotism are portrayed as the fullest expression of his free will. The "proof" of that individuality lay in the contrast between the American spy and the enemy Others that surrounded him, most forcefully shown in the Red Scare programs' portrayals of Communists as mindless drones. The representation of the ideal American agent is, as Dana Nelson puts it, "alter-referential"—the perceived *interiority* of the American self is constructed in discourses of *exterior* difference.[5] In other words, the agent is recognized as an ideal citizen by comparison to those who are not. In most discourses of nationalism, this referential loop closes, with the principal ideological effect of reinforcing the internal coherence and consistency of the American self. But in *Mission: Impossible,* with its anonymous agents, this referential logic never quite resolves; instead, the show turns its attention exclusively toward demonstrating the "infinite particularity" of the Other.[6] *Mission: Impossible* is organized around the voyeuristic pleasures of observing, scrutinizing, and eventually mimicking the Other—concretized both in the program's narrative structure and in its use of exhaustive research services to corroborate its representations of nonwhite cultures.

Mission: Impossible's practice of carefully researching its portrayals of other cultures was partly due to its attempts at realism and accuracy, but it was also influenced by significant changes within the television industry. The show was one of the first whose profitability to the studio depended heavily upon international distribution. Despite its popularity with domestic audiences, *Mission* was sold at or below cost to CBS. From its inception, *Mission: Impossible*'s producers sought to guarantee that the program would not offend international audiences, which led them to take great care researching the show's racial and cultural representations. The result is a strangely contradictory text; both virulently nationalistic and circumspect in its representations of the Other, *Mission: Impossible* offers a striking case study of how the decolonizing world was portrayed in American popular culture of the 1960s.

Anonymous Agents: The CIA and the IMF

We like to think that the CIA is awake and watching us. The CIA isn't saying.

—WILLIAM READ WOODfiELD,
MISSION: IMPOSSIBLE HEAD WRITER

When journalist Frederick Collins wrote in 1962 that the ideal FBI agent was a high-minded public servant with a "passion for anonymity," it was neither the first nor the last time the phrase was used to describe a government agent. Used by various writers, both in and out of the government, for some twenty or more years, the phrase was probably first attributed to Allen Dulles, CIA chief during the Eisenhower administration. By the time "passion for anonymity" appeared in the memoir of a retired CIA operative in 1968, it was without quotation marks or attribution; it had become part of the common sense of CIA life. It is perhaps fitting that the phrase's origins are murky; like an ideal agent itself, its effectiveness isn't marred by personality. Even more than the FBI, the Central Intelligence Agency shrouded its activities in secrecy, and demanded that its agents hide their professions from family, friends, and the press. According to Director Dulles, an effective spy was "not overambitious or anxious for personal reward in the form of fame or fortune" and was instead ready to toil in obscurity in service of his country.[7]

More than any other spy program of the period, *Mission: Impossible* seemed to follow through on this ideal. The veil of anonymity varied, however, from character to character. The team's white male agents—including Willy the strongman, Martin Landau as the team's master of disguise, and leader Dan Briggs (played by Steven Hill, replaced by Peter Graves as Jim Phelps) often passed unnoticed as endlessly malleable officers, diplomats, or tourists. Barbara Bain's character, Cinnamon, however, was often prominently on display, the spectacle of her sexuality mobilized as a mechanism of anonymity. And Barney Collier (played by Greg Morris, only the second African American actor in an ongoing dramatic role on U.S. television) was often literally hidden from view, his electronics and explosives expertise taking him into the dim recesses of both the buildings they infiltrated and the narrative itself. In later seasons, the cast changed several times, including at various times Leonard Nimoy, Lesley Ann Warren, Sam Elliott, and Lynda Day George. Seldom did we learn about the characters' personal lives or past, and the program included no serialized plot elements that tied one episode to the next. The team was assembled—with occasional guest stars as extra agents—for each individual mission, and upon its successful completion, the group disbanded once again. In a sense, the show offered a model of multicultural pluralism that reflected the shifting landscape of American television, but without the complexities of identity politics; stripped of history or context, the characters' identities were themselves technologies, implements to be mobilized in the service of the state.

When CBS began market research to test the viability of *Mission: Impossible* before it went on the air, a focus group was uncertain how to react. The CBS testers reported, "The program's opening was called 'confusing' by some of the viewers. They said that 'the beginning didn't explain whether they were good or evil' [and] 'I didn't know their goal, so how could I sympathize with them?' " Such viewers were unable to place the program's protagonists in a recognizable heroic narrative. In response, CBS recommended that "Dan Briggs should probably not continue as the program's lead. However, if he is to remain, an attempt should be made to make him more forceful and aggressive." Further, the network suggested exploring "in greater depth, the personalities of the team members," claiming that "the appeal of the program might be increased by distributing heroism among two or three central characters, rather than spreading it among five or six."[8]

Steven Hill was cut after the first season, though the stated reasons were contract disputes and on-set conflicts rather than his character's apparent lack of personality.[9] His replacement, Peter Graves, did, however, more conventionally fit the mold of the virile leading man. The other CBS recommendations regarding character development were largely ignored. Despite such concerns, the characters' anonymity and superficiality became one of its most popular aspects. One fan wrote an indignant letter to executive producer Bruce Geller when she read an article in the *Los Angeles Times* speculating that the characters might be given "more characterization" in the coming 1968 season. "If the audiences had wanted another *U.N.C.L.E.* or *I Spy, Mission: Impossible* wouldn't have caught on to begin with," she wrote. "Who CARES about character development??"[10]

One of the first season's episodes succinctly captures the curious flatness of the IMF's personalities. In "The Carriers," the self-destructing tape informs Briggs, "This is Janos Passik, an enemy expert on American traditions, slang, and customs. Passik is gathering some two hundred agents who are in final training, learning to act as Americans for a special operation." Passik's plot is to spread a septicemic plague throughout the United States, using his specially trained agents as carriers. In order to penetrate the operation, the IMF intercepts four new trainees and takes their places in Passik's group. When they arrive in the unnamed Iron Curtain country, they're taken to "Willow Grove," a mock American small town constructed as a training center for double agents. There, the Communist agents are trained to behave as Americans. Driving through the gates, we see housewives doing laundry, American Legion signs, garbage collectors, fathers playing horseshoes, basketball, and football, and sailors on leave walking the streets. In the episode, the IMF pretends to be clumsy outsiders and must be taught to act like "Americans."

After their induction, they are assigned new identities by Passik: Rollin is trained to be a hotdog vendor at a ballgame, guest star George Takei is to be a librarian, Barney is assigned to be a fry cook, and Cinnamon is indoctrinated in proper go-go dancing technique. The agents are uncomfortable, awkward in their new skins. This is, of course, part of the act; as double agents, they must appear inexperienced, unable to masquerade as Americans easily. But at the same time, the IMF team dons these markers of everyday American life with the same level of detachment as any other form of characterization. Receiving a hotdog, Rollin is the picture of all-American friendliness, but his flat smile mocks the possibility of earnest patriotism.

Mission: Impossible thus reduces all characterization to the play of surfaces; stripped of personal lives and histories, the IMF agents are completely malleable, able to step in or out of any given identity that might be required in their missions. Writing in the *Journal of Popular Culture* in 1967, Richard Carpenter commented,

> In a world where we are worried about retaining some semblance of individuality in the face of overwhelming problems, *Mission: Impossible* shows us characters overcoming impossible problems through the submergence of individuality into the activity of the group. It demonstrates by implication that technology and cooperation can overcome evil, that we can succeed if we will contribute our one special talent to the cause, forgetting any other interests we may have.[11]

This marked a significant departure from typical representations of spies. The agents of the IMF have so completely sublimated their own identities to the will of the group that they have no coherent selves; they have no personal identities outside their espionage practice.

Instead of patriotic national heroes, *Mission: Impossible* offers only infinitely adaptable functionaries of the state. In a sense, then, the show brings spy programs' uncertainty about the relationship between the ideal national agent and the state full circle. Rather than hinge its narratives on this uneasy conflation, *Mission: Impossible* dispenses with any conventional sort of "agency" at all. The spies of *Mission: Impossible* couldn't be more unlike Alexander Scott of *I Spy;* rather than historically founded subjects with personal lives that are crafted around dominant norms of citizenship, their individual pasts are as murky as the present they inhabit. As Geller once put it, they exist only for the "con"— their agency is founded only in action, stripped of historical significance, transformation, or national identification.

Exporting Difference

The actions of these anonymous mercenaries, whose lack of ethical restraint was perhaps the closest narrative corollary to the actual practices of the CIA during the 1960s, seems to have been a poor example of the kind of moral leadership that was increasingly called for in American television of the 1960s. FCC chairman Newton Minow said in his famous "vast wasteland" speech, "What will the people of other countries think of us when they see our Western bad-men and good men punching each other in the jaw in between the shooting? What will the Latin American or African child learn of America from our great communications industry? We cannot permit television in its present form to be our voice overseas."[12]

At the same time, federal agencies began to recognize that U.S. commercial television would likely have far more influence on international audiences than any government-sponsored media. In 1961 the Defense Department research director testified before the Senate, "We cannot consider our communications systems solely as civil activities. . . . We must consider them as essential instruments of national policy." And by 1968, U.S. syndicated television was airing in 102 countries, surpassing the reach of even the U.S. Information Agency (USIA). American commercial television, the USIA reported, was "setting the tone for television programming throughout the world."[13]

Within such a context, this internationally distributed narrative of American superiority was not without its critics. *Mission: Impossible* was more than just another violent American program; disavowed or not, its mercenaries were official representatives of the U.S. government. R. L. Shayon, television critic for *The National Review,* voiced these concerns in a scathing review:

> My candidate for this season's most harmful television program is *Mission: Impossible.* The viewer is invited to watch the exploits of a group of experts skilled in carrying out dangerous missions involving international violence. . . . The heroes of *Mission: Impossible,* for pay and at government instigation, interfere directly in the affairs of foreign nations with whom we are at peace and from whom no direct threat to our safety emanates.[14]

Indeed, *Mission: Impossible* represented the most aggressive and imperialist tendencies of 1960s U.S. foreign policy. Even as the CIA was coming under attack for its efforts throughout the 1950s and 1960s to subvert the governments of Iran, Angola, and Guatemala, *Mission: Impossible* showed the agency's tactics at work in an internationally distributed television program. Like many critics, Shayon was most concerned with what the show suggested to the presumptively naïve developing world:

Abroad, this series certainly will not win us friends. The British and French may be able to place it in context, assuming some separation of national policy from media behavior. But in emergent nations the viewers may say: "The Americans are telling us, in these programs, that this is the way to run a society. What is good for the big one is good for us: We will repeat their words but do their deeds.". . . In a world at the door of satellite communications, it is time to introduce some international dimensions of ethical sensitivity.[15]

Mission: Impossible did meet with occasional resistance on the global market. The series was briefly banned in Israel, though distributors managed to exploit regulatory loopholes to get it on the air—an action that prompted Israel's Theatre and Film Censorship Board to complain to the Knesset.[16] Despite the apparently reprehensible behavior of the show's agents, though, the program was quite popular internationally. Not entirely unpredictable, it was especially popular in Franco-controlled Spain, where it won the Golden Quixote award for the best series of 1967.[17] Desilu Productions—and later Paramount Television—distributed it throughout Europe as well as the Middle East, South America, and Africa. Although the show provoked some criticism in specific national settings, it was sold internationally from the first season, and eventually aired in ninety countries.[18] From its inception, the show's producers worked to make sure that *Mission: Impossible* would have a profitable future as a globally circulated television product.

Just as the 1960s was the "development decade" in terms of the United States' official policies of extending its reach to the far corners of the globe, so too was the period one of rapid international expansion for the television industry. According to a major UNESCO study of international syndication during the decade, it was in approximately 1962 that the number of television sets outside the borders of the United States surpassed those within. Much of the programming content on those new sets was provided by the U.S. television industry, which was able to sell packages of shows for far less than it would cost for comparable new local production. Nearly half the programming content in Latin America and Africa was American in origin, with some small countries importing nearly all of their television programming from the United States and Europe. In both Eastern and Western Europe, American television accounted for nearly a quarter of all television programming.[19]

The U.S. share of the international television market was particularly heavy in fictional series programming. In many countries, the only series programming on the air in the 1960s was foreign-produced, with nearly all of that coming from the United States. According to the UNESCO report, "In international television program production the United States has led markets in the mid-Sixties by exporting more than twice as many programs as all other countries combined. During the latter half of the '60s American TV program exports approached $100 million a year." Distribution numbers for specific programs are often difficult to trace, particularly during this early period, as distributors carefully guarded sales data about these new markets. Nonetheless, by most accounts, westerns and spy shows were among the most popular of all U.S. programs internationally, and many shows reached larger international audiences than domestic ones. *Mission: Impossible* was a top seller, reported in *Variety* as enjoying "record sales" abroad.[20]

Desilu and Paramount thus faced a curious challenge with the marketing of *Mission: Impossible*. This was the studio's most expensive program, budgeted at nearly $200,000 an episode. The show featured highly technical sets and costumes, and the per-episode shot count was often double that of a comparable hour-long drama due to its brisk editing rhythm and heavy use of cut-ins to show the technical details of equipment. As a result, the show nearly always went over budget. Even by the third season, when *Mission: Impossible*'s domestic success was proven, Paramount lost $830,000 on the program. One two-part episode, "The Bunker," was budgeted at $370,000 but reached a final tab of over half a million dollars.[21] In fact, Paramount nearly pulled the show from production after a reinvigorated fifth season in order to extract as much as possible from the series in off-net syndication. *Mission: Impossible* was sold for several times the going rate for one-hour syndicated material, and Metromedia TV had made the first syndication contract during the show's first season. As *Variety* reported on the series, "It's no secret that Par[amount] has had considerable red ink on the series because of deficit financing, plus a low price tag on the show its first few years. Studio has now begun an all out drive to sell the commitments on the series in the syndie field, and reports are it's doing very well."[22] This extremely expensive program was part of a growing trend within the TV industry; it would only generate a profit for the studio in syndication.

At the same time, however, this was a program about the violent and politically disruptive behavior of American mercenaries abroad—hardly model citizens. Nonetheless, the program's syndication was entirely international, since off-net domestic syndication would not begin until after the series was canceled. This created a serious marketing problem for all studios producing spy programs, as *Variety* noted in 1967:

> The spy-spoof show, loaded with political innuendo, is sometimes proving a headache to the Yank distributor who has to unload the show in European markets. . . . Segments can be marred by inadvertent references—visual or oral—to points which are taboo in many sensitive markets. . . . One hopeful sign for the future, however, is the noticeable switch in international video villainy from the dusky European to the Oriental.[23]

I Spy was one of the shows that most fully made the switch to Asian locations, and indeed its Asian racial stereotypes were far more overt and offensive than its portrayals of European cultures. But *Mission: Impossible* episodes were often set in Europe, as well as throughout the developing world. Instead of relocating the show's settings, the *Mission* producers developed a careful system of script research and supervision that negotiated its American nationalism with global sensitivities in ways that ensured its international marketability. In large part, the program's representations of national cultures were limited by the producers' economically driven decision to avoid arousing political tensions that might jeopardize sales.

Just prior to the development of *Mission: Impossible*, Peter Cary, director of European sales for Desilu, told *Broadcasting* that political sensitivities made certain topics unmarketable internationally:

> Programs that stress violence or ones with plots concerning the overthrow of governments or revolutions are definitely out. . . . War pictures are very tough to sell because the Europeans have had enough of war. . . . Anything that smacks of the Communist question or non-Communism is a very, very difficult product to sell [because] a lot of the countries that I do business with do business with Russia and they don't want to offend Russian officials at all. . . . In Spain you cannot get anything on that has anything to do with the church unless it's a purely religious-type show.[24]

Despite such potential obstacles, international distribution was not only appeal-ing, it was crucial to studio success. Fueled in part by the U.S. networks' invest-ments in the television industries of newly independent postcolonial nations, the international market for American television began to boom in the mid-1960s.[25] Peter Cary had his eyes on opening foreign television markets when he announced, "Greece initiated television, Turkey is opening up within the next year and two or three African countries are coming in real soon.... The future of syndication in foreign markets is extremely bright.'"[26]

Based on Desilu's own criteria for what sorts of representations might suc-cessfully become marketable programs, *Mission: Impossible* would seem to have been an unlikely candidate for international distribution—in Europe or any-where else. For how could the studio possibly package an American spy pro-gram in a way that would not offend local and national sensibilities? In a specific strategy to acquire international markets—as well as to appease those in the United States who criticized the show's apparent moral turpitude and its poten-tial to exacerbate strained foreign relations—the program's references to specific foreign countries were intentionally purged, and the program substituted instead fictional countries (such as Carpathia, Lubjanka, or Santa Costa) that were untraceable to a specific "real" point of origin. At the same time, though, each episode's cultural and linguistic references were precise and accurate. The resultant text, while staged as a nationalist conflict, disrupts the integrity of "nation" as a unifying source of narrative cohesion.

The program's producers enlisted the aid of an outside research company to warn them of instances when they might touch off controversies in particular countries. DeForest Research, a company specializing in media research ser-vices, carefully scrutinized each *Mission: Impossible* script before it went into production. Such services were (and are) commonly used by production com-panies to avoid inadvertently libelous references to real people, but here their services went much further. DeForest provided information on such varied topics as local customs and idiomatic expressions, proper quarantine proce-dure, techniques for handling infectious biohazards and radioactive elements, the epidemiology of the plague, consular etiquette, astrology, Swiss banking, and the circumstances of Hitler's death. Most important, though, was DeForest's monitoring of the national, cultural, and linguistic distinctions made by the program.

There was little confusion as to the meaning of the "Gellerese" warning signs in *Mission: Impossible.*

In episodes set in Eastern European countries, characters spoke a fictional language that featured traces of a variety of Germanic and Slavic languages, but which couldn't be traced to any single national tongue. Dubbed "Gellerese" after the show's executive producer and creator, Bruce Geller, the dialect was clearly meant to signify an Eastern European language while remaining recognizable to English-speaking audiences. "Gellerese" was composed entirely of cognates, liberally sprinkled with extra umlauts and circumflex accents. Some of the common words that appeared on street signs, documents, and in dialogue included Alarüm, Elevaten, Exterminador, Machina Werke, Secürit Clerenz, and Zöna Restrik.

A script about the resurgence of German Nazism, "The Echo of Yesterday," prompted this response from DeForest:

> In the past, the general policy of *Mission: Impossible* has been to fictionalize countries that the IMF operated in to avoid the repercussions, both foreign and domestic, which might result from the implication that the United States was, in fact, manipulating in the

politics and government of a specific country. In this script the references to Germany throughout might be too specific. We gather references are to be fictionalized.[27]

This particular script was a difficult one to revise, since it referred to a neo-Nazi leader as "the number one choice to become the next Fuhrer . . . with such a huge financial base there's no question that von Frank could be a second Adolf Hitler."[28] In order to mitigate this problem, the script was modified to exaggerate the neo-Nazis' delusional paranoia. The episode resolves with Martin Landau in disguise, this time as Adolf Hitler returning from the past, which provokes one of the neo-Nazis to murder von Frank in a paranoid rage. By shifting the context of the episode from the political conditions of 1960s Germany to a more idiosyncratic enclave of obsessive psychopaths, the producers preserved the international marketability that was one of their central concerns.

The producers also eliminated specific references to the social habits and monetary units that were associated with a single country. In one case, DeForest researchers wrote, "'A hundred drachma'—Correct plural: 'drachmas' or 'drachmae.' This unit of currency might tend to overly pinpoint Greece as the location of the story, which could perhaps cause international repercussions. Suggest: 'a hundred dinars.' The dinar as a unit of currency is used in Yugoslavia, Jordan, Tunisia, Kuwait, Iraq, and Iran."[29] A concrete example of *Mission: Impossible*'s internationalist tendency, this strategy of cultural regionalism allowed the producers to market the show without pinpointing an explicit enemy.

Mission: Impossible's unwillingness to identify or implicate specific nations did not extend to its representation of regional cultures. Indeed, the program's verisimilitude was based upon some level of realism, and its marketability depended upon a degree of cultural accuracy. As a result, the program coupled national anonymity with regional cultural specificity. In cases when a particular script's portrayal of a foreign setting might interfere with the show's marketability—particularly in the profitable markets of Western Europe—DeForest researchers were certain to comment. In their comments on a scene set in a European train yard, they advised,

> Railroad design, especially with rolling stock and locomotives, differs radically between Europe and North America. To use footage of

American railroad yards, rolling stock, Pullman cars, etc., in a purported European locale is ludicrous. Viewer reaction could be anticipated.... The usage of American railroads as European would mil-
itate against the sale of this show, and possibly the series, in Europe.[30]

In another instance, researchers commented on the unfeasibility of a plot turn
in which precious artifacts are sold to the British Museum. "Since the budget
for the British Museum is only 1,623,000 pounds annually, to suggest that the
Museum would currently have the funds and interest to purchase a ten million
dollar collection of Incan artifacts might be deemed ludicrous when the show
is syndicated in England."[31]

Similarly, in episodes set in regions that shared a common language—particularly Spanish or Arabic—linguistic specificity was used to legitimate the
program's portrayals. Many times, the researchers translated names and phrases
into correct Spanish, sometimes venturing into comic territory, as when they
observed that "Zack ... is not a Spanish name."[32] In another instance, the DeForest researchers were probably delighted to correct a scriptwriter's error in nam-
ing a Middle Eastern ruler King Ibn Borca:

> Borca in Arabic means: a lady's veil; ibn means: son of. "Son of a
> Lady's Veil" will be amusing to those who know any Arabic. Suggest:
> Ibn Baraka, which is a real Arabic name.... "Prince Fasar Borca":
> See above re Borca. Fasar is not a personal name in Arabic. It means:
> to examine a urine specimen.[33]

Similar care was taken in specifying the program's representations of religions.
In this same episode, the IMF was due to execute its plans in a holy city where
Muslims prayed around a large stone. DeForest researchers were quick to point
out that the episode as written could never be distributed in Islamic countries:

> Mecca is the only city in which there is a stone that is revered in the
> fashion depicted. To have Muslims praying in this fashion to a stone
> that is not Mecca is contrary to [network and National Association
> of Broadcasters] policy. Since it is *absolutely forbidden* for non-
> Muslims to enter Mecca, this entire program amounts to sacrilege. To
> avoid pin-pointing Mecca and possibly acrimonious repercussions
> affecting U.S.-Saudi Arabian relations, suggest delete "stone" and
> give city a name.[34]

Only occasionally, however, did the limits upon the program's representations come from concerns such as this about direct network or NAB (National Association of Broadcasters) reprisal. To be sure, *Mission: Impossible*, like other spy shows, caused a few raised eyebrows over its violence. In one of the most pointed network responses to a script, CBS Program Practices was concerned that an assassination scene was perhaps a bit too close to the headlines of the day: "The filmed scenes in the hotel corridor will not be reminiscent of the familiar scenes from the Robert Kennedy assassination."[35] But most of the directives issued by CBS Program Practices were scarcely different from those sent to other programs of the period; CBS simply demonstrated the U.S. networks' perennial concerns over sex and violence. Most of the Program Practices comments might just as easily be directed at a crime show: "To avoid excessive morbidity, we ask that the slain Connie's face not be seen as the flashback occurs. The business of the little girl screaming in terror should be deleted." Or the following: "Confirming our discussion with Mr. Lansbury, we will not see a picture of a 'lush full-bodied nude,' in Scene 53, page 22." Or, "Meredith's line: 'all those nights we would have spent making love,' will be deleted or modified to a less blunt expression.'" The network, in short, was principally concerned with FCC and NAB guidelines; the specific challenges of international marketability were beyond the network's area of concern.[36]

CBS was, however, anxious about referring to the Soviet Union even obliquely, and DeForest was instructed to monitor scripts for questionable inferences. When a script referred to missile bases being constructed in a Third World country, the DeForest researchers reported, "This line reinforces identification of Validin's country with the Soviet Union—only superpowers have the economic and military capability of building such bases. CBS Program Practices has asked that all countries mentioning such a situation be patently fictitious, as any identification with the Soviet Union could lead to international repercussions. Suggest delete 'missile.'"[37] This concern dovetailed more closely with those of Desilu/Paramount regarding international representations, since the studio sought to market the show not only in Western Europe, but in Eastern European countries that were partially open to U.S. imports, including Poland, Czechoslovakia, and Yugoslavia.

Thus in its representations of American agency, *Mission: Impossible* offered a much more complicated political landscape than that modeled by spy shows of less than a decade earlier. The most basic contours of that earlier landscape were recognizable, with the Soviet bloc roughly sketched out. But due both to broad changes in the American cultural climate of the 1960s and to the concrete pressures of international television syndication, this jingoistic program—dubbed "Mission: Immoral" by its critics—was perhaps uniquely hesitant to make blanket claims about the various menaces imagined to threaten the "American way of life."[38] The show's realism was generated not through the urgency of its political references, but through highly specific representations of cultures and technologies.

Mission: Impossible's truth claims about global cultural identities were further reinforced by its emphasis on the verifiable accuracy of its devices of manipulation. While *Mission: Impossible* did not claim to be reality-based in the same way as were the documentary melodramas of the 1950s, the activities of the IMF were always positioned as technologically feasible. Like the late-1950s show *The Man Called X, Mission* purported to give accurate lessons in spy technique. Technological and psychological verisimilitude was central to *Mission: Impossible*'s marketing strategy, as well as an important part of its fan culture. Unlike other narratives of techno-spies—particularly *The Man From U.N.C.L.E.* and *Get Smart,* which reveled in the absurd—*Mission: Impossible* claimed that its fantastic devices and ruses were always reproducible in the "real" world. In its press releases, Paramount told viewers and potential advertisers that *Mission: Impossible* was "technically possible":

> Probably no dramatic television series goes to the lengths that Paramount Television's *Mission: Impossible* does to eliminate faults—or "holes"—in the stories. "In particular," points out creator and executive producer Bruce Geller, "we consult with technical experts to verify that the mechanical and psychological ruses are, in fact, possible, because the success of the series is largely dependent on the credibility of the complex maneuvers of the Impossible Missions Force.... If we were to resort to solutions which are invalid, then there would be no real challenge to the audience."[39]

In some instances, the program gave itself credit for being more innovative and technically skilled than the industries whose products they emulated. Paramount made much of one episode in particular: "*Mission* technicians went to a local aerospace company and studied drawings and pictures of the intricate claws, each of which costs $70,000 and seven months to make. They built two working claws at Paramount in ten days for about $2,800, and aerospace officials refused to believe it could be done until they came to the studio to see the claws in action."[40] In large part, such claims to verisimilitude were highly exaggerated for the purposes of promotion. It seems unlikely in the extreme that the IMF's $2,800 claws would ever be used outside a soundstage, let alone in the radioactive environment they were apparently designed for.

Nonetheless, the program's technological realism became an important part of its fan culture. Many fans wrote to the producers to ask about particular devices, or to correct what they saw as minor errors. A group of law-enforcement students at the University of Maryland approached Geller, wanting to discuss how *Mission: Impossible* resembled other programs that were produced in cooperation with government agencies. Geller replied, "I frankly cannot see that it has any pertinence to police-community relationships as the series deals only peripherally with police and is a pure entertainment with no pretenses to be a documentary," but the program's claims of technological accuracy nonetheless provoked letters from fascinated fans across the country. A college professor wrote to the show to ask for information about the program's investigative methods to share with his criminology class, and a psychiatrist wrote to discuss techniques of psychological manipulation.[41]

Hy Gardner's nationally syndicated newspaper column, "Glad You Asked That," wrote to Bruce Geller, inquiring, "How many electrical engineers does *Mission: Impossible* employ to pull off all of those tricks that make the program so fascinating? Do all of the devices really work?"[42]

Geller responded, "We use a sizable but flexible number of Special Effects men on *Mission: Impossible.* . . . All of [the devices] will really work."[43]

Part of the appeal for fans was to attempt to unravel each episode's plot. When they encountered what they perceived to be errors, whether of political context, technology, or set design and props, they were quick to write. One fan wrote,

> I can successfully overlook the repeated use of Volvos, Mercedes, and Checker cars to represent East European makes, as I ignore the Danish submachine guns in the hands of what are supposed to be Communist troops. What is almost impossible to ignore are the natty, expensive-looking suits, shirts, and ties and Madison Avenue

type hair styles that would have any of the male characters spotted
as American actors in any foreign city. If realism is your goal, send
your wardrobe mistress shopping in Belgrade.[44]

Mission: Impossible's claims to technological accuracy, however, were at best a
tenuous means of maintaining dramatic realism. Indeed, these assertions of
accuracy—along with its agents' flat, deadpan delivery and wooden character-
izations—made it one of the most spoofed of its day. *Mission: Impossible* was
lampooned by *The Lucy Show* and *Mad* magazine, as well as by other spy programs; An episode of *The Avengers* was entitled "Mission: Highly Improbable,"
and a *Get Smart* episode entitled "The Impossible Mission" parodied the iconic
self-destructing tape sequence from the show.

Despite the program's artificiality, however, it continually reasserted that
each of its missions could be successfully executed. Operating in a fantastic world
and ranging over an artificial map of imaginary countries, the IMF enacted
through technology what "real" U.S. agents abroad in the late 1960s could not
do. With careful precision, split-second timing, and ingenious gadgets, the IMF
was able to stabilize a hostile world to make it a more secure place for the
United States.

The show was an assertion of feasibility, of the possibility of performing
the impossible: maintaining American military and political superiority in an
increasingly unmanageable international arena. As Bennett and Woollacott suggest in *Bond and Beyond*, the figure of the secret agent functions here "as a site
for the elaboration—or, more accurately, re-elaboration—of a mythic con-
ception of nationhood." It is no coincidence that such a recuperative gesture
appears in the midst of a national crisis over U.S. international authority over
Vietnam. For Bennett and Woollacott, such a crisis provides the fertile terrain
from which the idealized agent springs forth. They write of the crisis of British
military superiority provoked by the loss of the Suez Canal in 1957, "In the aftermath of the national humiliation of the Suez fiasco, Bond constituted a figure
around which, imaginarily, the real trials and vicissitudes of history could be
halted and put into reverse." At a historical moment at which American authority was similarly approaching a critical ebb point, *Mission: Impossible* emerges
as "an imaginary outlet for a historically blocked jingoism."[45]

The particular ways in which the agents of *Mission: Impossible* mobilize their
knowledges of cultural difference and their technological skill, however, don't

readily conform either to typical television narrative conventions or to normative discourses on American national identity. On the one hand, the show's virtually anonymous agents operate with neither serialized arcs of character development nor the emotional and psychological consistencies that familiarize audiences with the characters in nonserialized narrative programs. At the same time, however, *Mission: Impossible* treated its racialized others with careful specificity. The American-ness of the show's agents is anything but essential or innate; instead, it is only identifiable by contrast, forged in a complicated dynamic that depended upon their knowledge, and eventually assimilation and mimicry, of the identities of the Other. In this way, the program relies upon what Robyn Wiegman has called an "economy of visibility... a disproportionate system in which the universalism ascribed to certain bodies... is protected and subtended by the infinite particularity assigned to others." This system, Wiegman argues, "is contingent on certain visual relations, where only those particularities associated with the Other are, quite literally, seen."[46] In *Mission: Impossible*, agents' knowledge of the Other gives them the power to act in support of the interests of the American state. In this way, an apparently liberal recognition of difference—motivated by economic pressures of television syndication—functions simultaneously as a strategy of American nationalistic differentiation.

Significantly, though, agents Phelps, Hand, and Paris not only surveil racialized Others, they mimic them as well. A hallmark of the show is the use of seamless disguises by which IMF agents, the men "of a thousand faces," masquerade as those whom they're trying to manipulate. Transforming their bodies through makeup, costume, and masks, the agents of the IMF assume the identities of their enemies in order to complete their missions. Appearing as dictators, gypsies, clowns, dancers, acrobats, diplomats, and ghosts, the agents literally inscribe signifiers of alterity upon their bodies. The proliferation of difference is thus enacted upon the body of the American secret agent, where it can be caricatured and contained, but where it also haunts the American national subjectivity that seeks to define and delimit it.

The penultimate moment of many episodes was the infamous "peel-off"—the moment when a character whom we thought was a villain reaches to his neck, grasps a hidden flap, and "pulls off" his face. Underneath, of course, lurked the IMF agent. This dramatic moment, however, reveals nothing quite so much as the fact that there was precious little inside *to* reveal. This crucial instant—at

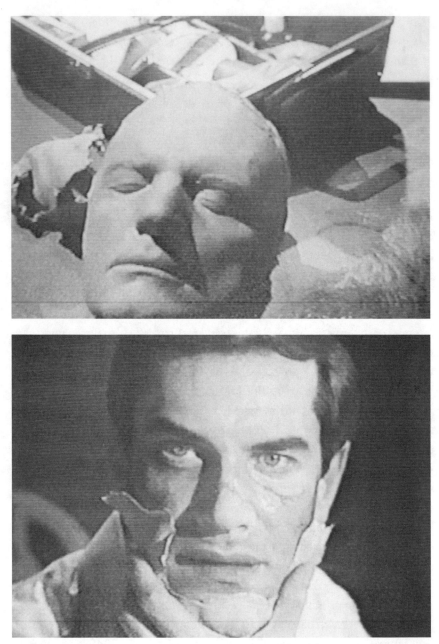

For the Impossible Missions Force, identities are simply layers of artifice, representations donned and shed at will in service of the mission. Here, a blank template lies waiting, while Rollin Hand transforms himself into a Latin American dictator and Cinnamon practices her go-go dancing skills so that she might impersonate an American woman.

which the irreducible "truth" of the agents' normative American identity is juxtaposed with the equally irreducible Otherness of their enemies—is nothing but another layer of disguise. National authority in the program depends not on the agents' stability and reliability as essential, "true" Americans, but on their ability to appropriate and embody difference. Their very identities become multiple and contingent, lacking the coherent fixity that historically has characterized the image of the masculinized American hero.

The show's repeated turn to masquerade as a mechanism for defining the limits of normative national identity parallels Philip Deloria's discussion of white Americans "playing Indian." From the Boston Tea Party to the Boy Scout movement to post–World War II American "pow-wows," this peculiar form of masquerade has become more prevalent during times of cultural instability and national transformation. As Deloria argues, "At the Boston Tea Party and elsewhere, Indianness provided impetus and precondition for the creative assembling of an ultimately unassemblable American identity." Such practices, Deloria suggests, are symptomatic of an ongoing instability regarding dominant conceptions of the ideal American subject; by "'playing Indian,' white Americans engaged in a still unfinished, always-contested effort to find an ideal sense of national Self."[47]

Not coincidentally, this practice of "playing Indian" became widespread and popular during the 1960s. Deloria links this to the generalized anxiety surrounding definitions of American national identity during the period. In light of the corporatization of America and the reduction of individuals—particularly men—to the "organization man" and the "man in the gray flannel suit," any sense of an American national community decayed "into a shallow conformism that turned individuals into automatons. For ironically, if the war had united Americans, it had also confirmed every antimodern anxiety about the meaninglessness of the individual Self." At such moments, according to Deloria, for white Americans, "the quests for personal substance and identity often involved forays into racial Otherness."[48] The Other was not only a symbol of a kind of primal authenticity no longer possible within industrialized American society; it also served to demarcate the boundaries of the ideal white American self.

Like other spy programs, *Mission: Impossible* engages an ongoing inquiry into the possibilities and limitations of ideal masculine citizenship. But *Mission:*

Impossible diverges in its inability to close the referential loop that defines that ideal subject in dialectic relations of cultural difference. The agents of the IMF, like those of the CIA itself, are driven by a "passion for anonymity"—a lack of self-presence, of individual identity. This, then, is the contradictory condition in which the program leaves its national agents. Unable to assert control over a politically and culturally complex world through legitimate military or diplomatic action, and unable even to identify with any clarity the national conflicts that make the secret agent necessary, the agents of the IMF are locked in a tenuous struggle that can only be accomplished by mimicking the identities and bodily markings of the Other. The program is marked by an unresolvable ambivalence in its attempt to narrate coherent and intelligible national identities for U.S. agents and the racialized Others it points out as enemies. As Michael Taussig writes, the "infernal American identity machine thus composes a mosaic of alterities around a mysterious core of hybridity seething with instability, threatening the First World quest for a decent fix of straightforward Othering."[49] Rather than supply that desired fix, *Mission: Impossible* registers the *impossibility* of forging a coherent national identity.

Vietnam, or The Agent Comes Home

The importance of the growing televisual spectacle of American failure in Vietnam cannot be underestimated as an influence on *Mission: Impossible*'s representations of American foreign policy and activity. In 1966, the year of the program's premiere, over 330,000 troops were engaged in Vietnam. That number rose to over half a million American soldiers in each of the next two years. *Mission*'s peak years of 1967 to 1971 had as their backdrop bloody protests over American foreign policy, news of American atrocities in Southeast Asia, inquiries into government deception over the Gulf of Tonkin incident and the My Lai massacre, and a growing sense that the war was unwinnable. The Vietnam War began to expose the impossibility of maintaining America's international power through frontal military assault. Within this context, *Mission: Impossible* offered a new model of American nationalism which was more interventionist and cynical, and which was based on deception and the appropriation of tactical disguise and trickery. Television representations of the Vietnam War, while it was happening, regularly featured the gruesome spectacle of bloody conflict—

brought into American living rooms nearly live and in color—coupled by a near disavowal of the war in fictional form. *Mission: Impossible,* with its re-interpretation of American foreign policy as a series of surgically clean, isolated interventions, was one of the few means by which the tensions surrounding Vietnam could be addressed within a televisual fictional narrative.

Film scholars have suggested that particularly in the peak years of the conflict the cultural anxieties surrounding the war made it virtually unrepresentable in narrative. Only one film that dealt explicitly with the experience in Vietnam was produced during the conflict *(The Green Berets),* and critics Linda Dittmar and Gene Michaud have suggested that "the growing criticism of this war both at home and abroad made it hard for Hollywood to produce a sequel to *The Green Berets,* while policymakers' determination to escalate the fighting allowed for only covert, highly mediated, and murky expressions of concern."[50] Instead, the war was transformed into a metaphoric presence, one that could be dealt with only through allegory. *Mission: Impossible* was just such a "covert, highly mediated" forum for dealing with the tensions surrounding the war.

One of the areas in which CBS Program Practices exerted its strongest edi-torial control was over the show's use of overtly militaristic images. More than other types of violence, military references were increasingly culled from the program. Just as film producers agreed during the early Cold War to fulfill what was seen by the State Department and the House Un-American Activities Committee as their responsibility to portray American values in a positive light,[51] so did the television industry impose limits upon its representations of the conflict in Vietnam. In one instance, Program Practices censors commented on a script, "we assume that the stills of 'Mass Death' will not be unacceptably shocking or repulsive."[52] Another episode, one of the very few that ever explic-itly mentioned Vietnam, featured a returned veteran suspected of going on a violent rampage. That script provoked an even sharper response from CBS: "As presently written, this script contains too much shock and terror, particularly for the new early-evening broadcast time.... In Seth's first speech, the phrase 'cooked in napalm' is too graphic and we ask that it be deleted."[53] In both of these instances, Vietnam is an unmentionable specter that cannot be invoked. The irony here, of course, is that such violent imagery had become a recurrent element of CBS's own news programming that aired every weeknight before primetime.

By *Mission: Impossible*'s fourth season, 1970–71, such concerns ultimately led to a major transformation in the show's representations of American mercenaries abroad. Turning away from international settings, the program instead became a domestic crime drama in which its agents' efforts were directed at controlling the operations of "the Syndicate." In part, this was due to the precarious balance the program struck between technological and cultural specificity and fictional license. The show's rigid regulation of international representations led to a level of repetition that the producers described as stifling. As the show's CBS liaison said of the program, "some Iron Curtain country would have to be the culprit. That was the trap. Far too many of these stories had been done in the previous broadcast year, and it hurt the series."[54] The vaguely European settings that were one of the program's most notable characteristics isolated it from the political context with which it was supposed to be engaged. Likely seeking both new opportunities for plot innovation and respite from criticisms of the IMF's geopolitical meddling, Paramount initiated a major change in the show's format. Where in 1969–70 all but two episodes were set in Europe or Latin America, virtually all of the show's final three seasons were set in domestic locations.

Mission: Impossible's creator, Bruce Geller, argued vehemently against this change to domestic settings, insisting that it was the international settings that made the show popular, and which made their missions outside the law and thus dangerous.

> With regard to credibility, the taped speech now reads, 'Conventional law enforcement agencies have been unable to...' Let's not fool ourselves. The FBI, Treasury Department, State and Local Law enforcement agencies *could* handle the criminal problems posed; they do it on every other show in Television....It doesn't ring true, all law enforcement agencies will be irritated, and the spectre of lack of due process (somewhat defensible in never-never lands) is going to haunt you.[55]

Nonetheless, the CBS vice president of programming insisted that the change be made, reportedly due to social pressures about television violence and criminality.[56]

Mission: Impossible never again achieved the high ratings of its first three seasons. The show's Nielsen shares fell off from a high of 39–41 for the first three seasons to numbers in the 25–30 range, falling from a top ten show to a middling performer. Furthermore, the international sales that had been a crucial source of revenue also slumped as the show was reoriented around domestic plots. Just when *Mission* had begun to develop an international fan culture to parallel those of its domestic audiences, its abandonment of international settings made it less appealing globally. "The show is now made cheaper," Geller charged in 1971, "but its foreign sales [have begun] to fall off and its ability to maintain a high license fee from the Network is irrevocably impaired."[57]

When *Mission: Impossible* turned toward domestic crime-fighting, it was the last of the widely popular American spy programs. The move effectively ended the spy cycle on American television (by 1973, even James Bond had become principally a crime fighter; *Live and Let Die* sends the British agent to Harlem to thwart a heroin ring).[58] Just a few years earlier the surging popularity of espionage had led the producers of domestic crime programs to reinvent their shows as spy dramas. The waning years of *Mission: Impossible*, however, signaled the final reversal of this trend; once mercenaries, the IMF were reinvented as clever cops. In part, of course, this kind of repetition and appropriation has continually marked American commercial television. But these shows' emergence from—and eventually collapse back into—domestic crime drama is more directly symptomatic of a cultural moment when the place of normative American national identity amid a burgeoning global culture was very much at question. *Mission: Impossible* embodies the tension between an expanding American presence in global affairs and growing evidence of the U.S. government's inability to contain and circumscribe political activity in the developing world. While in much 1960s television globalism was treated as an appealing and glamorous ideal, by the end of the decade glamour was replaced by cynicism. The agents of the IMF have no illusions about the morality of their actions. Instead, they simply do what spies have always done—use whatever tactics and resources are at hand to serve the political aims of the state.

Finally, *Mission: Impossible* pushes us to consider what happens when the cultural politics of difference collide with both market imperatives and nationalistic constructions of identity. Though the show's careful attention to issues of cultural difference was a significant departure from much programming of the period, *Mission: Impossible* does not advocate multiculturalism so much as it co-opts pluralism for state control. In the mid-1960s U.S. television producers were increasingly turning to the international market to recoup high production costs. And because international television was a key component of the Cold War struggle for nonaligned nations, they were also under scrutiny for their circulation of representations of America abroad. Furthermore, the specter of irreconcilable—and unwinnable—conflict in Vietnam, coupled with critical public reports of the CIA's global interventions, limited the range of representations of America's official agents. Within this context, *Mission: Impossible* emerges as a contradictory text—one that reproduces the kind of jingoistic nationalism that marked many of the televisual narratives of the previous decade while simultaneously being influenced by discourses of internationalism and multiculturalism.

Because the terms by which we construct and recognize difference are themselves predicated upon structures of inequality, simply identifying the "fact of difference" alone doesn't signal a cultural transformation. In light of the hierarchical structures of knowledge that *produce* difference, Christina Crosby argues that a progressive politics, "if it is to avoid the circularity of ideology, must read the processes of differentiation, not look for differences." In light of this, it seems crucial not just to identify the existence of cultural differences in such programs as *Mission: Impossible,* but rather to examine the systems of knowledge that shape how and why particular kinds of difference are made visible—in Robyn Wiegman's terms, to identify not just that which is visible, but the underlying processes of visibilization.[59] Espionage programs are, in various ways, centrally preoccupied with differentiating an ideal American self from its constitutive Others; they often develop highly elaborate mechanisms for this task. Within the narrative of *Mission: Impossible,* a kind of multicultural literacy makes it possible for the agents to carry out their covert missions. This literacy is mirrored by the show's international syndication efforts, which capitalized on cultural specificity not as an egalitarian gesture of goodwill, but as a strategy of market differentiation.

Still, *Mission: Impossible* was a moment in Cold War era television that disrupted what some historians have argued was a media culture characterized by uncomplicated narratives of American moral, political, and cultural superiority. J. Fred MacDonald has argued that television in the 1960s was highly politicized theater. . . . Americans saw the world divided into two incompatible camps. There were few gray areas in this dichotomy. On the other hand, areas of compromise were not required, for those video shows told audiences continually that Americans were always right, Americans never lost, and that as selfless rescuers of the world, Americans wanted little except a pat on the back, a kiss from a pretty girl, or a child's smile.[60]

In the case of *Mission: Impossible,* Americans may have been the rescuers of the Western world, but the methods by which they achieved those ends were far more complicated.

Instead, *Mission: Impossible* represents a shift in constructions of American Cold War identity, one in which the very coherence of "America" is revealed to be relational, situational, and characterized by political, cultural, and economic self-interest. This, then, may be part of the show's appeal internationally, just as it is clearly a part of the American cultural critiques of the show. While espionage programs explicitly explore issues of heroic nationalism and international paternalism, *Mission: Impossible* emerged at a time when the coherence of a singularly heroic American international stance began to become increasingly untenable. The show, then, represents a paradox; on the one hand, it constructs a political world cast in rigid terms of black and white, one in which the leadership of America—and the villainy of its antagonists—is firmly stated. But at the same time, *Mission: Impossible* shows that such an articulation of American identity is necessarily strategic, deceptive, and tentative.

Spurred on by the Kennedy and Johnson administrations' global paternalism, television producers extended the terrain of the Cold War by exporting pro-Western ideologies through American popular culture. In 1961 industry critic Leonard Goldenson wrote, "In Cuba we have seen how the battle for democracy can be lost. We are in grave danger of losing it in many countries of Latin America, Asia, and Africa. We must get our message of democracy to the uncommitted nations as soon as possible, then let them see us as we are, not as the Russians paint us to be."[61] Consistent with that goal, Robert Shayon lambasted *Mission: Impossible,* finding its representations reprehensible: "It is important to emphasize that the protagonists are not American agents in a time of war. Neither are they, in a time of peace, counteracting direct threats to our national security, as is done by CIA or FBI agents."[62] What Shayon was concerned about was that international audiences, particularly those in the developing world, might "incorrectly" assume that the show was a direct reflection of U.S. policy. What Shayon doesn't address, however, is that part of *Mission: Impossible*'s international appeal may have been precisely the sheer transparency of its agents' actions. Instead of camouflaging American foreign policy behind high-minded claims of democratic moral leadership, *Mission: Impossible* exposed it in its most interventionist and manipulative mode. While Shayon and other critics might have preferred a program about honorable American agents acting nobly, this show exposed the impossibility and artificiality of such an ideal.

Conclusion
Spies Are Back

NUMBER 6: What do you want?

NUMBER 2: Information.

NUMBER 6: Whose side are you on?

NUMBER 2: That would be telling. We want information! Information! Information!

NUMBER 6: Who are you?!

NUMBER 2: I am Number 2.

NUMBER 6: Who is Number 1?

NUMBER 2: You are Number 6.

NUMBER 6: I am not a number! I am a free man!!

— *THE PRISONER,* 1968

Longing on a large scale is what creates history. This is just a kid with a local yearning but he is part of an assembling crowd, anonymous thousands.

—DON DELILLO, *UNDERWORLD*

The most succinct expression of the 1960s TV spy's alienation from the state was not an American program but rather a short-lived British import that aired for a single summer season in 1968 on CBS. *The Prisoner,* created by and starring Patrick McGoohan, considers the consequences of a top secret agent's resignation from civil service. McGoohan had for several years been familiar to American audiences as British NATO spy John Drake in *Danger Man* and *Secret Agent. The Prisoner,* however, was a radical departure from other spy programs, for in it the ambivalent relationship between the agent and the agency completely ruptures. In the first episode, the agent (whom we assume to be Drake, although he is never named) storms into his London headquarters and resigns without an explanation. Returning to his apartment, he is drugged, abducted, and spirited off to a mysterious Orwellian town known only as "The Village."

The town is a bizarre self-contained enclave of service workers and a variety of former government officials: admirals, generals, diplomats, and lapsed spies of all nationalities. No one can leave the Village, and apparently none of its residents has the slightest clue where it is located. The town is guarded by mysterious hovering spheres that patrol the outskirts, incapacitating anyone who attempts to escape. The entire Village is covered by an elaborate surveillance network whose purpose is to extract information from those incarcerated there. Because the inhabitants carry sensitive information in their heads, they are deemed too dangerous to move freely in the outside world. Every comfort is provided them, but they are never allowed to leave. Furthermore, the inhabitants/inmates are stripped of their identities, assigned numbers instead. McGoohan's character, Number 6, continually tries to escape, but he is constantly thwarted by Number 2, the town's warden, cryptically played by a different actor nearly every week.

McGoohan conceived *The Prisoner*—which more closely resembled a *Twilight Zone* episode than other spy programs in overall tone—as a protest against the "numeralization, the loss of individuality which is happening to us all."[1] The world in which Number 6 finds himself is nightmarish; thwarted at every turn, he is desperate to escape. Each time he believes he is free, he finds himself the victim of yet another ruse to extract secret information.

His efforts culminated in the program's final episode, "Fall Out," one of the most highly experimental hours ever aired on U.S. commercial television, then or since. After outwitting the crafty Number 2, Number 6 is put through a series of tests before he is to be allowed to leave. He runs through an underground passage lined with jukeboxes blaring the Beatles song "All You Need Is Love," emerging into a large chamber. Workers and soldiers scurry about, and before him stands a robed judge and dozens of masked, Janus-faced figures as jury and Greek chorus. The judge applauds him, declaring, "He has gloriously vindicated the right of the individual to be an individual," which prompts the jury to start chanting, "I, I, I, I . . ." After a lengthy debate over Number 6's individuality, the judge declares him to be the new leader of the Village. Number 6 refuses, leading to a series of violent clashes and his escape. As the Village explodes around him, Number 6 flees with the help of a dwarf, as another prisoner dances wildly—and inexplicably—to the spiritual "Dem Bones." Arriving in London, Number 6 is apparently free, but the resolution of the episode, and the series, is ambiguous. Was this all yet another ruse, designed to lure him out to reveal the secrets hidden in his mind?

The Prisoner extends the basic conflicts inhering in spy narratives, imagining the predicament—for both the agent and the state—of a spy whose knowledge is too complete. Indeed, the notion of an all-knowing, independent secret agent is anathema to official intelligence operations. Such an agent ceases to be an asset and becomes instead a liability to the state; he literally becomes a man who knows too much. When the CIA issued its directives that ideal agents maintain a "passion for anonymity," it was not simply to allow them to pass undetected in open society. It was also an injunction against ambition and the comprehensive knowledge that might accompany it. Like blind men describing an elephant, no single agent could be allowed to know enough to threaten the agency's secrecy. As *The Prisoner* asserts in the most hyperbolic fashion, such state bureaucracies are often stultifying to those who operate within them. Dehumanizing and "numerifying," the modern state makes individuality a precarious proposition.

By the end of the 1960s, espionage was quickly waning on American television while the reputation of U.S. intelligence agencies plummeted. A few shows lingered into the 1970s; *Get Smart* eked out a final season on CBS after being dropped by NBC in 1970, and *Mission: Impossible*—whose agents redirected their efforts toward cases of organized crime and drug smuggling—remained on CBS until 1973. *The F.B.I.*—in effect the show NBC had worked so hard to create in the mid-1950s—was a fixture of ABC's Sunday night schedule until 1974, but it focused exclusively on domestic crime and avoided political intrigue. The handful of other copycat shows like *Amos Burke–Secret Agent* and *It Takes a Thief* similarly faded away. By 1973, even James Bond was chasing Harlem heroin dealers (in *Live and Let Die*). At the same time, the political opposition sparked by the antiwar movement helped lead to institutional reforms in the intelligence agencies. The *New York Times* revealed that the CIA under Nixon had continued its efforts to quell political dissent in the United States, and the CIA, NSA, and FBI were implicated by investigative committees in both bodies of Congress, as well as by a presidential commission.[2] Though they sounded like clever acronyms derived from 1960s spy television, COINTELPRO and Operation CHAOS (a name bestowed two years after the creation of *Get Smart*'s enemy agency, KAOS) were revealed to be the FBI's and CIA's illegal domestic surveillance operations. Fact had become stranger than fiction.

A reinvigorated popular skepticism toward state institutions may be one of the lasting discursive legacies of spy programs in particular, and of the general cultural reevaluation of the federal government and its policies during the late 1960s. In the earliest of the Red Scare programs, the nation, the state, and the individual agent occupied a common ideological ground. But as critiques of the federal government mounted—and as the representational logics of the spy shows themselves unraveled—the neat equation of nation, state, and agent failed. Compounding the crises in the intelligence agencies were a host of other dubious federal interventions, from Vietnam and Watergate to Iran-Contra, each of which made it increasingly difficult to imagine that a narrative of state authority could ever speak univocally for the nation and its citizens. It has been some three decades since espionage programs captured the popular imagination and airwaves. As if to prove conclusively that the Cold War was gone and forgotten—its fears vanished like a bad dream—we might look no further than UPN's ill-fated 2000 revival *Secret Agent Man*, whose apolitical pastiche of 1960s spy narrative elements didn't survive a mid-season culling.

Espionage-related programs were scarce throughout the 1980s and 1990s. One exception was the Reagan-era *Scarecrow and Mrs. King* (CBS, 1983–87), rare in its uncomplicated renewal of anxieties of Cold War infiltration. The show united a proto-soccer mom with a mysterious government agent whom she eventually married, bringing its conflation of domesticity and nationalism to a neat resolution. More common, though, were programs that played upon popular skepticism about the state and its covert powers. Among the most prominent of these was the popular series *The X-Files* (Fox, 1993–2002). Extending the logic of *The Prisoner*, *The X-Files* posits two renegade agents acting both against and within the hierarchy of the FBI. The show's premise is that agents Mulder and Scully explore cases "outside the Bureau mainstream," which leads them to question the basic underlying principles motivating the Bureau's actions. They themselves are under continual scrutiny, for as they get closer to the secret cabal of conspirators that constitute a U.S. shadow government, they grow increasingly skeptical about the state they serve. Similarly, the USA cable network's adaptation of the 1993 film *La Femme Nikita* (USA, 1997–2001) sketched an ambivalent relationship between Nikita and the organization within which she worked.

In the fall of 2001, though, three major espionage programs premiered in prime time, set against the backdrop of a major national crisis whose implications are still unraveling. This curious convergence was eerily prescient. Not only were the events of September 11, 2001, seemingly the stuff of Hollywood, but the ensuing debates—about American citizenship, patriotism, and identity, as well as about the role of intelligence agencies in a democratic society— reopened lingering tensions that were at the heart of Cold War spy narratives. *Alias, 24,* and *The Agency* were nearly derailed by the September attacks on the World Trade Center and Pentagon. In the immediate weeks after the attacks, network premiere schedules were rolled back across the board, and several films and television programs were postponed. *The Agency,* the program most directly modeled on the practices of the real CIA, canceled its pilot episode, which was to have dealt with a bomb attack sponsored by Osama bin Laden, and the pilot of *24* was re-edited to remove a shot of a 747 exploding in mid-air (TV ads and film trailers including the image were quickly pulled from circulation, as well). Critics suspected that both shows might die a quick death due to the shifting cultural climate of the fall, but producers insisted that *24* would be a public forum for the processing of the collective crisis.[3] Similarly, within two months of the attacks, *The Agency* was promoted as offering a documentary glimpse into the real practices of the CIA agents who were even now protecting our vital interests and saving American lives.[4]

These shows revived discourses about nationalism, civic authority, and agency that had lain largely dormant in espionage-related programs for decades. In a practice reminiscent of the earliest semidocumentary crime and espionage dramas of the 1950s, *The Agency* worked with CIA liaison Chase Brandon, who supervised the show's portrayals of the agency's work; in exchange, the program was given unprecedented access to CIA locations, the use of official seals and props, and a powerful marketing ploy. According to producer Wolfgang Peterson, "I think we show things as realistically as you possibly can, not just to make straight heroes out of these people but to just show their work."[5] Though the show occasionally explored the moral ambiguities of intelligence work, *The Agency's* forthright confidence in the ultimate value and necessity of the CIA earned it the approbation of some critics. The *New York Times* reported that "CBS clearly has become an agency booster," and FAIR founder Jeff Cohen editorialized in the *Los Angeles Times* that so as long as CBS and the CIA remain wedded, we can expect more episodes like last Thursday's, in which the CIA director's lying under oath to the Senate is portrayed as the correct and ethical choice. But don't expect hard-hitting episodes on the CIA's past alliance with terrorists such as Osama bin Laden. Or on the agency's role in the bombing of the pharmaceutical factory in Sudan and the Chinese Embassy in Serbia.[6]

Less reliant on official endorsement than *The Agency,* 24 and *Alias* articulate their protagonists' agency instead through domestic life and family relationships. In a telling move, 24's narrative arc was altered after 9/11 to make the impending crisis personal rather than public; Fox Entertainment president Gail Berman said, "The show is a mano a mano battle. The man has a particular problem in his division. A very personal problem."[7] This reduction of political conflict to the personal may have helped the network avoid arousing grisly memories of mass slaughter, but it also invoked a familiar set of narrative conventions that conflate the personal and the national. In both 24 and *Alias,* nationalism reconciles (or attempts to reconcile) the public with the private, the political with the personal, the broadly social with the psychological. These contemporary containment narratives activate powerful discourses of national identity and its relationship to psychosocial trauma that were at the heart of the hyperbolic anti-Communist programs of the Red Scare.

24 is structured by the crisis provoked when the private and public, the home and the state, collide. Jack Bauer, the show's protagonist, is successful only inasmuch as he can simultaneously manage both his home life and his professional responsibility to prevent assassinations and terrorist attacks. While his mobility across those spheres continually reaffirms his narrative authority, similar movements by the show's female characters—his daughter's transgressive teenage rebellion, his wife's infidelity and mobilization of her sexuality, his coworker Nina's symbolic invasion of his home through an affair and eventual betrayal, another female coworker's treason committed to provide for her infant son—are portrayed as dangerous and/or traitorous. As the series progresses, the plot becomes ever more complicated; warned of an internal government conspiracy to aid the assassins, Jack finds he can ultimately trust no one. Jack's answers can't simply be found in external physical action, so instead 24 seeks resolution by turning inward to the family. Leslie Hope, who played

Teri Bauer, said of *24*, "It's not a stinging expose on the CIA as much as how does one man try to save his family, his daughter, his relationship, the candidate, his morality and his way of life."[8] Indeed.

Like *24*, *Alias* immerses itself in the familial longings of its protagonist.[9] Double agent Sidney Bristow, we quickly learn in the opening minutes of the pilot episode, really just wants to be a girl—to settle into a coherent community of close friends and family. Sidney is the most dynamic and autonomous female spy on network television since Diana Rigg and Honor Blackman migrated to American shores in *The Avengers,* but the show's persistent relocation of Sidney to the domestic sphere resonates with some of the most retrograde appropriations of femininity in the service of nationalism. She is only truly at ease when she can settle back into the comforting gender-normative relationships of her *Felicity*-meets-*Friends* home life. Sidney's nagging anxieties about her parents—a cold absentee father (also a counterspy) and a traitorous, murdering mother—further mitigate her potentially radical gender-bending. What she most desperately seeks is her family. Like the three-lived Herb Philbrick fifty years earlier, Sidney's most unnerving crises occur when her multiple worlds collide. Unlike *I Led 3 Lives* and *24*, though, the home isn't a cherished sanctum protected by a father's diligent public service; instead, the home in *Alias* is a principal source of conflict.

The 2001–2 season finale ("Almost Thirty Years") brings the national directly into contact with the familial. Trying to unravel a labyrinthine plot led by a mysterious figure known only as "the Man," Sidney is captured by a diabolical Russian agent whom she believes to be the malevolent mastermind. When challenged, however, he bleakly admits, "I am not the Man." A shadowy figure emerges from a darkened room, and Sidney can barely squeak, "Mom?" Not only has Irina Derevko abandoned the family and committed murder and treason, she has become "the man"—the horrifying phallic mother returned as if from the dead.

The show's second season becomes an extended—and sometimes comically awkward—family reunion, as Sidney's mother surrenders to the government and offers her assistance in thwarting SD-6's plans. Irina is confined to a high-security cell where she stays sharp by catching flies in midair and performing yoga and calisthenics, and from which she doles out trickles of crucial information that guarantee her usefulness and her life. The simmering tensions boil over during what amounts to a dysfunctional family vacation; the three are sent to central Asia to intercept a nuclear arms exchange. There, a small miracle occurs—Sidney finds herself at the center of a family whose mission and motives are, for the briefest instant, congruent with those of the nation she serves. As she tells her friend Will,

> It seemed impossible that two people with so much deceit between them could ever find a way to breathe the same air. Then all of a sudden, there we were, just the three of us, walking down a dirt road in Kashmir. We were out there working as a team. It was comforting. We were ambushed, and we fought back. We survived.

Even the skeptical Jack for a moment accepts his estranged wife; he deactivates a C4-laden diamond necklace that encircles Irina's neck as both figurative and literal leash, and she uses it as an impromptu grenade in the firefight. For a moment frozen in Sidney's idealized slow-motion flashback, the family stands united, repelling threats both personal and political in a hail of bullets and high explosives.

In many respects, though, *Alias* offered more complex gender discourses than much of the rest of American commercial media of the time. Coverage of the 2001 attacks has often reverted to a simplistically gendered tale of American heroism, in which women signify solely grief and/or consolation. Press accounts of surviving families have focused heavily on widows, and a month after the attacks Laura Bush was featured on the cover of a national weekly magazine as "Comforter-in-Chief."[10] The same week, *Wall Street Journal* columnist Peggy Noonan declared,

> Men are back. A certain style of manliness is once again being honored and celebrated in our country since Sept. 11. You might say it suddenly emerged from the rubble of the past quarter century, and emerged when a certain kind of man came forth to get our great country out of the fix it was in. I am speaking of masculine men, men who push things and pull things and haul things and build things.[11]

For Noonan, this resurgence of all things macho came not a moment too soon.

> I was there in America, as a child, when John Wayne was a hero, and a symbol of American manliness. He was strong, and silent. And I was there in America when they killed John Wayne by a thousand cuts. A lot of people killed him—not only feminists but peaceniks, leftists, intellectuals, others.

Noonan dismissively feminizes her objects of scorn; among those "others" are "small, nervous, gossiping neighborhood commentators," orthodontists, and Woody Allen. Her contempt is rationalized by a nostalgic longing for an imaginary past in which stable gender norms ensured a continuity between one's daily life and the actions of the state. As Susan Jeffords writes of Richard Nixon's and Robert Bly's dire pronouncements about the lack of patriarchal leadership, her statement links the "crisis of a nation with the crisis of manhood." Like Ronald Reagan (in whose administration Noonan served) such figures operate as what Jeffords calls "sites of national fantasy," for they "combine for many Americans the national and the individual, the public and the personal, the global and the local."[12]

Similarly, it's worth considering the family of Johnny "Mike" Spann, the first American casualty of the U.S. military action in Afghanistan. Spann, a former Marine and member of the CIA's paramilitary Special Operations Group, was killed in a prison uprising in November 2001. He was widely eulogized, praised by CIA director George Tenet as "an American hero, a man who showed passion for his country and his Agency through his selfless courage." The agent's widow, Shannon Spann, quickly became a symbol of sacrifice, appearing throughout the news media and attending the 2002 State of the Union speech as President George W. Bush's guest. The White House described her as "the wife of Johnny Michael 'Mike' Spann. . . . Shannon and Mike had been married for two years. She is raising their three children."[13] The Spanns seemed to fit precisely the prescriptive mold of American family life suggested by Noonan—that of a martyred hero and his supportive family. But these accounts overlooked a more complex portrait; Shannon Spann was herself a CIA agent, and the couple had met during their training at the agency.

Spann's hometown paper wrote nearly a year later, "She told friends she had joined the State Department in 1999. But she really was jumping out of airplanes, learning how to use firearms and studying the famed 'sources and methods' curriculum at the Central Intelligence Agency. Only her family and two close friends knew she was a spy-in-training."[14] Her painful experience as a widow generated understandable sympathy and attention, but the public portrait of Shannon Spann largely ignored this aspect of her life. When they identified anything about her beyond her family identity, most press accounts referred to her as a "CIA employee," conjuring images of an anonymous position in the secretarial pool. A former law school dean described by friends as more likely to read foreign policy journals than *Vogue,* Spann has since returned to the CIA, though the media exposure surrounding her husband's death made it impossible for her to work covertly. While on one level the press accounts of the Spann family are accurate—Shannon Spann is indeed a widowed mother of three, struggling to reassemble her family after a profound personal loss— the gendered discourses of nationhood, martyrdom, and sacrifice mobilized around her are intensely reductive. War is both gendered and gendering; in linking the national to the personal, its narratives hinge upon essential, "true" masculinity and femininity. As in television narrative, so too in public discourse— it is remarkably difficult to imagine a feminine agent of the nation.

These containment narratives reactivate dimly remembered but still pressing questions surrounding the nature and demands of citizenship in a time of constraint; by doing so, they also invite us to rethink the cultural politics of the Cold War. What does it mean to be an agent? A citizen? More broadly, what does "Cold War" mean today? In the strictest sense, the Cold War refers to a relatively bounded historical period, circa 1947–89, in which the United States engaged in an ongoing political, military, economic, and cultural conflict with (principally) the Soviet Union. That Cold War had a number of important highlights: the public dramas of the Berlin airlift and the Cuban missile crisis; proxy wars in Korea and Vietnam; simmering conflicts in Africa, the Middle East, and Latin America; détente; remilitarization; a crumbling Wall. These conflicts were marked also by cultural parallels in the United States: the Red Scare of the 1950s; a culture of containment that circumscribed American definitions of family, of legitimate political expression, and of personal identity; a postwar baby boom that fed a burgeoning youth culture; a civil rights movement that was inextricable from the decolonization of the developing world; the popularization of the feminist movement; the rapid expansion, diversification, and eventual globalization of mass media, such that television became Americans' principal means of interacting with the world outside their physical and figurative borders.

But if we take "cold war" more broadly, as metaphor, we might think about its chill as an ongoing condition that mediates between the politics of the state and the cultures of our everyday lives. Most of the time, this connection is fuzzy at best. The official responsibilities of citizenship seem more of a bureaucratic burden than a personal responsibility; the notion of a military draft seems as anachronistic as butter rationing, and jury duty is an oft-ignored chore. Furthermore, the immediate consequences of geopolitics on our everyday lives seem ambiguous at best for most Americans—though the events of September 2001 brought the outside world crashing in. But at moments of instability or crisis, discourses of nationalism knit the self to the state. Sometimes the calls to vicarious participation are crudely economic—as with the "Keep America Rolling" zero percent loan financing promotion offered by General Motors and matched by other automobile manufacturers in October 2001. Sometimes, too, our popular culture explicitly addresses us citizens, as with the September 21, 2001, celebrity telethon simulcast by the top four broadcast networks and their cable partners. More often, though, the linkages between the self and the state aren't so clearly articulated. Instead, our sense of national identity is but vaguely felt, an untapped reservoir of attachment. In that sense, we might think of "cold war" as an ongoing ideological undercurrent, a mechanism of both participation and constraint that emerges in explicit form only in moments of crisis.

As with all expressions of nationalism, the cultural logics of the Cold War require an externalized Other, though the actual source of threat is seldom clearly defined. Frederick Dolan writes, "In the world of the Cold War, loci of agency can never be fixed; the answer to 'Who's *they*' is endlessly deferred."[15] These externalized threats, murky and inchoate, ultimately collapse inward; the specter of an unknowable foe prompts a contorted attempt to clarify the definition of the national self. The enemy can only be known by what s/he is not: a "true" American. Hence the reactionary definitions of heroism and patriotic sacrifice, the troubling language of the "homeland" (dare we call it heimat?) with its xenophobic exclusionism, and the reclassification of suspicious citizens as "enemy combatants" in order to retract what were once considered inalienable rights.[16] Hence, too, the Total/Terrorism Information Awareness program—a latter-day HUAC with unprecedented electronic surveillance tools—that promises to ferret out the enemy agents within our midst.

Though spy narratives concern themselves directly with the relationship between the self and the state, they are ultimately unlikely sites for the elaboration of pure, essential national identities. The self/Other differentiating process crumbles in the moral ambiguities of espionage. Dolan calls it (borrowing from John Le Carré's novel of the same title) a "looking glass war . . . organized around the fear of phantasms and the need to clarify them, but always vitiated by a mingling of the antagonists' identities that insinuates itself into the very core of the conflict."[17] Espionage narratives generate their own skepticism— for how, given their multiple layers of deceit and subterfuge, can they represent a foundational, idealized nation? These programs' discourses of nationalism are profoundly fragile, teetering on the edge of representational collapse. The spy is an unlikely figure of national identification, as suited for parodic or skeptical critique as for patriotic retrenchment.

The spy programs discussed here are thus far from univocal. The preceding chapters have addressed espionage television's major discursive elements—the jingoistic Red Scare, parodic critique, civil rights and citizenship, and 1960s internationalism—fairly discretely, using individual programs to illuminate particular discourses over others. This is not to say, however, that *I Led 3 Lives* was always and only a mouthpiece of the FBI, or that *Get Smart* didn't maintain some affection for the nation-state whose policies it lampooned. The episode in which Max and the Chief are called into active duty in the Navy closes, after all, with an awkwardly patriotic moment. Surrounded by military hardware (a rarity itself, since such a display necessitated a high degree of Navy involvement) the CONTROL agents share a salute with the naval captain who helps them complete their mission. As they fly off the deck of an aircraft carrier in a borrowed Navy helicopter, the *Get Smart* theme swells on the soundtrack, reorchestrated as a military march. The converse is true as well; comic and ironic moments lurked in even the most serious episodes of many programs. Building upon Bill Cosby's principal fame as a comedian, *I Spy* was often comic in tone. Nonetheless, the humorous banter shared by Kelly and Scotty wasn't directed at the government, but rather forged a bond of camaraderie that helped to endorse Cosby's character as a new black citizen. Whether explicitly comic or sternly patriotic—or more often something in between—when considered in the aggregate, these programs were important sites for grappling with contentious issues of nationalism and citizenship.

Though often deeply ambivalent, Cold War spy programs were also among the period's important points of popular engagement with the practices of the federal government. These TV programs exposed those operations to public scrutiny in a way that was not always possible in other media. A 1966 issue of the *Saturday Evening Post* included a pair of contradictory and revealing articles: The first, "Would You Believe Don Adams," was a profile of the star of *Get Smart*. "To the television viewer who watches NBC's *Get Smart* each Saturday night," the *Post* reported, "the following terms for its hero come to mind: Fool. Schlemiel. Dope."[18] The article didn't comment broadly on the content of the program, instead drawing a playful sketch of Adams and his private life. Printed back to back with the Adams profile was a photograph of a stern-faced General Westmoreland, the U.S. commander in Vietnam, illustrating an article entitled, "Why We Can Win in Vietnam." The article began,

> With American policy under attack and the U.S. military strategy criticized as a failure, a veteran reporter argues forcefully that victory is in sight. . . . No one analyzes the present strategy of our brilliant field commander in Vietnam, General William C. Westmoreland. No one refers in any way to what is currently happening on the battlefield. Yet the battlefield is where our own best hope of victory lies.[19]

In the pages of the *Saturday Evening Post*, these contradictory national figures nearly—but don't quite—meet, separated by more than just the paper on which they are printed. In these articles, the heroic general and the bumbling but charming comic represent two apparently incompatible poles of American masculinity, worlds apart in tone, manner, and political import. In *Get Smart* itself, however, such figures are regularly brought together, but inverted: it is the generals and admirals who are bumbling and ineffectual leaders, while the nation's future lies in the hands of Maxwell Smart, Agent 86.

These shows also chart the growth of a distinctly televisual mode of referentiality. As their strategies of realism generally moved away from direct state influence and toward a more general referencing of political and cultural events, spy shows bespoke the importance of television itself in crafting a national community. While all cultural texts are situated in particular social and historical contexts, espionage programs encouraged a particularly dynamic and intertextual form of reading on the part of their audiences. Their topicality increasingly became linked to their referencing of the media culture of which they were a part. A show like *I Spy* could only be understood in dialogue with the mediated images of the civil rights movement that aired alongside it; it offered a new narrative framework within which to address the national crises surrounding racial integration.

The more comic programs even more explicitly referenced media events. It is difficult to find an episode of *Get Smart* that doesn't simultaneously spoof both the federal government and a popular media figure, either fictional or real. In the Navy episode, Max paces the deck spinning a pair of steel balls in his hand in a dead-on impression of Humphrey Bogart in *The Caine Mutiny*. Other popular films and programs parodied by *Get Smart* included *The Fugitive, The Treasure of the Sierra Madre, Rear Window, Ironside,* and nearly every other spy program on the air. Both *The Man from U.N.C.L.E.* and *Get Smart* regularly featured prominent actors and celebrities—from James Caan and Janet Leigh to Johnny Carson and Don Rickles—in guest appearances. As the third season of *U.N.C.L.E.* began, it showed Illya sitting happily before a television, watching *The Girl from U.N.C.L.E.* In these shows, the cultural experiences shared by audience members are not specific political conflicts, but a set of intertextual media references; these shows encapsulate the growing importance, from the 1950s to the 1960s, of television itself as the preeminent site for the elaboration of a shared national culture.

The national is founded on the historical. That is, the maintenance of normative national identity requires an ongoing historical practice by which a coherent shared past is suspended in the collective historical imaginary. But this collectively shared past is not itself a direct product of the state. Instead, it is generated through the embrace of, and engagement with, a shared popular culture—mediated and otherwise. From their earliest 1950s incarnations to their virtual demise by the end of the 1960s, Cold War espionage programs increasingly engaged televisual literacy itself as a marker of the national community. Over these two decades, spy programs thus also chart a shifting relationship between the nation and the state. Just as their claims of authority were unraveling in the late 1960s, so too had unraveled the notion that the nation and the state might be synonymous terms.

When in 1966 *Esquire* evoked for its readers the irresistible but impossible "daydream" of the spy's mythic power, it lamented the failing premise that masculine agency, the state, and the national might fold neatly in upon one another.[20] This central premise, so crucial to the early Cold War, had frayed beyond repair. The cultural conditions that in 1953 allowed an idealized figure like Herb Philbrick simultaneously to embody state politics, national history, and patriarchal authority had by the late 1960s radically shifted. The state had not ceased to be a powerful political institution, national identity had not somehow become detached from discourses of historical continuity, and masculinity had not surrendered its privileged social position. Rather, espionage programs—once a crucial site for the expression of authoritative will—could no longer harness these diverging discourses within a tightly enclosed narrative. And indeed, it had been a tight fit all along; the rigid matrix of nation, state, and agent was from its inception an impossible proposition.

Notes

Preface

1. Raymond Williams, *Television: Technology and Cultural Form* (London: Schocken Books, 1975).

2. David Lowenthal, *The Past Is a Foreign Country* (London: Cambridge University Press, 1988).

3. Hayden White, *The Content of the Form: Narrative Discourse and Historical Representation* (Baltimore: Johns Hopkins University Press, 1990).

4. Carlo Ginzburg, "Microhistory: Two or Three Things That I Know about It," *Critical Inquiry* 20 (Autumn 1993): 21.

5. Michel Foucault, *The Archaeology of Knowledge and the Discourse on Language,* trans. A. M. Sheridan Smith (New York: Pantheon, 1972), 10.

6. Ginzburg, "Microhistory," 24.

Introduction

1. "Spies, Science, and Sex: The American Daydream," *Esquire,* September 1965, 79.

2. Ibid.

3. Frank Krutnik, *In a Lonely Street: Film Noir, Genre, Masculinity* (New York: Routledge, 1991), 202.

4. The notion that a common set of ideological problematics are "worked through" a series of interrelated texts is explored in detail by Tony Bennett and Janet Woollacott, *Bond and Beyond: The Political Career of a Popular Hero* (New York: Methuen, 1987), 4–7.

5. In the *Beverly Hillbillies* episode "Double Naught Jethro" (original airdate, March 3, 1965), Jethro Bodine decides to try his hand at espionage, rigging his truck as a spy-mobile and his shoe as a secret communicator; In "The Private Eye" (original airdate, October 6, 1965), he returns to spycraft to foil a bank robbery plot. The 1966 season premiere of *Gilligan's Island* pitted Gilligan against a look-alike secret agent ("Gilligan vs.

Gilligan," original airdate, Sept. 12, 1966), and other episodes featured exploding brief-cases and other spy gadgets.

6. Robert Weincek, "A Historical, Descriptive, and Analytical Study of British Television Espionage Programs That Appeared on American Television during the Seasons 1961–1969," master's thesis, University of Southwestern Louisiana, 1987, 1–3. In 1966, the British were exporting more in total sales to U.S. television markets than they were purchasing—an unprecedented reversal of economic tides. Spy programs, principally *The Avengers*, but also *The Saint* and *Secret Agent* were a significant part of this deficit. As British filmed production accelerated in the mid-1960s, production costs in the United States were simultaneously rising rapidly as networks began to switch to all-color formats. In 1965, for example, average British program imports ranged from $30–60,000 per episode, with *The Avengers* being sold to ABC for $40,000 per episode. This was cheaper by half than typical U.S. programming of the era, and was an even bigger bargain in contrast to the two most popular and expensive spy shows of the mid-1960s, *I Spy* and *Mission: Impossible*, both of which had typical per-episode costs of $200,000 or more.

7. Quoted in Michael Kort, *The Columbia Guide to the Cold War* (New York: Columbia University Press, 1998), 24.

8. The causes and implications of the Cold War are sources of ongoing debate. Among the overviews that summarize the conflict are H. W. Brands, *The Devil We Knew: Americans and the Cold War* (New York: Oxford, 1993); and Lary May, ed. *Recasting America: Culture and Politics in the Age of Cold War* (Chicago: University of Chicago Press, 1989). In *America's Half-Century: United States Foreign Policy in the Cold War* (Baltimore: Johns Hopkins University Press, 1989), Thomas McCormick locates the origins of the Cold War principally in U.S. efforts to expand global markets; arguing a similar point is Walter LeFeber, *America, Russia, and the Cold War: 1945–1992* (New York: McGraw Hill, 1993), though Robert Pollard strenuously defends U.S.-led economic multilateralism in *Economic Security and the Origins of the Cold War, 1945–1950* (New York: Columbia University Press, 1986). John Lewis Gaddis is among the most prominent of the antirevisionists; he argues that the Cold War was a period of relative peace principally due to U.S. containment policies that thwarted Soviet expansionism (John Lewis Gaddis, *We Now Know: Rethinking Cold War History* [New York: Oxford University Press, 1998], and *The Long Peace: Inquiries Into the History of the Cold War* [New York: Oxford University Press, 1987]). Kort's *The Columbia Guide to the Cold War* gives a useful timeline and thumbnail summaries of major events, and includes an extensive annotated bibliography.

9. Kim E. Nielsen, *Un-American Womanhood: Antiradicalism, Antifeminism, and the First Red Scare* (Columbus: Ohio State University Press, 2001); Ward Churchill, Jim Vander Wall, and John Trudell, *The COINTELPRO Papers: Documents from the FBI's Secret Wars against Dissent in the United States,* 2d ed. (Boston: South End Press, 2002).

10. Among the several histories of the cultural implications of McCarthyism and the Red Scare are Albert Fried, ed., *McCarthyism: The Great American Red Scare: A Documentary History* (London: Oxford University Press, 1996); M. J. Heale, *McCarthy's Americans: Red Scare Politics in State and Nation, 1935–1965* (Atlanta: University of Georgia Press, 1998); Richard Fried, *Nightmare in Red: The McCarthy Era in Perspective* (London: Oxford University Press, 1991); H. W. Brands, *The Devil We Knew: Americans and the Cold War* (New York: Oxford University Press, 1993).

11. Robert Vaughn, *Only Victims: A Study of Show Business Blacklisting* (New York: Putnam, 1972), 37.

12. Classics professor Bernard Knox (hundreds of scholars were also tainted by HUAC's investigations) later reflected, "How, I wondered, could *anyone* be a *premature* anti-Fascist? Could there be anything such as a premature antidote to a poison? A premature antiseptic? A premature antitoxin? A premature anti-racist? If you were not premature, what sort of anti-Fascist were you supposed to be?" Bernard Knox, "Premature Anti-Fascist." Abraham Lincoln Brigade Archives, Bill Susman Lecture Series. King Juan Carlos I of Spain Center, New York University, 1998, http://www.alba-valb.org/lectures/1998_knox_bernard.html.

13. Stephen J. Whitfield argues that the Cold War had broad public support. In 1949 70 percent of Americans disagreed with Truman's pledge that he wouldn't authorize a first strike. Within two years, nearly half of those polled supported the use of nuclear weapons in Korea as well. To some, the policies of containment and deterrence were anything but aggressive; in 1949, Truman's own secretary of the navy called instead for a preemptive strike to eliminate the Soviet threat, which he claimed "would win for us a proud and popular title—we would be the first aggressors for peace" (Stephen J. Whitfield, *The Culture of the Cold War* [Baltimore: Johns Hopkins University Press, 1996], 6).

14. Robert Griffith, *The Politics of Fear: Joseph R. McCarthy and the Senate* (Boston: University of Massachusetts Press, 1987).

15. See, for example, Elaine Tyler May, *Homeward Bound: American Families and the Cold War Era* (New York: Basic Books, 1988); Alan Nadel, *Containment Culture: American Narratives, Postmodernism, and the Atomic Age* (Durham, N.C.: Duke University Press, 1995); Nina Liebman, *Living Room Lectures: The Fifties Family in Film and Television* (Austin: University of Texas Press, 1995); Stephanie Coontz, *The Way We Never Were: American Families and the Nostalgia Trap* (New York: Basic, 1992).

16. Paul Boyer, *By the Bomb's Early Light: American Thought and Culture at the Dawn of the Atomic Age* (Chapel Hill: University of North Carolina Press, 1994); Walter Hixson, *Parting the Curtain: Propaganda, Culture and the Cold War, 1945–1961* (New York: Palgrave Macmillan, 1998).

17. Nadel, *Containment Culture*; Betty Friedan, *The Feminine Mystique* (New York: Norton, 1963); Daniel Horowitz, *Betty Friedan and the Making of* The Feminine Mystique:

The American Left, the Cold War, and Modern Feminism (Boston: University of Massachusetts Press, 2000); Joanne Meyerowitz, *Not June Cleaver: Women and Gender in Postwar America, 1945–1960* (Philadelphia: Temple University Press, 1994).

18. Mary Dudziak argues this point in *Cold War Civil Rights: Race and the Image of American Democracy* (Princeton, N.J.: Princeton University Press, 2000). She insists that the civil rights movement must be understood not just alongside, but intertwined with, U.S. foreign policy of the Cold War.

19. Warren Hinckle, Robert Scheer, and Sol Stern, "The University on the Make," *Ramparts* (April 1966).

20. Aniko Bodroghkozy, *Groove Tube: Sixties Television and the Youth Rebellion* (Durham, N.C.: Duke University Press, 2001), 162.

21. Vaughn, *Only Victims*, 277.

22. Kathryn S. Olmsted, *Challenging the Secret Government: The Post-Watergate Investigations of the CIA and FBI* (Chapel Hill: University of North Carolina Press, 1996); Angus Mackenzie, *Secrets: The CIA's War at Home* (Berkeley: University of California Press, 1997).

23. Thomas Rosteck, *See It Now Confronts McCarthyism: Television Documentary and the Politics of Representation* (Tuscaloosa: University of Alabama Press, 1994); The historical drama *You Are There* (CBS, 1953–57) was one of the many programs that was an outlet for blacklisted writers; the series premise and most episodes were the work of Walter Bernstein and Abe Polansky, who saw the show as a critical response to the excessive conformism of the period (Walter Bernstein, *Inside Out: A Memoir of the Blacklist* [New York: Knopf, 1996]). Frederick Ziv, the producer of some of the period's most virulent anti-Communist spy dramas, acknowledged just before his death that he had regularly hired blacklisted writers. Though virtually impossible to trace conclusively, this at least invites the possibility that, as Tom Doherty writes, "Like moles burrowing from within, they commented on their own dilemma, doubtless savoring the irony of using the premiere anticommunist series on television to critique anticommunist paranoia" (Thomas Doherty, "At Last Count, I Led 3 Lives," paper presented at Society for Cinema Studies annual conference, Chicago, March 9–12, 2000).

24. Frederick Dolan, *Allegories of America: Narratives, Metaphysics, Politics* (Ithaca, N.Y.: Cornell University Press, 1994), 61.

25. David Brown, *Contemporary Nationalism: Civic, Ethnocultural, and Multicultural Politics* (New York: Routledge, 2000), 1; Benedict Anderson, *Imagined Communities*, 2d ed. (London: Verso, 1991); Slavoj Zizek, "Enjoy Your Nation as Yourself!" *Tarrying with the Negative: Kant, Hegel, and the Critique of Ideology* (Durham, N.C.: Duke University Press, 1993), 202.

26. Brown, *Contemporary Nationalism*, 51, 52.

27. Monroe Price, *Television, the Public Sphere, and National Identity* (London: Oxford University Press, 1995), 4; Maurizio Viroli, "Republican Patriotism," in *The*

Demands of Citizenship, ed. Catriona McKinnon and Iain Hampsher-Monk (New York: Continuum, 2000), 273.

28. Nancy Fraser, "Rethinking the Public Sphere: A Contribution to the Critique of Actually Existing Democracies," in *Habermas and the Public Sphere,* ed. Craig Calhoun (Cambridge: MIT Press, 1992), 109–43; Margaret Canovan, "Patriotism Is Not Enough," in *The Demands of Citizenship,* ed. McKinnon and Hampsher-Monk, 278, 291.

29. Anthony Smith argues that this is in fact the central process of establishing modern nationalisms. See Anthony Smith, *National Identity* (Las Vegas: University of Nevada Press, 1991), and *Theories of Nationalism* (London: Duckworth, 1983).

30. George Mosse, *Nationalization of the Masses: Political Symbolism and Mass Movements in German from the Napoleonic Wars through the Third Reich* (Ithaca, N.Y.: Cornell University Press, 1975).

31. Price, *Television,* 246.

32. Andrew Parker, Mary Russo, Doris Sommer, and Patricia Yaeger, *Nationalisms and Sexualities* (New York: Routledge, 1992), 5; Ernest Gellner, *Nationalism* (New York: New York University Press, 1997), 101.

33. Anderson, *Imagined Communities.*

34. Michele Hilmes, *Radio Voices: American Broadcasting, 1922–1952* (Minneapolis: University of Minnesota Press, 1997).

35. Nadel, *Containment Culture;* Liebman, *Living Room Lectures;* George Lipsitz, "The Meaning of Memory: Family, Class, and Ethnicity in Early Network Television," in *Time Passages: Collective Memory and American Popular Culture* (Minneapolis: University of Minnesota Press, 1990), 39–75. Also influential has been Mosse's *Nationalism and Sexuality: Middle-Class Morality and Sexual Norms in Modern Europe* (Madison: University of Wisconsin Press, 1988), which focused more directly upon the ongoing relevance of reproduction and sexuality to the formation of national identity. Among the most influential historians of the Durkheim myth and symbol school, Mosse suggested that nations cannot be understood solely through their official political culture, but must also be analyzed through more dispersed sites of cultural exchange. The nation and the state are not synonymous, although institutions of state power nearly always claim to be working in the interests of the nation. And while the state may speak with a fairly univocal voice, enacting its will through official agencies and policies, the nation has no such stability. Instead, national identity is under constant transformation, subject to processes of hegemonic negotiation. This climate of contest and debate surrounding definitions of national identity has led scholars to revise significantly Mosse's close alignment of the national character with the political goals of the state. In an influential 1992 anthology, Parker et al. began with the title of Mosse's book, but pluralized it to *Nationalisms and Sexualities,* hoping to move beyond the "trans-historical, supra-national, or self-identical categories" that characterize his work, writing that there is "no 'nationalism in general' such that any single model could prove adequate to its myriad and

contradictory historical forms" (Parker, Russo, Sommer, and Yaeger, *Nationalisms and Sexualities*, 2).

36. Dana Nelson, *National Manhood: Capitalist Citizenship and the Imagined Fraternity of White Men* (Durham, N.C.: Duke University Press, 1998), 28.

37. Engin Isin, *Being Political: Genealogies of Citizenship* (Minneapolis: University of Minnesota Press, 2002), 35–36.

38. Nan Enstad, "Fashioning Identities: Cultural Studies and the Historical Construction of Political Subjects," *American Quarterly* 50 (Dec. 1998): 745, 748, 774.

39. E. Ann Kaplan, *Looking for the Other: Feminism, Film, and the Imperial Gaze* (New York: Routledge, 1997), 32.

40. Herman Gray, "Remembering Civil Rights," in *The Revolution Wasn't Televised: Sixties Television and Social Conflict*, ed. Lynn Spigel and Michael Curtin (New York: Routledge, 1997).

41. John Caughie, *Television Drama: Realism, Modernism, and British Culture* (London: Oxford University Press, 2000), 112, 122.

42. Dolan, *Allegories of America*, 2–3.

1. Documentary Melodrama

1. "Fatal Ferret," review of Gordon Young, *The Cat with Two Faces* (New York: Coward-McCann, 1957), in *Time*, Feb. 24, 1958, 104.

2. "Spies in Russia Told All," *U.S. News and World Report*, Apr. 6, 1951, 13–15.

3. For an overview of espionage films, see Larry Langman and David Ebner, *Encyclopedia of American Spy Films* (New York: Garland, 1990).

4. Krutnik, *In a Lonely Street*, 202.

5. In 1954 the Sylvania Award for "most outstanding program on television" was given to *Medic;* see *Broadcasting and Telecasting*, Dec. 6, 1954, 79. *Dragnet* promotion kit, 1952–53, "Audience Promotion Files," Box 138, NBC Collection, State Historical Society of Wisconsin (hereafter SHSW).

6. Memo to station publicity managers, Exploitation Section, NBC Press Department. "*Victory at Sea* Exploitation Manual," Audience Promotion Files: *Victory at Sea*, Folder 6, Box 138, NBC Collection, SHSW.

7. "Greaza's 'Chief' Status on 'T-Men in Action' Brings Some Carryovers to His Real Life, Too," press release, Continuity Acceptance Program Files, "Treasury Men in Action, 1951–4," Folder 27, Box 152, NBC Collection, SHSW.

8. Advertisement, *Broadcasting*, Aug. 17, 1953, 42.

9. John Corner, *Television Form and Public Address* (New York: St. Martin's Press, 1995), 27, 31, 77.

10. In 1952 Sylvania gave *Treasury Men in Action* its award for "Best Documentary Melodrama." "NBC Wins Seven Sylvania Television Honors," press release, Dec. 11, 1952, Folder 2, Box 323, Doris Ann Papers, NBC Collection, SHSW.

11. Sonia D'Artois, as told to Anne Fromer, "I Was a Woman Spy," *Coronet,* May 1954, 159–70; "Onetime Spy Tells His Story: How U.S. Press Was Infiltrated by Communists," *U.S. News and World Report,* July 8, 1955; "The Crime of the Century," *Reader's Digest,* May 1951, 149–68.

12. "Most Wanted Story," *Time,* Jan. 14, 1957, 59; Clarence Budington Kelland, "Spy and Counterspy," *Saturday Evening Post,* Sept. 5, 1953, 36–99 (part 3 of 8).

13. See, for example, May, *Homeward Bound;* Nadel, *Containment Culture;* Liebman, *Living Room Lectures.*

14. "Most Wanted Story"; J. Edgar Hoover, "What Makes an FBI Agent," *Coronet,* June 1955, 110–14; J. Edgar Hoover, foreword to Don Whitehead, *The FBI Story: A Report to the People* (New York: Random House, 1956), xi.

15. *Treasury Men in Action* aired on ABC for one season in 1951, was then picked up by NBC for two seasons, and returned to ABC in 1954 in its final season. When it returned to ABC, *Treasury Men* was shot on film in order to take advantage of the new syndication market for rerun programs.

16. Advertisement, *Broadcasting and Telecasting,* Dec. 6, 1954.

17. Stockton Helfrich, memo re: "Treasury Men in Action," May 29, 1951, Continuity Acceptance Program Files, "Treasury Men in Action, 1951–4," Folder 27, Box 152, NBC Collection, SHSW.

18. "Greaza's 'Chief' Status on 'T-Men in Action' Brings Some Carryovers to His Real Life, Too."

19. "The Case of the Honorable Men," *Treasury Men in Action* script by Alvin Boretz, Jan. 21, 1954, Script 130, Box 14, Folder 7, Alvin Boretz Papers, SHSW.

20. "Agent to Receive Treasury Award on 'T-Men' Telecast Based on Bootleg Case," press release, Continuity Acceptance Program Files, "Treasury Men in Action, 1951–4," Folder 27, Box 152, NBC Collection, SHSW.

21. "The Case of the Iron Curtain," *Treasury Men in Action* production #16, script by Alvin Boretz, Folder 13, Box 14, United Artists (UA)/Ziv Script Collection, SHSW.

22. "If any scripts come your way on the 'Federal Bureau of Investigation' or the 'FBI,' please check us on them promptly so that we can be sure, to quote Howard Monderer [from the NBC legal department], to take appropriate action if said 'words or initials are used in a manner reasonably calculated to convey the impression that the broadcast or telecast is approved, endorsed or authorized by the Federal Bureau of Investigation'"; Stockton Helfrich, CART Report 11, November 1954, "1954 CART Reports," M95–101, Folder 7, Box 1, NBC Collection, SHSW.

23. NBC's chief censor wrote, "Management advises us that any references to the Central Intelligence Agency or the Secret Service in script material requires clearance with those bodies. We have had subsequent discussion with both the man in charge of Public Relations for the Treasury Department and the office of General Bedell Smith at Central Intelligence. In each case the result has been a little more clarification on how to

implement the policy. Please, therefore, bear very definitely in mind that this department should be checked so that we in turn can get to the gentleman mentioned for
guidance." Stockton Helfrich, CART Report 17, June 7, 1951, 4, "1951 CART Reports,"
M95–101, Folder 4, Box 1, NBC Collection, SHSW.

24. It seems more likely that the networks were afraid of ruffling feathers than that
the federal agencies were concerned about false representation, though FBI director
J. Edgar Hoover was more reluctant to embrace television. See Stockton Helfrich, memo
re: "Treasury Men in Action," May 29, 1951, in Continuity Acceptance Program Files,
"Treasury Men in Action, 1951–4," Folder 27, Box 152, NBC Collection, SHSW.

25. Review, *Treasury Men in Action*, in *Variety*, Sept. 2, 1953.

26. Charles Barry, draft of letter to Lou Nichols, assistant to the director, Federal
Bureau of Investigation, approximately June 29, 1953. The draft was likely written by
William McAndrew of NBC. The final letter was sent by Charles Barry to FBI Director
J. Edgar Hoover on June 30, 1953. "FBI Project," Folder 24, Box 367, Charles Barry Papers
(hereafter Barry Papers), NBC Collection, SHSW.

27. Charles Barry, memo to John Herbert, Aug. 28, 1953, Folder 24, Box 367, "FBI
Project," Barry Papers.

28. Charles Barry, memo to S. L. "Pat" Weaver, Dec. 3, 1953, Barry Papers.

29. Adrian Samish, letter to Louis Nichols, assistant to the director, FBI, Aug. 12,
1953, Barry Papers.

30. Ibid.

31. Ibid. Samish wrote that NBC "would clear with you the names and professional
background of all men who might be seriously considered for positions in the perma-
nent NBC unit."

32. Ibid.

33. Samish, who was to be executive producer of the series, wrote that "I argued
against Mr. Nichol's views as strongly as I could, but considering that I was talking to
J. Edgar Hoover's right hand man, but it's kinda like talking to the army . . . you have to
do it their way, or you can't do it at all." Adrian Samish, memo to Charles Barry, Aug. 19,
1953, Barry Papers.

34. *Spies Confidential,* a *Confidential Magazine* Special Report, 1960.

35. Ladislas Farago, *War of Wits: The Anatomy of Espionage and Intelligence* (New
York: Funk and Wagnalls, 1954), vi.

36. Maurice Unger, letter to Eddie Davis, Dec. 19, 1955, in "*The Man Called X:* Correspondence, Outlines, 1955–1957," Folder 11, Box 29, UA/Ziv Production Files, Series
7.7, SHSW (hereafter "*Man Called X* Correspondence" file).

37. "Although some of the espionage weaknesses in this script have been corrected,
Farago thinks it is inconceivable that an espionage agent of X's ability could ever be
handled in the manner that he is by a free-lance swindler like Voydan. Also, contrary to
espionage technique, all the agents get arrested." Richard Dorso, letter to Jon Epstein, re:

MCX 4B, Dec. 12, 1955, in "*Man Called X* Correspondence" file. In another letter regarding the same episode, Dorso wrote, "Farago points out in this script that once again X acts like a stupid agent rather than a bright one. Not only is he not smart but, in addition, he is passive. Instead of X doing things, in this script he is in the position of people doing things to him which really can only occur because of acts he commits which no good intelligence officer would." Richard Dorso, letter to Jon Epstein, re: Espionage Facts, Nov. 29, 1955, in ibid.

38. If the Ziv producers' comments are any indication, Farago certainly seemed to enjoy his position: "Mr. Farago called this morning. . . . He is happy. He is fascinated. He is grateful. He actually giggled over the phone." Jon Epstein, letter to Eddie Davis, Apr. 17, 1956, in ibid.

39. Richard Dorso, letter to Jon Epstein, Feb. 16, 1956, in ibid.

40. Ibid.

41. See Liebman's *Living Room Lectures*, as well as Mary Beth Haralovich, "From Sitcoms to Suburbs," in *Private Screenings: Television and the Female Consumer*, ed. Lynn Spigel and Denise Mann (Minneapolis: University of Minnesota Press, 1992).

42. Lynn Spigel, *Make Room for TV: Television and the Family Ideal in Postwar America* (Chicago: University of Chicago Press, 1992).

43. See, for example, Nadel, *Containment Culture*, and May, *Homeward Bound*.

44. Maurice Unger, letter to Eddie Davis, Nov. 3, 1955, in "*Man Called X* Correspondence" file.

45. *The Man Called X*, episode 5b, "Extradition Story," Dec. 10, 1955, Folder 4, Box 116, UA/Ziv (hereafter UA/Ziv) Collection Series 7.2, SHSW.

46. *The Man Called X*, episode 3b, "The Ballerina Story," Dec. 3, 1955, Folder 3, Box 116, UA/Ziv 7.2, SHSW.

47. Harry Truman, address before a joint session of Congress, Mar. 12, 1947. Available at: gopher://gopher.law.cornell.edu:70/00/foreign/historical/truman.txt. Accessed Aug. 21, 1998.

48. Richard Dorso, letter to Maurice Unger, Nov. 8, 1955, in "*The Man Called X:* Correspondence" files.

49. For an overview of this period of U.S.-Iranian history, see, for example, Yonah Alexander and Allan Nanes, eds., *The United States and Iran: A Documentary History* (Frederick, Md.: University Publications of America, 1980).

50. Synopsis, *The Man Called X* episode #10b, "Provocateur," Jan. 6, 1956, Folder 10, Box 116, UA/Ziv 7.2, SHSW.

51. Dorso, letter to Unger, Nov. 8, 1955.

52. Maurice Unger, letter to John Sinn, Nov. 11, 1955, in "*Man Called X* Correspondence" file.

53. *The Man Called X* script, episode 12b, "U.S. Planes," Folder 13, Box 116, UA/Ziv 7.2, SHSW.

54. Jon Epstein, letter to George Callahan, Jan. 6, 1956, "*Man Called X* Correspondence" file.

55. John Sinn, letter to Richard Dorso, Nov. 4, 1955, in ibid.

56. William Boddy, *Fifties Television: The Industry and Its Critics* (Urbana: University of Illinois Press, 1990), 159.

57. *The Man Called X*, episode 5b, "Extradition Story."

58. Script Notes: Tag Scene, Nov. 15, 1955, "*Man Called X* Correspondence" file.

59. "Television: The New Cyclops," *Business Week*, Mar. 10, 1956, 76–104. See also Spigel, *Make Room for TV.*

60. Thurman Arnold, "Mob Justice and Television," *Atlantic Monthly*, June 1951, 68–70; Ring Lardner Jr., "TV's New 'Realism,'" *The Nation*, Aug. 13, 1955, 132–34.

61. For a further discussion of the transition from New York–based live anthology drama to Los Angeles–filmed production, see Boddy, *Fifties Television.*

62. "Slice of Life," *Time*, Aug. 2, 1954.

63. Bruce Bliven, "Why Let Red Lies Go Unchallenged?" editorial, *Saturday Evening Post*, Sept. 5, 1953, 10.

64. "Slice of Life."

65. Corner, *Television Form and Public Address*, 27.

2. *I Led 3 Lives* and the Agent of History

1. Liebman, *Living Room Lectures.*

2. The program used several slightly different versions of this introductory voice-over. This particular version was used in later episodes that were not based specifically on Philbrick's autobiography.

3. Maurice Unger, memo to Jon Epstein, Aug. 19, 1953, Folder 14, Box 28, UA/Ziv 7.7, SHSW.

4. *Broadcasting*, Aug. 17, 1953, 42.

5. A promotional film shown by salesmen to local broadcasters and advertisers begins with the claim, "This is an introduction to the timeliest, most powerful television show ever to be presented to an American audience." Memo, "Tentative Layout of Presentations Film on *I Led 3 Lives*," June 6, 1953, UA/Ziv 7.7, 28–10. Sponsors apparently responded quite favorably to the program. The advertising manager of Phillips Petroleum, a major sponsor, wrote, "The interest of this audience has been reflected in favorable customer comments to our Phillips 66 dealers and distributors. And the dealers themselves have taken time to express their satisfaction by writing to us in praise of the show. Many of these letters not only praise the entertainment value of *I Led 3 Lives* but comment on its excellent public service features." Quoted in Morleen Getz Rouse, "A History of the F. W. Ziv Radio and Television Syndication Companies: 1930–1960," Ph.D. diss., University of Michigan, Ann Arbor, 1976, 357.

6. Dennis Rinzel, "A Description of the Ziv Television Series: *I Led 3 Lives*," M.A. thesis, University of Wisconsin, Madison, 1975, 88. Rinzel's thesis is a valuable resource for investigating the series. He conducted several interviews with key production personnel in the 1970s, and his exhaustive research about Ziv sales strategies and local ratings is excellent.

7. Rouse, "History of the F. W. Ziv Radio and Television Syndication Companies," 358.

8. Rinzel, "Description of the Ziv Television Series," 135.

9. *Broadcasting*, Aug. 8, 1953, 42; Rinzel, "Description of the Ziv Television Series," 105.

10. Rinzel, "Description of the Ziv Television Series," 104, 105.

11. Hayden White, "The Historical Event," in *The Persistence of History: Cinema, Television, and the Modern Event*, ed. Vivian Sobchack (New York: Routledge, 1996), 19.

12. Herbert Philbrick, *I Led 3 Lives: Citizen, "Communist," Counterspy* (New York: McGraw Hill, 1952), 83.

13. Joan Hawkins, "*Red Nightmare:* Propaganda and the Crisis in American Masculinity," paper presented at 1996 Console-ing Passions Conference, Madison, Wis., Apr. 27, 1996.

14. Philbrick, script notes, undated, Folder 10, Box 28, Folder 10, UA/Ziv 7.7, SHSW.

15. Bob Friedheim, memo to Maurice Unger, Sept. 10, 1953, in ibid.

16. Philbrick, *I Led 3 Lives*, 256.

17. May, *Homeward Bound*, 113.

18. Philbrick, *I Led 3 Lives*, 77.

19. William Whyte, *Organization Man* (New York: Simon and Schuster, 1956), 11, 263.

20. Maurice Unger, notes on pilot episode, Apr. 30, 1953, Folder 11, Box 28, UA/Ziv 7.7, SHSW.

21. Philbrick, *I Led 3 Lives*, 90. For an account of the discourses of white suburban retreat that marked the periods after both world wars, see Gwendolyn Wright, *Building the Dream: A Social History of Housing in America* (Boston: MIT Press, 1981).

22. Philbrick, "How It All Began," p. 8, Folder 14, Box 28, UA/Ziv, 7.7, SHSW.

23. In 1951 FBI director J. Edgar Hoover publicly praised Herb's wife for coping with the pressures of her husband's work. His letter to Eva paid homage to her personal sacrifices, proclaiming, "The victories of the Philbrick adventure were undoubtedly attributable in no small part to the additional responsibilities assumed by you and to your loyal and faithful devotion to (your husband) and to your country. You must have endured endless suffering. . . . I want to commend you for a task well done and to extend my sincerest appreciation." Cited in *New York Herald Tribune* brochure, Folder 14, Box 28, UA/Ziv 7.7, SHSW. Tom Doherty's research into Philbrick's FBI file suggests that "Hoover took pains to disassociate himself and the agency, at least officially, from the series, emphasizing that Philbrick had never been a true FBI agent but only a civilian informant"; Doherty, "At Last Count, I Led 3 Lives." Hoover's hesitance is at least in part

due, as Doherty suggests, to his guarded control of his own imprimatur, though in other cases Hoover was quite willing to use popular media to promote both himself and the Bureau's anti-Communist investigations. Hoover was likely more skeptical about television than other media, and his reluctance may also have been related to the FBI's negotiations with NBC over an officially sanctioned FBI series which were ongoing during the period of *I Led 3 Lives*' preproduction and first season. The NBC project was developed not by a budget syndicator but by the nation's preeminent network and it was in both the network's and the FBI's interests for such a show to be an exclusive glimpse into the Bureau.

24. Philbrick, untitled memo, Dec. 2, 1953, Folder 10, Box 28, UA/Ziv 7.7, SHSW.

25. Liebman, *Living Room Lectures*, 25.

26. Philbrick, *I Led 3 Lives* (1952).

27. Nadel, *Containment Culture*, 4.

28. Stuart Hall, "The Rediscovery of 'Ideology': Return of the Repressed in Media Studies," in *Culture, Society, and the Media*, ed. Tony Bennett et al. (New York: Methuen, 1982).

29. Nadel, *Containment Culture*, 6.

3. The Irrelevant Expert and the Incredible Shrinking Spy

1. "Slice of Life."

2. Harry Ackerman, undated personal notes, Folder 1, "*Behind Closed Doors*, General #1," Box 1, Harry Ackerman Papers (hereafter Ackerman Papers), Accession 4876, University of Wyoming American Heritage Center.

3. Similar arrangements were common at United Artists (which acquired Ziv in 1959), 20th Century-Fox, and MGM, who co-produced or distributed programs created by Desilu, Four Star, T & L/Three F, Quinn Martin Productions, and others. For a further discussion of the development of Hollywood studio television production, see Mark Alvey, "The Independents: Rethinking the Television Studio System," in *The Revolution Wasn't Televised*, ed. Spigel and Curtin, 139–58, as well as Thomas Schatz, "Desilu, I Love Lucy, and the Rise of Network TV," and David Marc, "The Screen Gems Division of Columbia Pictures: Twenty-Five Years of Prime-Time Storytelling," both in *Making Television: Authorship and the Production Process*, ed. Robert J. Thompson and Gary Burns (New York: Praeger, 1990).

4. Alvey, "The Independents: Rethinking the Television Studio System," as well as Christopher Anderson, *Hollywood TV: The Studio System in the Fifties* (Austin: University of Texas Press, 1994).

5. "Standard Opening" (distributed to writers), Folder 1, Box 1, Ackerman Papers.

6. All in Box 1 of the Ackerman Papers: Kingman T. Moore, Meeting Report, Whitehall Pharmaceutical, Bates and Co., Screen Gems. Sept. 24, 1958, Folder 1; Harry

Ackerman, teletype to Ralph Cohn, May 12, 1958, Folder 2, "*Behind Closed Doors,* General #2"; Jay Michaels, letter to Sam Gallu, July 14, 1958, Folder 1; Harry Ackerman, letter to Lynn Poole, Aug. 4, 1958, Folder 1.

7. *Behind Closed Doors* Platform Outline, Screen Gems, July 29, 1958, Folder 3, "*Behind Closed Doors,* General #3," Box 1, Ackerman Papers.

8. The quandary producers faced was that historical incidents gave better opportunities for dramatic action (and historically accurate documentarism), but seemed of less interest and relevance to audiences who expected the show to deal directly with current events. Most Cold War spy cases were passive and dull in comparison to wartime exploits. Kingman T. Moore, Meeting Report, Whitehall Pharmaceutical, Bates and Co., Screen Gems, Oct. 22, 1958, Folder 1, Box 1, Ackerman Papers.

9. Burt Hanft, teletype to John Mitchell and Harry Ackerman, Oct. 31, 1958, and Ellis Zacharias, letter to Harry Ackerman, Screen Gems, Aug. 4, 1958, both in Folder 1, Box 1, Ackerman Papers.

10. Dancer-Fitzgerald-Sample (Liggett and Myers' agency), letter to Harry Ackerman, Aug. 26, 1958, Folder 1, Box 1, Ackerman Papers. The actor in question here is Bruce Gordon.

11. Kingman T. Moore, Meeting Reports, Whitehall Pharmaceutical, Bates and Co., Screen Gems, Oct. 1 and 22, 1958, Folder 1, Box 1, Ackerman Papers.

12. Jay Michaels, General Artists Corporation-TV, letter to Harry Ackerman, Oct. 31, 1958, Folder 1, Box 1, Ackerman Papers.

13. John Bushnell, NBC Continuity Acceptance, CART Report, *Behind Closed Doors* Episode #4359, "Flight to Freedom," NBC Continuity Acceptance Department, Aug. 22, 1958, Folder 1, Box 1, Ackerman Papers.

14. Harry Ackerman, teletype to Ralph Cohn, Aug. 22, 1958, Folder 1, Box 1, Ackerman Papers.

15. Michaels, letter to Ackerman.

16. In 1962, for the first time there were more TV sets outside the United States than within; see Kaarle Nordenstreng and Tapio Varis, *Television Traffic—A One-Way Street?: A Survey and Analysis of the International Flow of Television Programme Material* (Paris: United Nations Educational, Scientific, and Cultural Organization [UNESCO], 1974), 31. Noting this study, William Boddy argues that international telefilm syndication was becoming increasingly lucrative by the late 1950s: "It was in the late 1950s and early 1960s that foreign program sales exploded, and by then the networks and large telefilm producers dominated a huge international market for American television programming"; Boddy, *Fifties Television,* 142.

17. Jay Michaels, letter to Irving Briskin, July 8, 1958, Folder 1, Box 1, Ackerman Papers.

18. Ratings quoted in teletype from Ralph Cohn to Harry Ackerman, Oct. 3, 1958, Folder 1, Box 1, Ackerman Papers.

19. Moore, Meeting Report, Oct. 22, 1958.

20. Selmer L. Chalif, executive director, Screen Gems, internal memo to Harry Ackerman et al., Oct. 23, 1958, Folder 1, Box 1, Ackerman Papers.

21. "It would be a *must* to show the figure of Zacharias sitting at the desk and stamping papers with 'Top Secret' or 'Ready to be Released' to give the show the authenticity it needs so badly." Dancer-Fitzgerald-Sample, letter to Ackerman, Aug. 26, 1958.

22. Richard A. R. Pinkham, vice president for radio-television, Ted Bates and Company, letter to Harry Ackerman, Oct. 16, 1958, Folder 1, Box 1, Ackerman Papers.

23. Pinkham insisted upon securing *BCD*'s place as the agency's preeminent narrative program: "Bates has thirteen film shows on the air this year, and this is the *only one* that I am really concerned about. With *21* about to be replaced with a new live game show, we must have a highly commercial show at 9:00 pm, or we will have a real bomb on our hands." Ibid.

24. Cohn, teletype to Ackerman, Oct. 3, 1958.

25. See Krutnik, *In a Lonely Street*, 202–8.

26. Chalif, memo to Ackerman.

27. Gene Plotnik, memo to Harry Ackerman, Oct. 16, 1958, Folder 1, "*Behind Closed Doors,* General #1,"Box 1, Ackerman Papers.

28. Ibid.

29. Plotnik wrote, "It seems that more effective validation must be built directly into the show. Since Zacharias is the source, his direct corroboration, both before and after the drama, might help convince.... I think any further supporting testimony, on screen, whenever obtainable, of actual public figures who might be expected to have had a direct knowledge of the situation described, would further help this gnawing disbelief." Ibid.

30. "Both Mr. Pinkham and Mr. Rogers stressed strongly the thesis that the series must be keyed to action and not just intellect. While the basic top level theme of a show can be an interesting intellectual idea of espionage or counter-espionage, the presentation level of the actual script must be one of action, not one of complicated situations and talk." Moore, Meeting Report, Oct. 1, 1958.

31. Harry Ackerman, teletype to Ralph Cohn, Oct. 3, 1958, Folder 1, Box 1, Ackerman Papers.

32. Initially, correspondence with federal agencies was handled by Gallu, but direct interaction between the production company and the agencies led to confusion and inconsistencies. After the pilot was nearly scuttled by communication problems, information was subsequently channeled through Columbia's PR department. Harry Ackerman, memo to Sam Gallu, Sept. 29, 1958, Folder 1, Box 1, Ackerman Papers.

33. Donald E. Baruch, production branch chief, Audio-Visual Division, Office of News Services, Office of the Assistant Secretary of Defense for Public Affairs, letter to Gallu Productions, Oct. 22, 1958, Folder 1, Box 1, Ackerman Papers.

34. All in Box 1 of the Ackerman Papers: J. Raymond Bell, Allied Public Relations, letter to Harry Ackerman, Folder 1; Harry Ackerman, teletype to Ralph Cohn, Aug. 18, 1958, Folder 2; Charles T. Newton, manager of communication, Convair Astronautics, letter to Arthur Frankel, resident counsel, Screen Gems, May 16, 1958, Folder 2.

35. Jay Michaels, Report of Meeting with the Office for Eastern European Affairs, U.S. State Department, July 7, 1958, Folder 2, Box 1, Ackerman Papers.

36. Ibid.

37. "For our own guidance, I would suggest that stories which concern points under negotiation between the US and USSR be held back until our diplomatic corps has reached agreement with Russia." Ibid.

38. Such concerns were consistent with the strategies of the recently formed U.S. Information Agency, the principal international propaganda unit of the State Department and the CIA. These concerns weren't lost on Screen Gems, who observed, "From the above, we can conclude that our State Department is more concerned with the feelings of neutral nations than with the USSR. Thus, any stories which could be effectively misused by Radio Moscow worry our people." Ibid.

39. Harry Ackerman, memo to Irving Briskin, Sept. 2, 1958, Folder 1, Box 1, Ackerman Papers.

40. Chalif, letter to Ackerman.

41. "For the present Pinkham felt stories about espionage and counter-espionage with action and easy understanding were more highly preferable to stories of revelations which require complex exposition. At a later date, stories which were unique and thought-provoking could well be included." Ibid.

42. Most episodes were produced for between $40,000 and $50,000, although at least two ("Enemy on the Flank" and "The Nike Story") were over $60,000. Ackerman, teletype to Screen Gems New York, Nov. 13, 1958, Folder 2, Box 1, Ackerman Papers.

43. "*Behind Closed Doors* could find its compelling area of acceptability in a considered blending of realism and fiction so long as the heart of each program was an incident, event, or action close to the minds and emotions of the American people, and easily recognizable and identifiable." Chalif, letter to Ackerman.

44. Ackerman, teletype to John Mitchell, Nov. 3, 1958, Folder 2, Box 1, Ackerman Papers.

45. Ackerman, teletype to Burt Hanft, Screen Gems New York, Nov. 10, 1958, Folder 2, Box 1, Ackerman Papers.

46. For more discussion of 1950s science-fiction films in the context of the Cold War, see Cynthia Hendershot, *Paranoia, the Bomb, and 1950s Science Fiction Films* (New York: Popular Press, 1999); Jerome Shapiro, *Atomic Bomb Cinema: The Apocalyptic Imagination on Film* (New York: Routledge, 2001); and Vivian Sobchack, *Screening Space*, 2d ed. (New Brunswick, N.J.: Rutgers University Press, 1997).

47. Albert Taylor, memo to Maurice Unger, July 18, 1958, Folder 3, "*World of Giants*— 'Teeth of the Watchdog' scripts and annotations," Box 206, UA/Ziv 7.2, SHSW.

48. Ibid.

49. Robert Corber, *In the Name of National Security: Hitchcock, Homophobia, and the Political Construction of Gender in Postwar America* (Durham, N.C.: Duke University Press, 1993), 63, 222. Corber argues that though the politicization of homosexuality in the Cold War was consistent with the political right, it was liberals' reclamation of the consensual "vital center" that most forcefully linked heterosexuality with normative American national identity.

50. Susan Sontag, "Notes on Camp," *Against Interpretation and Other Essays* (New York: Dell, 1966), 283.

51. Boddy, *Fifties Television,* 161.

52. Harry Ackerman, letter to Dave Nyren, Dancer-Fitzgerald-Sample, Apr. 10, 1959, Folder 2, Box 1, Ackerman Papers.

4. Parody and the Limits of Agency

1. Frederick L. Collins, *The FBI in Peace and War,* 2d ed. (New York: Ace Books, 1962), 21. The first edition of this book, published in 1943, was adapted for radio and ran on CBS for fourteen years (1944–58).

2. Daniel O'Hara, *Radical Parody: American Culture and Critical Agency after Foucault* (New York: Columbia University Press, 1992), 18–21.

3. Ibid., 21.

4. Tom Schatz, *Hollywood Genres: Formulas, Filmmaking, and the Studio System* (New York: Random House, 1981). Also see John Cawelti, *The Six-Gun Mystique* (Bowling Green, Ohio: Bowling Green University Press, 1970); Will Wright, *Sixguns and Society: A Structural Study of the Western* (Berkeley: University of California Press, 1975); E. Ann Kaplan, *Women in Film Noir* (London: BFI, 1978); Christine Gledhill, *Home Is Where the Heart Is: Studies in Melodrama and the Woman's Film* (London: BFI, 1987); Stephen Neale, *Genre* (London: BFI, 1980).

5. Tom Schatz writes in *Hollywood Genres* that generic texts "examine and affirm 'Americanism' with all its rampant conflicts, contradictions, and ambiguities. Not only do genre films establish a sense of continuity between our cultural past and present, but they also attempt to eliminate the distinctions between them. As social ritual, genre films function to stop time, to portray our culture in a stable and invariable ideological position" (31). Much of the enduring ideological pull of the western genre, for example, is this ability to operate somehow outside of time, to portray a culture in static, idealized state. The spy programs of the 1950s attempt precisely such an ideological operation, by positing an idealized American citizen who is uncompromisingly patriotic and devoted to preserving the continuity of the state. But espionage programs cannot "stop time," for equally important to these shows is their engagement with contemporary political realities; these shows oscillate uncomfortably between the timely and the timeless.

6. Rick Altman argues directly against this evolutionary model, arguing instead that Hollywood genres are always in process—but in ways that may be contradictory and nonlinear. See Rick Altman, *Film/Genre* (London: BFI, 1999). For another extended discussion of genre criticism, see Stephen Neale, *Genre and Hollywood* (New York: Routledge, 2000).

7. Ancillary merchandise required virtually no investment by the studio; marketing and development costs were borne by the toy manufacturers and comic-book publishers, who generally paid from 2 to 10 percent in royalties. The merchandise leader in this area in the early 1960s was the James Bond film franchise, which netted $50 million per year. "Smash! Batman Is Hit on the Retail Scene; He Outsells Agent 007," *Wall Street Journal*, Mar. 9, 1966; "The Story of POP: What It Is, and How It Came To Be," *Newsweek*, Apr. 25, 1966, 54; "Batman Zooms in as Big Contender in Merchandising," *Advertising Age*, Jan. 10, 1966.

8. Friedan, *The Feminine Mystique*. Also May, *Homeward Bound*.

9. John Fiske, *Understanding Popular Culture* (Sydney: Allen and Unwin, 1989), 103.

10. Dan Harries, *Film Parody* (London: BFI, 2000), 7, 26. Linda Hutcheon, *A Poetics of Postmodernism* (London: Routledge, Kegan and Paul, 1988). For an extended discussion of the historical treatment of parody in literary criticism, as well as its place in the development of poststructuralist and postmodern critical theory, see Margaret Rose, *Parody: Ancient, Modern, and Post-Modern* (London: Cambridge University Press, 1993).

11. Caughie, *Television Drama*, 140.

12. Ibid., 151.

13. Ibid., 164.

14. Fredric Jameson, "Postmodernism and Consumer Society," in *The Anti-Aesthetic: Essays on Postmodern Culture*, ed. Hal Foster (Seattle: Bay Press, 1983), 114. Also, see Jameson's *Postmodernism, or the Cultural Logic of Late Capitalism* (Durham, N.C.: Duke University Press, 1992).

15. Caughie, *Television Drama*, 215.

16. Robert Anderson, *The U.N.C.L.E. Tribute Book* (Las Vegas: Pioneer Books, 1994), 15.

17. Toby Miller, *The Avengers* (London: BFI, 1997), 97, 102, 107.

18. NBC, *The Man from U.N.C.L.E.* promotional booklet, c. 1964, reprinted in Anderson, *The U.N.C.L.E. Tribute Book*, 27.

19. Ibid., 28.

20. Ibid., 17.

21. Ibid., 111.

22. John Hill, *The Man from U.N.C.L.E.'s ABC's of Espionage* (New York: Signet Books, 1966), rear cover.

23. Ibid., i, x.

24. Review, *The Man from U.N.C.L.E.*, *Variety*, Sept. 30, 1964.

25. "Inside *U.N.C.L.E.*," *Newsweek*, July 5, 1965, 54.

26. Vaughn speculated that his father would likely have been listed in *Red Channels*, even though he had regularly appeared on the radio crime dramas distributed by one of the publication's authors. Robert Vaughn, *Only Victims: A Study of Show Business Blacklisting* (New York: Putnam, 1972), 277.

27. Dwight Whitney, "The Other Bobby in American Politics," *TV Guide*, Feb. 24, 1968. Also see John B. Murray, *Robert Vaughn: A Critical Study* (London: Thessaly Press, 1987).

28. Vaughn, *Only Victims*.

29. Whitney, "The Other Bobby in American Politics."

30. Marcia Borie, "U.N.C.L.E. Bobby—Robert Vaughn goes to Washington to 'babysit' for Robert Kennedy's kids—and enjoys the wildest weekend of his life!" *TV Radio Mirror*, July 1966.

31. Don Freeman, "The Man from U.N.C.L.E.," *Saturday Evening Post*, June 19, 1965, 75–79.

32. David Ragan, "Ridgefield's Robert Vaughn: He Confounds the Experts," *Fairfield County Magazine*, June 1982.

33. Whitney, "The Other Bobby in American Politics"; Freeman, "The Man from U.N.C.L.E.," 77; Ragan, "Ridgefield's Robert Vaughn."

34. Alan Nadel, "The Invasion of Postmoderism: The Catch-22 of the Bay of Pigs and Liberty Valance," chapter 6 of *Containment Culture*.

35. Mario Amaya, *Pop as Art: A Survey of the New Super-Realism* (London: Studio Vista, 1965), 11.

36. For a further discussion of the relationship between Pop Art and American culture of the period, see, for example, Christin Mamiya, *Pop Art and Consumer Culture: American Super Market* (Austin: University of Texas Press, 1992).

37. Anderson, *The U.N.C.L.E. Tribute Book*, 32; Miller, *The Avengers*, 25.

38. P. M. Clepper, "Stars Coming for Mayor's Party," *St. Paul Sunday Pioneer Press*, Dec. 5, 1965.

39. Lynn Spigel and Henry Jenkins, "Same Bat Channel, Different Bat Times: Mass Culture and Popular Memory," in *The Many Lives of the Batman: Critical Approaches to a Superhero and His Media*, ed. Roberta Pearson and William Ulricchio (New York: Routledge, 1991).

40. "Dozier's 'Batman' to Wink at That Unserved Minority—the 'Camp' Set," *Daily Variety*, Dec. 15, 1965, 42.

41. "The Story of POP," 54.

42. Shana Alexander, "The Feminine Eye: Don't Change a Hair for Me, Batman," *Life*, Mar. 11, 1966.

43. Bill Boichel, "Batman: Commodity as Myth," in *The Many Lives of the Batman*, ed. Pearson and Ulricchio, 10.

44. "'Super Camp' Batman Flies High Again" *Los Angeles Times*, Dec. 14, 1965, sec. V, 18.

45. Spigel and Jenkins, "Same Bat Channel," 125.

46. *Newsweek*, Apr. 25, 1966; *Life*, Mar. 11, 1966.

47. Psychiatrist Fredric Wertham, who had with his book *Seduction of the Innocent* led the attack on comic books a decade earlier, insisted that the "adventures of the mature Batman and his young friend Robin [were] like a wish dream of two homosexuals living together." Quoted in "The Story of POP," 58.

48. Quoted in "Pravda Meets 'Batman' Head On," *New York Times*, Apr. 30, 1966.

49. "The Story of POP," 58.

50. Moe Meyer, ed., *Politics and Poetics of Camp* (New York: Routledge, 1994).

51. When the program later entered syndication, it was appropriated by slash fiction writers, who generated fan fiction that explored the relationship between the two agents.

52. Sasha Torres argues a similar point about *Batman* in "Pop, Camp, and the Batman Television Series," in *Pop Out: Queer Warhol*, ed. Jennifer Doyle, Jonathan Flatley, and José Esteban Muñoz (Durham, N.C.: Duke University Press, 1996), 238–55.

53. This critical foregrounding of social contradictions is central to most definitions of queer camp. See, for example, Jack Babuscio, "Camp and the Gay Sensibility," in *Gays and Film*, ed. Richard Dyer (London: British Film Institute, 1977), 40–57.

54. In addition to Toby Miller's *The Avengers*, James Chapman also offers a discussion of the program that situates the show's shifting narrative address from drama to ironic humor in relation to the development of postmodern aesthetics and to "a contradictory image of modern womanhood that both celebrates female empowerment and yet at the same time attempts to establish control mechanisms whereby women can be kept in their place" (57). James Chapman, "*The Avengers*: Television and Popular Culture during the 'High' Sixties," in *Windows on the Sixties: Exploring Key Texts of Media and Culture*, ed. Anthony Aldgate, James Chapman, and Arthur Marwick (London: IB Tauris, 2000), 37–69.

55. Julie D'Acci, "Nobody's Woman?: *Honey West* and the New Sexuality," in *The Revolution Wasn't Televised*, ed. Spigel and Curtin, 81.

56. Moya Luckett, "Sensuous Women and Single Girls: Reclaiming the Female Body on 1960s Television," in *Swinging Singles: Representing Sexuality in the 1960s*, ed. Hilary Radner and Moya Luckett (Minneapolis: University of Minnesota Press, 1999), 280.

57. Quoted in John Peel, *Files Magazine: The U.N.C.L.E. Files—The Girl from U.N.C.L.E.* (Canoga Park, Calif.: Psy Fi Movie Press, 1985), 46.

58. Anderson, *The U.N.C.L.E. Tribute Book*, 45.

59. Donna McCrohan, *The Life and Times of Maxwell Smart* (New York: St. Martin's Press, 1988), 3.

60. Ibid., 15, 46. NBC dropped the program in its final year, when it was picked up by CBS.

61. Ibid., 25.

62. Ibid., 46, 48.

63. Ibid., 61.

64. Ibid., 107.

65. Linda Dittmar and Gene Michaud, eds., *From Hanoi to Hollywood: The Vietnam War in American Film* (New Brunswick, N.J.: Rutgers University Press, 1991).

66. "Inside the CIA," *New York Times*, Apr. 26–29, 1966.

67. John Smith, *I Was a CIA Agent in India* (New Delhi: New Age Press, 1967), 4.

68. Patrick Garvey, *CIA: The Myth and the Madness* (New York: Saturday Review Press, 1972), 7, 10.

69. David Wise and Thomas Ross, "The Spies on Our Side," *Saturday Evening Post* 240 (Nov. 4, 1967): 56.

70. "The CIA, or Who Was That Dictator I Seen Ya With?" Students for a Democratic Society, Chicago, c. 1968.

71. "The CIA and 'The Kiddies,'" *Newsweek*, Feb. 27, 1967.

72. Todd Gitlin and Bob Ross, "The CIA at College: Into Twilight and Back," pamphlet, Liberation Press and Students for a Democratic Society, Chicago, originally published in *Village Voice*, July 6, 1967.

73. "The CIA and 'The Kiddies.'"

74. "When the 'Cover Was Blown,'" *U.S. News and World Report*, Mar. 13, 1967, 97.

75. "The CIA and 'The Kiddies.'"

76. "How to Care for the CIA Orphans," *Time*, May 19, 1967, 42–43.

77. "Playing It Straight: Who Did What and Why for the CIA?" *The New Republic*, Mar. 4, 1967, 4–10.

78. "The CIA, or Who Was That Dictator I Seen Ya With?"

79. Mauldin cartoon, syndicated by *Chicago Sun-Times*, reprinted in *Newsweek*, Feb. 27, 1967.

80. Bodroghkozy, *Groove Tube*, 172. Bodroghkozy's excellent discussion of *The Mod Squad* situates it in the context of more outspoken and ideologically critical programs like *The Smothers Brothers Comedy Hour*, perhaps the most politically radical network television program of the era.

81. John Tulloch, *Television Drama: Agency, Audience, and Myth* (London: Routledge, 1990), 246.

82. For a further discussion of parody and canonization, see Harries, *Film Parody*.

83. Linda Hutcheon, *A Theory of Parody: The Teachings of Twentieth-Century Art Forms* (Urbana: University of Illinois Press, 1985), 32.

84. Ernest Gellner, *Nations and Nationalism* (Ithaca, N.Y.: Cornell University Press, 1983), 1.

5. *I Spy* a Colorblind Nation

1. Wayne Shorter, quoted in liner notes to *Speak No Evil*, Blue Note Records, 1964. Original cover art and photograph by Reid Miles.

2. Manning Marable, "Race, Identity, and Political Culture," in *Black Popular Culture*, ed. Michele Wallace (Seattle: Bay Press, 1992), 292.

3. Aniko Bodroghkozy suggests that though critical discussions of TV and relevance generally center on the Norman Lear and MTM productions of the early 1970s, the practice began earlier; she argues that *The Mod Squad* (which premiered in 1968) similarly attempted to grapple with pressing social concerns, providing a forum within which conflicting perspectives on the youth and antiwar movements found public voice. Bodroghkozy, *Groove Tube*.

4. Brenda Gayle Plummer, *Rising Wind: Black Americans and U.S. Foreign Affairs, 1935–1960* (Chapel Hill: University of North Carolina Press, 1996), 278. In a nationally televised speech delivered on September 24, 1957, President Eisenhower declared, "In the South, as elsewhere, citizens are keenly aware of the tremendous disservice that has been done to the people of Arkansas in the eyes of the nation, and that has been done to the nation in the eyes of the world. At a time when we face grave situations abroad because of the hatred that Communism bears toward a system of government based on human rights, it would be difficult to exaggerate the harm that is being done to the prestige and influence, and indeed to the safety, of our nation and the world. Our enemies are gloating over this incident and using it everywhere to misrepresent our whole nation. We are portrayed as a violator of those standards of conduct which the peoples of the world united to proclaim in the Charter of the United Nations. There they affirmed 'faith in fundamental human rights' and 'in dignity and worth of the human person' and they did so 'without distinction as to race, sex, language or religion.'"

5. "Worldwide Reactions to the Alabama Events," USIA report #IRI/A-RO-2–61. May 29, 1961, Folder S-17–61, Box 20, RG306, USIA, Office of Research, Special Reports 1953–63, National Archives II, College Park, Md.

6. Carl Rowan, "No Whitewash for U.S. Abroad," *Ebony*, August 1965, 56.

7. "African Reaction to the Alabama Events" USIA report #IRI/AA-RO-55–61. June 6, 1961, Folder S-18–61, Box 20, USIA, Office of Research, Special Reports 1953–63, RG306, National Archives II.

8. Plummer, *Rising Wind*, 195.

9. Vaughn, *Only Victims*, 221.

10. Paul Gilroy, *The Black Atlantic: Modernity and Double Consciousness* (Cambridge: Harvard University Press, 1993), 112.

11. Plummer, *Rising Wind*, 222–23.

12. Stanley Karnow, "Bill Cosby: Variety Is the Life of Spies," *Saturday Evening Post*, Sept. 25, 1965, 86.

13. Cal Wilson, a writer for *Soul*, quoted in Richard Lemon, "Black Is the Color of TV's Newest Stars," *Saturday Evening Post*, Nov. 30, 1968, 84.

14. Robyn Wiegman, *American Anatomies: Theorizing Race and Gender* (Durham, N.C.: Duke University Press, 1995), 11, 15.

15. "The Race Race," *Newsweek,* May 15, 1965, 74–75.

16. These series were also related to the surge in documentary programming that followed the critiques most succinctly expressed in Newton Minow's "vast wasteland" speech. See, for example, Michael Curtin, *Redeeming the Wasteland: Television Documentary and Cold War Politics* (New Brunswick, N.J.: Rutgers University Press, 1995).

17. By 1968 Bill Cosby himself hosted a seven-part CBS series entitled "Of Black America" that questioned the logic of liberal integrationism. In the series, which followed the assassination of Martin Luther King Jr. by just a few months, Cosby steps out of the easily accessible role of Scotty and insists that audiences recognize the ongoing inequalities that structured black American life.

18. Joan Barthel, "What a TV Producer Produces," *New York Times Magazine,* Nov. 21, 1965, 38.

19. Ibid., 152.

20. "Color Him Funny," *Newsweek,* Jan. 31, 1966, 76.

21. Herman Gray, "Remembering Civil Rights," in *The Revolution Wasn't Televised,* ed. Spigel and Curtin, 353.

22. Richard H. King, *Civil Rights and the Idea of Freedom* (New York: Oxford University Press, 1992), 6.

23. Ibid., 7, 115, 117.

24. Ibid., 150, 153, 160, 184.

25. "Color Blind Comic," *Newsweek,* May 20, 1968, 97; "An Electronic Mark Twain," *Life,* Mar. 15, 1968, 37; C. H. Simonds, "Primarily a Guy," *National Review,* Oct. 4, 1966, 1007–8.

26. Sut Jhally and Justin Lewis, *Enlightened Racism: The Cosby Show, Audiences, and the Myth of the American Dream* (Boulder, Colo.: Westview Press, 1992). It is not uncommon for American conservatives to appropriate black figures who can be fitted to the civil rights subject mold. In 1994, for example, the right-wing think tank the Heritage Foundation published *The Conservative Virtues of Dr. Martin Luther King* by Robert Woodson and William J. Bennett, secretary of education during the first Bush administration (Washington, D.C.: The Heritage Foundation, 1994).

27. "Dick Gregory Is a 'Serious' Comic," *Chicago Daily Defender,* Oct. 9, 1965, 4.

28. Lillian S. Calhoun, "Fast Rising Comedian Bill Cosby Talks about His Different Approach to Comedy," *Chicago Defender,* Aug. 1–7, 1964, 4. "'If I go on Groucho's show, he knows I won't have any racial material and there'll be no racial material from him. So he can't exploit racial incidents. Not that he would anyway, as he doesn't need to do that,' Cosby added quickly."

29. "Color Blind Comic," 97.

30. In the mainstream press, Cosby was promoted (and seemed to promote himself) as colorblind. In *Ebony,* however, he was a bit more critical. He said, "I think we

must realize that unless a show is an educational program out of black America, you're not going to find reality. I mean, how much does a Gomer Pyle tell it like it is? We must remember that all of these things have to do with fantasy and they all have to be entertaining." "The Pleasures and Problems of Being Bill Cosby," *Ebony*, July 1967, 148.

31. The 1960s were a period of considerable growth in black American travel, both within and outside the United States. Travel promoters called black tourism "The Billion Dollar Sleeping Giant," suggesting that "Negro Americans with money now look to far away places. They are now thinking of Europe, Africa, Hawaii, Mexico, Nassau, Jamaica." A research report circulated to travel agents and tour operators asked, "Can you afford to ignore these people?" Clarence Markham Jr., "Economic Impact of the Negro Traveler," a research report prepared by *Negro Traveler and Conventioneer Magazine*, Travelers Research Publishing Co., Chicago, 1968, 6.

32. Tourism promoters from a variety of places contacted 3F Productions, from the Jamaica Tourist Board to the Virginia Skyline Caverns in Shenandoah National Park.

33. John Scuoppo, vice president of promotion, Desilu, letter to Fine and Friedkin, July 17, 1967, Folder 6: NBC, "*I Spy*, 1967/68," Box 10: "National Broadcasting Company, *I Spy*, Ephemera and Correspondence Related to the Production of *I Spy*," UCLA Department of Special Collections, University Research Library, Los Angeles (hereafter UCLA DSC).

34. According to the 3F translator, "They make reference to 'The Name of the Game' where also the plot is to assassinate an ex-president Norteamerican. It appears the plot is based on Johnson's trip to Mexico last year, and they cannot tolerate that throughout the world ignorant people could think Mexico is a country where that type of assassination plots against foreign political people are allowed and even less in the case of President Johnson who is identified by name and the head of the neighbor country. Unless the personality of Johnson is substantially changed and the script submitted again for approval they will not give authorization." "Censor Objections to Scripts Submitted," undated Mexican censorship report, Folder 4: "Mexico, *I Spy*, 1967/68," Box 10, UCLA DSC.

35. Mary Beth Haralovich notes that the show's representations of Mexico were generally more tempered than those of other countries (particularly China); Mexico was "presented as our friendly neighbor to the south, a haven for U.S. spies on vacation." Haralovich, "*I Spy*'s Living Postcards: The Geo-Politics of Civil Rights," in *Television, History, and American Culture: Feminist Critical Essays*, ed. Mary Beth Haralovich and Lauren Rabinovitz (Durham, N.C.: Duke University Press, 1999), 100.

36. "Typographical Errors on I Spy Scripts," memo, Jan. 31, 1967, Folder 1: "I Spy 1967/68, Greece/Morocco," Box 10, UCLA DSC.

37. Political instabilities in Greece interfered with the production schedule. Mike Fenton wrote, "Let's all hope that King Constantine is able to solve his problems so that we can, in fact, shoot the nine episodes of *I Spy* which we have scheduled for Greece."

214 Notes to Chapter 5

Cable to Henry Willson, Creative Management Associates, Apr. 21, 1967, Folder 2: "*I Spy* 1967/68 Cables," Box 10, UCLA DSC.

38. Friedkin to Leonard, Oct. 16, 1967, Folder 8: Overseas Correspondence, Friedkin/ Leonard/Fine, *I Spy,* 1967/68, UCLA DSC.

39. In "Sparrowhawk," the agents escort an Arab prince who wants to experience the pleasures of Las Vegas, while in "A Day Called 4 Jaguar," they search the Mexican jungle for an elusive Russian Air Force officer.

40. Robert Franklin Williams, *Negroes with Guns* (repr., Detroit: Wayne State University Press, 1998); Timothy Tyson, *Radio Free Dixie: Robert. F. Williams and the Roots of Black Power* (Chapel Hill: University of North Carolina Press, 1999).

41. "Punching Brag," *Newsweek,* Mar. 18, 1963, 93; "Cassius Clay Visits with Only Man Ever to Beat Him in Ring," *Chicago Defender,* Apr. 18–24, 1964, 20.

42. "$100 Misunderstanding?" *Newsweek,* Feb. 24, 1964, 58; "And I'm Already the Greatest!" *Newsweek,* Mar. 9, 1964, 50.

43. Malcolm X, quoted by Huston Horn, "The First Days in the New Life of the Champion of the World," *Sports Illustrated* 20, no. 10 (Mar. 7, 1964): 57.

44. John R. McDermott, "A Man-Child Taken in by the Muslims," *Life* 56, no. 10 (Mar. 6, 1964): 38–39.

45. Jim Murray, "The Drubbing," *Sports Illustrated* 22, no. 23 (June 7, 1965): 53.

46. "And I'm Already the Greatest!"

47. C. Chander, "Resents Boxing Czar's Threat to Cassius Clay," letter to editor, *Chicago Defender,* Apr. 18–24, 1964, 11. "When it came out that a day before the match Liston's company, Inter-continental Promotions, Inc., had paid $50,000 for the right to promote Clay's next fight if he won the championship and to name his opponent, Sen. Philip Hart, Michigan Democrat, threatened a Congressional investigation," in "And I'm Already the Greatest!"

48. "Cassius X," *Newsweek,* Mar. 16, 1964, 74.

49. Muhammad Ali, quoted by Horn, "The First Days in the New Life of the Champion of the World."

50. "The Black Muslim Hope," Scorecard, *Sports Illustrated* 20, no. 11 (Mar. 16, 1964): 8.

51. Because he left the Nation of Islam in March 1964, Malcolm X didn't accompany Ali on the trip. Instead, Ali's guide and traveling companion was Herbert X, son of Nation of Islam founder Elijah Muhammad.

52. "Muhammad Ali in Africa," photo essay, photographer Gerry Cranham, *Sports Illustrated* 20, no. 22 (June 1, 1964): 20; "Champ's African 'Love Affair,'" *Ebony,* Sept. 1964, 85; "The 400 Blows," *Newsweek,* Dec. 6, 1965, 64; "Early End for Early Bird," *Newsweek,* Aug. 15, 1966, 79; Norman Mailer, *The Fight* (Boston: Little, Brown, 1975), 78.

53. "Alas Poor Cassius!" *Ebony,* July 1965, 144.

54. Martin Kane, "The Greatest Meets the Grimmest," *Sports Illustrated* 21, no. 44 (Nov. 1, 1965): 36.

55. Floyd Patterson, "Cassius Clay Must Be Beaten," *Sports Illustrated* 21, no. 41 (Oct. 11, 1965): 79.

56. Ibid.; "Poetic Knockout," *Sports Illustrated* 21, no. 44 (Nov. 1, 1965): 10.

57. Floyd Patterson, with Milton Gross, "I Want to Destroy Clay," *Sports Illustrated* 21, no. 16 (Oct. 19, 1964): 44; "Big Fight," *Sports Illustrated* 21, no. 48 (Nov. 29, 1965): 22; Kane, "The Greatest Meets the Grimmest."

58. This is a clear example of *I Spy*'s use of NBC documentary and news programming resources. NBC had exclusive North American rights to the 1964 Olympic broadcast, which were carried via satellite from NHK, the Japanese national television service.

59. Gilbert Rogin, "Not a Great Fight, But It Was a Real One," *Sports Illustrated*, Dec. 6, 1965, 108.

60. Dan Jenkins, editorial co-chairman, NATAS, letter to Sheldon Leonard, Feb. 16, 1967, Folder 6, "Miscellaneous, *I Spy*, 1967/68," Box 10, UCLA DSC.

61. Dorothy Farley, NAACP Freedom Fund Committee chairman, Beverly Hills–Hollywood Branch, letter to 3F Productions, July 24, 1967, in ibid.

6. Agents or Technocrats

1. Jay Dratler, "List of Books," Folder "Manuscript: OSS," Box 31, Jay Dratler Papers (hereafter Dratler Papers), Accession 2/71, University of Wyoming American Heritage Center.

2. Jay Dratler, Prospectus Breakdown, Feb. 3, 1967, Dratler Papers.

3. Jay Dratler, "OSS Notes," Apr. 13 and May 18, 1967, Dratler Papers.

4. Susan Jeffords, *The Remasculinization of America: Gender and the Vietnam War* (Bloomington: Indiana University Press, 1989), and *Hard Bodies: Hollywood Masculinity in the Reagan Era* (New Brunswick, N.J.: Rutgers University Press, 1994).

5. Nelson, *National Manhood*.

6. Wiegman, *American Anatomies*.

7. Collins, *The FBI in Peace and War*, 21. Lyman B. Kirkpatrick Jr., *The Real CIA* (New York: Macmillan, 1968), 2; Paul H. Jeffers, *The CIA: A Close Look at the Central Intelligence Agency* (New York: Lion Press, 1970), 119–20.

8. "Report on Viewer Reactions—Program Analysis," CBS Television Network Research Department, Program Analysis Division, Report 28–66, May 5, 1966, Folder, 7, Box 30, Bruce Geller Papers (hereafter Geller Papers), SHSW.

9. Bernard Weitzman, vice president, Desilu Productions, letter to Steven Hill, June 28, 1966, Folder 7, Box 30, Geller Papers.

10. Hal Humphrey, "Mission: Impossible," *Los Angeles Sunday Times Television Weekly*, Aug. 27, 1968; Patty Drake, fan letter to Bruce Geller, Aug. 23, 1967, Folder 1: "Fan Mail," Box 31, Geller Papers.

11. Richard Carpenter, "*I Spy* and *Mission Impossible:* Gimmicks and a Fairytale," *Journal of Popular Culture* 1, no. 3 (Winter 1967): 290.

12. Curtin, *Redeeming the Wasteland*, 89.

13. Lawrence S. Wittner, *Cold War America: From Hiroshima to Watergate* (New York: Praeger, 1974), 121, 317.

14. Robert Lewis Shayon, "Mission: Immoral," *Saturday Review*, Nov. 19, 1966, 34.

15. Ibid.

16. Script notes, Feb. 14, 1971, Folder 8, Box 31, Geller Papers.

17. Certificate signed by Manuel de la Rosa Uclés, general secretary, Circulo de Escritores de Television (TV Writers Club), May 20, 1968, Folder 1, Box 31, Geller Papers.

18. Patrick J. White, *The Complete* Mission: Impossible *Dossier* (New York: Avon, 1991), 426.

19. Nordenstreng and Varis, *Television Traffic*, 12, 31, 40.

20. Ibid., 20, 33, 40; White, *The Complete* Mission: Impossible *Dossier*, 156.

21. White, *The Complete* Mission: Impossible *Dossier*, 208.

22. "CBS 'Mission' May Quit While Ahead So Par-TV Can Recoup from Syndie," *Variety*, Jan. 27, 1971, 1.

23. "Spy Spoofs Run Political Risks on Global Sales," *Variety*, Feb. 15, 1967, 27.

24. "Times Rough, but Outlook Bright for Foreign Syndication" *Broadcasting* 70, no. 18 (May 2, 1966): 66.

25. NBC, for example, had installed and maintained a thirteen-station network in Saudi Arabia. See Curtin, *Redeeming the Wasteland*, 78.

26. "Times Rough, but Outlook Bright for Foreign Syndication," 66.

27. DeForest Research, "Research on 'The Echo of Yesterday,'" Oct. 12, 1967, Folder 5, Box 15, Geller Papers.

28. Ibid.

29. DeForest Research, "Research on 'The Heir Apparent,'" May 9, 1968, Folder 6, Box 17, Geller Papers.

30. DeForest Research, "Research on 'The Train,'" Feb. 2, 1967, Folder 5, Box 11, Geller Papers.

31. DeForest Research, "Research on 'Trek,'" May 31, 1967, Folder 5, Box 13, Geller Papers.

32. DeForest Research, "Research on 'Fakeout,'" Aug. 9, 1966, Folder 1, Box 5, Geller Papers.

33. DeForest Research, "Research on 'The Slave, Part One,'" July 25, 1967, Folder 3, Box 14, Geller Papers.

34. Ibid.

35. Gerald Hirsch, CBS Program Practices Report, "Mindbend," June 8, 1971, Folder 9, Box 31, Geller Papers.

36. CBS Television Network Program Practices reports (all in Geller Papers): "Homecoming," May 11, 1970, Folder 6, Box 27; "The Brothers," July 15, 1969, Folder 1, Box 25; and "The Controllers," May 26, 1969, Folder 3, Box 23.

37. DeForest Research, "Research on 'The Bunker, part 1,'" Nov. 1968, Folder 5, Box 22, Geller Papers.

38. Shayon, "Mission: Immoral."

39. "*Mission: Impossible* Technically Possible," Paramount Television Sales promotion materials, undated, Folder 1, Box 31, Geller Papers.

40. "Prop-Special Effects Experts Are Responsible for Technical Excellence of Mission Series," Paramount Television Sales promotion materials, undated, in ibid.

41. Bruce Geller, letter to Angie Stavron, University of Maryland, Dec. 16, 1971, and Carole J. Pickelsimer, letter to Bruce Geller, Jan. 13, 1970, both in ibid.

42. Hy Gardner, letter to Bruce Geller, Oct. 3, 1969, in ibid.

43. Bruce Geller, letter to Hy Gardner, Oct. 6, 1969, in ibid.

44. Idan Simowitz, letter to Bruce Geller, Jan. 23, 1971, in ibid.

45. Bennett and Woollacott, *Bond and Beyond*, 28, 29.

46. Wiegman, *American Anatomies*, 6.

47. Philip Deloria, *Playing Indian* (New Haven: Yale University Press, 1998), 5, 9.

48. Ibid., 130, 132.

49. Michael Taussig, *Mimesis and Alterity: A Particular History of the Senses* (New York: Routledge, 1993), 143.

50. Linda Dittmar and Gene Michaud, *From Hanoi to Hollywood: The Vietnam War in American Film* (New Brunswick, N.J.: Rutgers University Press, 1990), 2. See also Julian Smith, *Looking Away: Hollywood and Vietnam* (New York: Scribner's, 1975); David Whillock, "The Fictive American Vietnam War Film: A Filmography," in *America Rediscovered: Critical Essays on Literature and Film of the Vietnam War*, ed. Owen Gilman and Lorrie Smith (New York: Garland, 1990).

51. Dittmar and Michaud, *From Hanoi to Hollywood*, 2.

52. John Kaye, CBS Television Program Practices memo, re: "Operation Rogosh," June 7, 1966, Folder 5, Box 3, Geller Papers.

53. Donald Gotschall, CBS Television Program Practices memo, re: "Homecoming," May 11, 1970, Folder 6, Box 27, Geller Papers.

54. White, *The Complete* Mission: Impossible *Dossier*, 275.

55. Bruce Geller, letter to Bruce Lansbury and Lawrence Heath, June 18, 1971, Folder 8, Box 31, Geller Papers.

56. Ibid.

57. Bruce Geller, letter to Frank Koninsberg, International Famous Agency, Feb. 17, 1971, Folder 1, Box 31, Geller Papers.

58. James Chapman places *Live and Let Die* in the context of the cycle American blaxploitation films of the early 1970s, arguing that the film attempted to exploit the commercial appeal of black action films while invoking racist stereotypes through an antimiscegenation narrative about Bond's rescue of a young white virgin from the thuggish—and not overly bright—black villain, Mr. Big. James Chapman, *License to Thrill:*

A Cultural History of the James Bond Films (New York: Columbia University Press, 2000), 163–72.

59. Christina Crosby, "Dealing with Differences," in *Feminists Theorize the Political,* ed. Judith Butler and Joan Scott (New York: Routledge, 1992), 140; Wiegman, *American Anatomies,* 6.

60. J. Fred MacDonald, *Television and the Red Menace: The Video Road to Vietnam* (New York: Praeger, 1985), 200.

61. Curtin, *Redeeming the Wasteland,* 83.

62. Shayon, "Mission: Immoral."

Conclusion

1. "The Private I," *Time,* June 21, 1968, 65.

2. Seymour M. Hersh, "Huge C.I.A. Operation Reported in U.S. against Anti-War Forces, Other Dissidents in Nixon Years," *New York Times,* Dec. 22, 1974, 1; Katherine S. Olmstead, *Challenging the Secret Government: The Post-Watergate Investigation of the CIA and FBI* (Chapel Hill: University of North Carolina Press, 1996); U.S. Commission on CIA Activities within the United States (Rockefeller Commission), *Report to the President* (Washington, D.C.: GPO, 1975); U.S. Senate Select Committee to Study Governmental Operations with Respect to Intelligence Activities (Church Commission), *Final Report,* 94th Cong., 2d sess., Senate Report No. 94–755, 6 vols. (Washington, D.C.: GPO, 1976).

3. See, for example, Joanne Weintraub, "Real World May Prove Too Much for *24,*" *Milwaukee Journal Sentinel,* Nov. 5, 2001; Michael Hill, "It's a New Day for Hour One of *24,*" *Washington Post,* Nov. 4, 2001, Y07.

4. All of the current spy shows were predicted to have excellent domestic and international sales potential. For example, *24* was successfully marketed at the international TV sales conference MIPCOM 2001, and was expected to gross over $1 million per episode in international distribution. See, for example, Jerry Rice, "Scripted Series Take a Run at Reality," *Variety,* Oct. 1–7, 2001, 58.

5. Charlie McCollum, "National Crisis Overshadows Three Television Premises," *San Jose Mercury News,* Sept. 14, 2001.

6. Jeff Cohen, "*The Agency* on CBS: Right Time but Wrong Show," *Los Angeles Times,* Oct. 8, 2001.

7. "Secrets and Spies," *TV Guide,* Oct. 29, 2001.

8. Janet Weeks, "*24,*" *TV Guide,* Nov. 3, 2001, 16.

9. The early critical enthusiasm for these shows (and particularly for *24*) began to wear off as the melodramatic elements have become more prominent. Given its development by the same production team that created the college drama *Felicity, Alias* has been viewed with some skepticism all along. Initially *24* was promoted—and received

by most popular critics—as "quality" television, reinforced by its sophisticated narrative structure, a noted film actor as star, and its unusual use of advance trailers in movie theaters. By midseason, though, both shows were scoffed at by critics: "These two shows are not distant critical cousins. That bloodline hinting at implausible fluffery runs through both. . . . *The Sopranos* and *West Wing* shouldn't lose sleep worrying about losing Emmys"; Tim Goodman, "Both *24* and *Alias* Deliver the No-brainer Thrills," *San Francisco Chronicle,* Feb. 19, 2002. The critical hierarchy that places the more overtly masculinist *24* over *Alias* mirrors the privileged status ascribed to noir over melodrama, though the two forms are closely intertwined. Elizabeth Cowie argues against the common bifurcation between film noir and melodrama: "The connection between film noir and melodrama has been made by a number of writers, but usually in order to distinguish film noir as a form of male melodrama, in contrast to the woman's film and female melodrama." Critics have often treated these as "parallel genres," but Cowie argues that she wants "to examine the melodramatic in film noir in order to overturn this rigid sexual division, not to affirm it." Elizabeth Cowie, "Film Noir and Women," in *Shades of Noir,* ed. Joan Copjec (London: Verso, 1993), 129–30.

10. *US Weekly,* Oct. 15, 2001.

11. Peggy Noonan, "Welcome Back, Duke: From the Ashes of Sept. 11 Arise the Manly Virtues," *Wall Street Journal,* Oct. 12, 2001.

12. Jeffords, *Hard Bodies,* 12.

13. Bob Drogin, "CIA Officer Is First U.S. Combat Casualty," *Los Angeles Times,* Nov. 29, 2001; George Tenet, director of Central Intelligence, "Statement on the Death of a CIA Officer in Afghanistan," Nov. 28, 2001, http://www.cia.gov/cia/public_affairs/press_release/archives/2001/pr11282001.html; Office of the President of the United States, "Guest List," http://www.whitehouse.gov/stateoftheunion/guest.html.

14. Valerie Godines, "Widow Shows Her Resolve," *Orange County Register,* Sept. 15, 2002.

15. Dolan, *Allegories of America,* 62.

16. Peter Blickle, *Heimat: A Critical Theory of the German Idea of Homeland* (New York: Camden House, 2002).

17. Dolan, *Allegories of America,* 63.

18. Gene Smith, "Would You Believe Don Adams?" *Saturday Evening Post* 239 (June 4, 1966): 32.

19. Joseph Alsop, "Why We Can Win in Vietnam," *Saturday Evening Post* 239 (June 4, 1966): 27.

20. "Spies, Science, and Sex: The American Daydream," *Esquire,* May 1966, 79.

Index

Avengers, The, xxi, xxii, 81, 96, 97, 182,
    209n54; export of, 192n6; institutional
    hierarchy of, 82; *Mission: Impossible*
    and, 164

Bailey, Stu, xxi
Bain, Barbara, 150, 167
Baker, Josephine, 114, 116
Barry, Charles C., 1, 11, 12, 198n26
Barrymore, Lionel, 145
Batman, 96, 209nn47, 52; Pop and, 89;
    popularity of, 89, 90, 91; representa-
    tional history of, 90
Bauer, Jack, 181
Bauer, Teri, 182
Bay of Pigs, xxi, xxvi, 46, 75, 106, 108
BCD. See *Behind Closed Doors*
Beatles, 177
Behind Closed Doors (BCD), xix, xxix,
    xxxvi, 2, 48, 71, 72, 84, 100, 144, 204n23;
    documentarism and, xx, 50–63; pro-
    duction of, 51, 59; syndication of, 58
Behind Closed Doors (Zacharias and
    Farago), 2, 14, 50
Being Political (Isin), xxxiii–xxxiv
Belafonte, Harry, 120
Berlin Wall, xxvi
Berman, Gail: on *24*, 181
Beverly Hillbillies, 191n4
Bewitched, xxi, 50
Bhabha, Homi, xxxv
Big Story, The, 3
Bill Dana Show, The, 100
bin Laden, Osama, 180, 181
Black action films, 217n58
Black activists, 117, 118, 123
Black Atlantic, The (Gilroy), 117
Black civil subject: Ali as, 134–43
Blacklisting, xxiv–xxv, xxvii, xxviii, 23,
    86, 194n23
Blackman, Honor, 182
Black Muslims, 134, 139
Black Panthers, 132
Black Power, 122, 128
Blacks. *See* African Americans
Bliven, Bruce, 24

Bly, Robert, 184
Boda, Balint, 14
Bodine, Jethro, 191n4
Bodroghkozy, Aniko, xxvii, 211n3; on *Get
    Smart*, 111; on *Mod Squad*, 210n10
Bogart, Humphrey, 189
Bond, James, 82, 103, 118, 144, 147, 172, 178.
    See also James Bond films
Bond and Beyond (Bennett and
    Woollacott), 81, 164
Bono, Sonny, 91, 92, 93
Borge, Victor, 95
Boston Blackie, 15
Brandon, Chase, 180
"Bridge of Spies" (*I Spy*), 129
Briggs, Dan, 150
Briskin, Irving: on *BCD*, 49
Bristow, Sidney, 182
Broadcasting: Cary in, 156
Broderick, Edwin R., 30
Brooks, Mel: *Get Smart* and, xxxvi,
    99, 100
Brown, David, xxix, xxx
Burdett, Winston, 1, 6
Bureaucracy, feminized, 32–37
Burke's Law, xxi, 145
Burn after Reading (Farago), 14
Burns and Allen, 4
Bush, George W., 184
Bush, Laura, 183
Butler, Judith, xxxiv

Caan, James, 189
Caine Mutiny, The, 189
Calhoun, John, 22
California Democratic Party, 86
Campbell's Soup, 13
Canovan, Margaret, xxxi
Carlson, Richard, 22, 39
Carmichael, Stokely, 114, 116, 122
Carpenter, Richard, 152
Carré, Mathilde, 1
"Carriers, The" (*Mission: Impossible*), 151
Carroll, Leo G., 83–84
Carson, Johnny, 189
Cary, Peter, 156

Michael Kackman is assistant professor in the Department of Radio–Television–Film at the University of Texas, Austin.